THE SECTARIAN COLLEGE

AND

THE PUBLIC PURSE

Fordham--A Case Study

By

Walter Gellhorn

and

R. Kent Greenawalt

1970
OCEANA PUBLICATIONS, INC.
Dobbs Ferry, New York

Preface

This work was commissioned by Fordham University. In not the slightest degree, however, has it been controlled or tinted by anyone connected with that institution. We, the authors, were asked to examine the University in any respect and to whatever extent we might choose, and then to make appraisals and recommendations that might or might not be palatable to Fordham. The University sought a wholly detached judgment about its educational and legal posture. That is precisely what we have attempted to supply.

In the main, our comments concerning the Fordham scene speak as of the close of the academic year 1967-1968. At that time, we believe, our descriptions and evaluations completely corresponded with the facts. But Fordham has by no means stood still while we have been completing our comments on it. It is a dynamic institution, constantly undergoing change. Without reference to the opinions we ourselves had been forming about desirable directions of development, Fordham pushed forward in many of those very directions—on its own initiative, not ours.

Thus, for example, even before this study had been presented in mimeographed form to the trustees of Fordham University, they had already taken steps to enlarge their number, to assure their control over the appointment of top-level administrators including the president, and to surrender their power to discriminate on religious grounds when admitting students (a power, we add, that in any event had long since decayed from disuse). Further significant changes have been made in the University since this report was prepared. Indeed, these changes have been deemed significant enough by the New York State Department of Education so that, shortly before this book went to press, the Department declared Fordham to be eligible for funds available only to nonsectarian universities. We have not attempted to alter our textual discussion to include changes occurring since our factual investigation was completed, though by footnotes

iii

and a descriptive epilogue we have sought to help bring the reader more nearly up to date. We stress, however, that this volume is not a newspaper purporting to present up-to-the-minute news, but rather a case study.

A word is in order here about how the book is put together. Its primary focus is upon what kinds of alterations Fordham and other Catholic and non-Catholic religious institutions of higher learning may have to undertake in order to be considered nonsectarian. Although we have tried to analyze in some depth the extent to which sectarian and independent institutions may be treated differently under the law, we believe that many of our readers will not be interested in pursuing that subject at length. Thus, we have included as Chapter II a summary of our conclusions about the denominational university under the law and have reserved more extensive consideration for the appendices.

Our work has been unstintingly aided by every member of the Fordham community whom we consulted, as well as by numerous scholars in other Catholic and secular institutions, academic administrators, and federal and state officials. Because a full listing of indebtednesses would be too lengthy, we name former President Leo McLaughlin, former Executive Vice President Timothy S. Healy, former Executive Vice President John J. Meng, and Michael J. Sheahan, Secretary of the Board of Trustees of Fordham University, as having been especially helpful in assuring that our inquiries within the University were not treated as intrusions. The Gerli Foundation supported our study by a generous grant to Fordham. Professors Clark Byse of Harvard University Law School, George R. LaNoue of Teachers College, Columbia University, Leonard F. Manning of Fordham University Law School, Leo Pfeffer of Long Island University, and Harold M. Stahmer, Jr. of the University of Florida kindly read the initial draft of this volume. We benefited from the informed criticisms and suggestions of these able scholars, but of course we do not suggest that they are in any sense responsible, individually or collectively, for what now appears.

WALTER GELLHORN
R. KENT GREENAWALT

March 1, 1970

iv

Table of Contents

Introduction

by

Timothy S. Healy, S.J.

In 1948 Fordham University formally filed with the New York State Department of Education a description of itself as a "religious institution." At that time World War II was over and the cold war had barely begun. The majority of Fordham's undergraduates were veterans and the University in its structure and its offerings was substantially as it had been in the late 1930's. Twenty years later, after Marshall McLuhan, two small wars, and one ecumenical council, Fordham just as formally requested that its self-description as a religious institution be withdrawn, and that its only denomination be that of "independent university." How profound and vast a change these twenty years represent is, on one legal front, the burden of the study which Professors Gellhorn and Greenawalt present here.

By the middle of the 1960's, it was obvious that all of private higher education was in serious financial difficulty. It was also fairly obvious that it was very much in the enlightened self-interest of states like New York to prevent the collapse of the private sector, even if that prevention involved direct subsidy of operational budgets. The Bundy Commission, appointed by Governor Rockefeller, adopted just this view and urged, bravely given the political climate, that State aid be extended to all private colleges and universities in the State which could qualify academically, even those associated with religious denominations.

For those of us who were involved in Catholic higher education, the Bundy Commission's report presented rather special problems. There seemed little chance of the repeal of New York's constitutional bar against the use of public funds for any school "wholly or in part under the control or direction of any religious denomination." On the other hand, if State aid were to be given to every university except Fordham, it seemed best to face that fact and its obvious conclusion by seeking to incorporate the University as swiftly as possible into the State or City University systems and forego by choice an independence which was effectively doomed.

The dilemma was sharply horned, and sitting in the middle of it was uncomfortable. As usual, any university has a superfluity of constitutional experts—law, like morals, being something on which any academic worth his salt feels free to comment. The rhetoric rolled back and forth, but the dilemma remained. In addition, time was clearly running out, and if the University was to continue to grow and develop, some clarification of at least the gross outlines of its future had to be forthcoming.

It was clear that there were very few studies of the Church-State question as it pertained to higher education. For this reason, the President of Fordham, Rev. Leo McLaughlin, S.J., began a series of discussions with the Dean and several faculty members of Fordham's Law School. At first the intention was to have a legal study done in the Law School itself. The discussions, however, made it clear that it would be better for Fordham if the study were done by someone outside the University, both for public objectivity, and to make certain that its view of the University was tinged with neither faculty myopia nor alumni nostalgia. Professor Gellhorn of Columbia was approached and he agreed to accept the commission.

It was Fordham's hope that there was (even in the totally polarized legal area of Church and State) a fair and equitable middle ground where a Catholic university could stand, fulfilling completely the demands for freedom, objectivity, and quality which the State imposed, and at the same time not disavowing its own tradition and history. The question it addressed to counsel could be variously stated. "How can Fordham secularize itself?" was one way of putting it, but a way calculated to raise the hackles of alumni and others whose reading of the word "secular" placed it squarely under the strictures of the *Syllabus of Errors*. The University's opponents were going to read the question, no matter what the study said, as "How can Fordham raid the public treasury for religious purposes?" We felt there was no real need to deal with this objection based as it was on pre-judged motives. The most satisfactory statement was the simplest, "How can Fordham gain parity before the law with other private universities in New York State?"

It ought to be underlined here that in asking the question, Fordham had to be prepared to accept an answer. If it were negative, then the University had only two choices: either accept its second-class citizenship and gradually die by strangling all its growth—a process, given the financial pressures of the 1960's, likely to be more painful than prolonged; or seek with all deliberate speed to incorporate itself into some public or other private system which could guarantee its future only by completely denying its past.

There was, of course, to all this a clear element of Caesar's wifery. Because of its past Fordham had to achieve a state of purity which would have staggered the Vestals. Fordham had been through this experience before—in its application for a chapter of Phi Beta Kappa. It was told on its first go around that a chapter could not be granted until the fraternity felt certain that the University could not be seduced back into its habits of the 30's and "big-time" football. That the fraternity had recently seen, without any audible public murmer, one of its chartered institutions make the football coach president seemed curiously irrelevant to the discussion. As Professors Gellhorn and Greenawalt put it, "Persuading others that . . . alteration has in fact occurred may require more powerful proofs than would be demanded if the institutional past were not casting a shadow upon the present" (p. 100). One is reminded of the story of Noel Coward who once tried to send a telegram signed Fiorello LaGuardia. He was informed that that was illegal. "Very well," he said, "just sign it, Noel Coward." When he was told that he couldn't do that either, he protested, "But I am Noel Coward." "In that case, sir," came the answer, "you can sign it Fiorello LaGuardia." There are times when university presidents need a sense of humor.

Many of the changes and restructurings this report recommended were already well under way by 1967. Beyond their clear legal importance was a much clearer educational and social imperative. The diversification of the Board of Trustees was an example of this, as was the swiftly developing ecumenical nature of the University's offerings and faculty in theology. Another whole series of reasons, springing much more from the recommendations of the Second Vatican Council than from the piety of Senator Blaine, were operative in the major changes Fordham helped build into the education of young Jesuits. There were, however, multiple enlightenments and ironies connected with this study and with its historic sequel. One of them is striking. In order to confirm the findings of this report that ". . . Fordham has done enough . . . to show . . . that neither faculty members who are theologians and philosophers, nor students who take their courses, are doctrinally shackled" (p. 96), the State Department of Education sent as an on-site visitor to Fordham a distinguished Protestant professor of theology from Chicago. No cavil is intended against either his qualifications or his integrity. But one can imagine the public outcry that the presence of a Jesuit on the Columbia University campus, with the same investigative, not to say inquisitorial, mandate would have aroused.

On one point in this study I would like to exercise the Introducer's privilege of raising a question. Professors Gellhorn and Greenawalt mention what they discern as the growing belief that ". . .concern with students' religious activity should be transferred wholly from the university to the churches" (p. 103). As long as we are dealing with activity, the statement seems unexceptionable. But beneath activity lies being, and here we may be on shakier ground. As it stands, the statement is a clear echo of the received wisdom, the posture of total objectivity and neutrality so cherished by academic America. At this moment, however, students are in loud cry against that same objectivist stance and are equally loudly accusing the university of lying when it claims to be neutral. One need not accept the distinction between neutrality of intent and neutrality of effect to be aware that this particular protest is leading the university into new and strange dimensions. It would be presumptuous to claim that universities like Fordham which have preserved intact their commitment to traditional judgments of value could respond to this new demand much more adequately than the most doctrinairely objectivist institution. But it does not seem in any way unrealistic to speculate on the possibility that part of the answer to this new demand may lie along the traditional lines which universities like Fordham have preserved.

In a very real sense the cry of the individual student may have a direct echo in the society at large. What Fordham is fighting for is the chance to be herself, legally as well as in reality. That fight in the larger pluralistic world of American higher education may well be the fight for freedom of religion itself. In that context, a wiser voice than mine can speak.

> To affirm freedom of religion in society is to affirm a secular value. Together with truth, justice, and civic friendship, freedom is one of the quaternity of secular values which define the bases, the goals, the spirit, and the methods of secular society. More than that, to affirm freedom of religion in society is to affirm the value of religion in and for the secular society. More precisely, it is to affirm the paradox which the shallow Age of

Reason, with its geometric mentality, wholly failed to see—namely, that without religion society cannot progress toward a healthy secularity but must inevitably regress along the line of history that leads from the laicist totalitarianism of Jacobin ideology to the even more bleak and inhuman totalitarianism of today, within which the values of truth, justice, love, and freedom have reached the most advanced stage of corruption that history has ever seen.

(John Courtney Murray, S.J., *The University in the American Experience*, New York, Fordham University Press, 1966, p. 7.)

One last word should be added. It was my privilege to work with both the authors of this study during the weeks they spent on the Fordham campus. Together we had moments of probing question and answer, some moments of puzzlement and confusion, and some moments of sheer fun. I join Professors Gellhorn and Greenawalt in hoping that our shared labors will be of some use well beyond the range of Fordham's problems, which now appear to be happily and legally solved. This Introduction would be radically incomplete did I not also pay tribute to the skill, the integrity and the growing sympathy with which Professors Gellhorn and Greenawalt pursued their not always uncomplicated task.

Timothy S. Healy, S.J.
Vice Chancellor for Academic Affairs
City University of New York.

CHAPTER 1

The Problems to be Considered

This volume has a seemingly narrow focus, since it discusses in detail the problems of a single university. But the discussion has extremely broad implications. Its purpose is to identify precisely, so far as possible, measures that a prominent church-related university might have to adopt were it to shed identification as a religious institution in the conventional sense and, instead, gain acceptance as a completely independent institution of higher learning. The advice given to the university now under special consideration cannot be extended without modification to all church-related colleges and universities because they vary too greatly, one from another, in their traditions, structures, and activities. Nevertheless the suggestions made in later chapters concerning Fordhams University's situation probably have relevance as well to other academic institutions, especially those linked with Roman Catholicism.

THE ECONOMICS OF THE SECTARIAN UNIVERSITY

The present inquiry into institutional characteristics and the means of changing them has been stimulated by economic considerations. Like all academic enterprises, church-related colleges—those "having definite present-day connections with religious bodies"[1]— need more money if they are to thrive. Though constituting close to forty percent of American institutions of higher education, they enroll less than twenty percent of present day students. Their share of total enrollment, moreover, has been declining at an accelerating pace.[2]

---

[1] M. M. Pattillo, Jr. and D. M. MacKenzie, Chuch Sponsored Higher Education in the United States 20 (Am. Council on Educ. 1966).

[2] Id. at 16. And see also J. W. Evans, "Catholic Higher Education on the Secular Campus," in R. Hassenger ed., The Shape of Catholic Higher Education 275 (U. of Chicago, 1967): "In 1963, Catholic colleges and universities had enrolled 366,000 students. Twice that number of Catholics attended non-Catholic institutions. By 1985 the trend was expected to increase the ratio by as much as eight or nine to one. By the end of the present century only one out of twenty-five Catholic college students was expected to be enrolled in a Catholic institution."

Lacking large endowments, most church-related colleges have been mainly dependent upon income from tuition fees.[3] Pressed by steeply mounting costs, some have been forced to raise tuition so sharply that many of the students they most desire to attract have for this reason, among others, gone elsewhere.[4] Though not peculiar to Catholic institutions, this problem is most emphatically shared by them. Impecunious Catholic students in ever larger numbers have entered tax-supported institutions or secular institutions that can afford to give financial aid to deserving scholars.[5] Numerous Catholic colleges have too few students to be viable either economically or academically.[6] In fact, the mortality rate among Catholic institutions has been especially high because their financial capabilities have not fulfilled their founders' optimistic hopes.[7] In 1963-1964, the latest year for which figures are now available, tuition payments covered only 31 percent of the operating expenses of America's private colleges, taken as a whole.[8] Tuition fees account for a larger share of Catholic institutions' total current resources, but, even so, the discrepancy

---

[3] Fordham University, which is more generously endowed than most Catholic institutions, depended on student tuition and fees for 71.6 percent of its total income in 1966-1967. Endowment provided only 1.4 percent of the university's income. Fordham University Financial Report for the Year Ended June 30, 1967, at p. 7.

[4] Compare C. Jencks and D. Riesman, The Academic Revolution 328, 383-84, 402-04 (Doubleday, 1968).

[5] A recent report of the United States Office of Education, "Projection of Educational Statistics to 1976-77," Pub. No. OE 10030-67 (1968), at 90, 93 suggests that this is likely to be an irreversible trend. The cost of attending a private four-year college is expected to be about 30 percent higher in 1976-77 than it is today; the cost of attending a public institution is expected to increase about 20 percent.

[6] The National Catholic Educational Association recorded 165 Catholic colleges with enrollments under 100 in 1965. "They cannot provide adequate faculty or curricula, or key facilities such as libraries." J. W. Trent, Catholics in College 274 (U. of Chicago, 1967). The Education Directory listed 368 Catholic colleges in 1966; a fifth of these enrolled fewer than 100 students and only a quarter of them enrolled more than 1,000. Id. at 45. "Almost every metropolitan area contains a number of small Catholic colleges, each of which has its own library and laboratories, struggles for adequate faculty, and replicates most of the curricula of the others." Id. at 310.

[7] Many Catholic colleges are newcomers; 139 of them admitted first students between 1950 and 1965. Trent, note 6 above, at 274. Compare "The Changing World of Catholic Education," Columbia College Today, vol. XIV, No. 1, at p. 24 (1966): "Catholic colleges are unusual in that they come and go. They have a high mortality rate of 70 percent. Of the 147 new colleges founded between 1850 and 1900, only 45 still stand. One-fourth of all the existing Catholic institutions have been founded since 1940. Unlike the parochial schools and contrary to common belief, they receive almost no support from the bishops and are financed as private institutions . . ."

[8] K. A. Simon and W. V. Grant, Digest of Educational Statistics 1967, at p. 88 (U.S. Off. of Educ. 1967).

between what students can afford to pay and what the Catholic colleges must expend is very considerable.[9] It is likely to become much wider as time passes. The gap must somehow be filled by means other than constantly greater tuition charges.

The worsening economic plight of most privately conducted universities and colleges in this country has aroused urgent advocacy of federal or state aid, in the form of direct grants of public money. Thus, for example, powerfully persuasive reports by both the American Council on Education and the Association of American Universities have recommended that the federal goverment pay a portion of academic operating expenses.[10] And in New York a prestigious study group under the chairmanship of McGeorge Bundy, president of the Ford Foundation, concluded in 1968 that "limited direct state aid to the private institutions is necessary. . . . We see the need as critical. Even though the gap to be filled represents less than 5% of the aggregate anticipated operating budgets, that small margin frequently determines whether the institution can maintain a competitive faculty salary scale or keep its campus in repair."[11]

---

[9] In 1966-67, Fordham University's operating deficit—that is, the gap between current expenditures and current income—amounted to $1,080,988. Fordham Univ. Financial Report for the Year Ended June 30, 1967, at p. 1. Student payments in that year amounted to 67 percent of expenditures; during the immediately preceding five years the average had been 76.5 percent. Id. at 8. In the spring of 1968, Fordham was in a "difficult and critical" financial situation, according to its administration. Among steps taken to meet the crisis were a $300 rise in tuition, voted toward the close of 1967, and a freeze on faculty hiring. The Ram, vol. 50, no. 16, April 26, 1968, p. 1, col. 1. A further tuition increase of $200 has been authorized for undergraduate freshmen for the autumn of 1969. Compare R. F. Drinan, The Constitution, Governmental Aid and Catholic Higher Education 11 (Nat. Cath. Educ. Assn., 1968): "Even if . . . federal appropiations for all colleges increase dramatically, no foreseeable annual federal subsidy can really solve the principal problem of the private college, the problem of the annual deficit resulting merely from mounting operating costs. If, for example, in 1970 the federal government appropriated five billion dollars (or about twice its commitment in 1967) for the 8,000,000 students expected to be in college in 1970, the total sum available to colleges would be only $625 per student—or less than 50 percent of the loss sustained by a good college for every person enrolled."

[10] Am. Council on Educ., "Higher Education and National Affairs" (Feb. 18, 1967); Assn. of Am. Universities, "Federal Financing of Higher Education" (June 24, 1968). For a carefully documented analysis of the rising cost of operating private colleges and universities, see "On Financial Prospects for Higher Education," 54 AAUP Bull. 182 (1968).

[11] Select Committee on the Future of Private and Independent Higher Education in New York State, "New York State and Private Higher Education" 46 (1968). The Committee unanimously rejected the "argument that all institutions of higher education having any religious connection should be ineligible. We think this kind of rigidity flies in the face of both logic and experience. History demonstrates that there is no automatic connection between the presence or absence of religious affiliation and the presence or absence of those qualities which make a college or university a major instrument of public service."

Are public grants to church-related universities and colleges permissible? Would they be regarded as an aid to education? Or would they be deemed to be an aid to religion? These are important legal questions, which will be discussed in later pages. Respected authorities have argued in support of both the desirability and the constitutionality of public subventions of church-related higher education.[12] Their views may ultimately prevail, but probably in only a piecemeal fashion and assuredly after lengthy and heated controversy that will have emotional as well as legal components.[13]

Moreover, state constitutional provisions, including those of New York, tend to go beyond the federal Constitution in specifically limiting the expenditure of public moneys in aid of educational institutions that have religious ties. The New York Constitution declares explicitly that neither the state nor any of its subdivisions may directly or indirectly support "any school or institution of learning wholly or in part under the control or direction of any religious denomination, or in which any denominational tenet or doctrine is taught . . ."[14] Somewhat similar limitations upon the expenditure of public funds in aid of denominational academic undertakings appear in a majority of the state constitutions.[15] Paths around these restraints may con-

---

[12] See, e. g., L. F. Manning, "Aid to Education—Federal Fashion," 29 Fordham Law Rev. 495 (1961), and "Aid to Education—State Style," 29 Fordham Law Rev. 525 (1961); R. F. Drinan, "Does State Aid to Church-Related Colleges Constitute an Establishment of Religion?—Reflections on the Maryland College Cases," 1967 Utah Law Rev. 491 (1967). And see also D. A. Giannella, "Religious Liberty, Nonestablishment, and Doctrinal Development," Part II, 81 Harvard Law Rev. 513, 581-90 (1968); "Statutory Note on Higher Education Facilities Act," 77 Harvard Law Rev. 1353 (1964).

[13] Compare F. M. Hechinger, "Education: Aid and Church-Related Schools," N. Y. Times, June 13, 1965, Sec. 4, p. 8, col. 1, discussing bills (later substantially enacted in the Higher Education Act of 1965) to provide federal funds to support university activities in urban slums, to improve academic libraries, to facilitate student and faculty exchanges between high prestige institutions and colleges which "are struggling for survival," and to provide tuition grants. "Most of the provisions of these bills have wide, enthusiastic support," Mr. Hechinger wrote. "Fear of a last-minute upset is based largely on the controversy over separation of Church and State. Although loans and grants for the construction of college facilities go, under legislation passed in 1964, to Church-related colleges, a substantial body of opinion continues to be concerned that the separation principle and possibly the Constitution itself are being violated."

[14] N. Y. State Const., Art. XI, Sec. 3. For discussion of this provision's background and application, see Inter-Law School Committee Report, "The Problem of Simplification of the Constitution" 115-133 (N. Y. Legis. Doc. No. 57, 1958); N. Y. State Commission on the Constitutional Convention, "Individual Freedoms" 21-30 (1967).

[15] See D. A. Degnan, "Secularizing Catholic Colleges," 118 America 696 (1968); A. P. Stokes and L. Pfeffer, Church and State in the United States 420-425 (Harper & Row, 1964); Index Digest of State Constitutions 370-371, 852-853, 904-905 (Columbia Univ. 1959, Supp. 1964).

ceivably be found.[16] But circumvention will inevitably engender warm debate and, in all probability, long litigation.[17] Protracted dispute does not create an atmosphere conducive to academic planning and achievement. Another possibility is repeal of these constitutional provisions, but the issue is highly charged and opponents of change will not give way easily. Whether and when elimination or alteration will occur in most states is impossible to predict with confidence.

In the meantime, legislators are likely to believe themselves precluded from bolstering necessitous denominational institutions. In 1968, for example, the New York legislature, heeding advice that the Empire State's preponderantly private system of higher education might collapse unless public moneys were pumped into academic treasuries, enacted a program of direct payments to colleges and universities. The new law specified, however, that state aid apportionments could go only to applicant institutions "eligible for state aid under the provisions of the constitution of the United States and the constitution of the state of New York."[18] Thus the legislature gave notice that universities with close church connections, no matter what be the extent of their contribution to the education of New Yorkers and no matter what be the depth of their financial need, might perhaps be barred from receiving grants like those given to, say, Cornell or New York University.

Even had the legislature been unmindful of the state constitution's limitations, the promise of open-handed state aid would probably have been less than wholly fulfilled. This was made clear in 1967, when the Attorney General ruled that a distinguished professorship, paid for in part by public funds, could not be assigned to Fordham, though the authorizing statute had not differentiated between denominational and other institutions.[19]

Pressures to extend aid to all institutions of higher learning have been gaining substantial support in American opinion and in

[16] See, e. g., Opinion of the Justices to the Senate, March, 27 1968, 236 N.E. 2d 523 (Mass., 1968), holding that a special authority set up by the Commonwealth of Massachusetts might permissibly help in financing construction projects in church-related colleges, despite a constitutional ban on state financial aid.

[17] A New York statute directing that public authorities provide school books to children in private as well as in public schools was enacted on June 1, 1965; its validity was not finally determined until June 1968. N. Y. Laws 1965, ch. 230, Education Law Sec. 701; Board of Education v. Allen, 392 U.S. 236 (1968).

[18] New York Laws 1968, ch.677, Education Law Sec. 6401.

[19] See Education Law Sec. 239; Letter to Commissioner James E. Allen, Jr. from Attorney General Louis J. Lefkowitz, Sept. 13, 1967.

legislative halls. As yet, nevertheless, the pressures have been too weak to surmount the barriers of constitutional restraints and traditional resistance to public subvention of denominational undertakings. True, public moneys have become available to some extent for specific purposes apart from general operations. In 1966-67, for example, Fordham received federal help toward construction of a new chemistry building in the total amount of $1,005,000; by contract or grant it also received from governmental sources $145,540 to launch an "Upward Bound" program for disadvantaged youths, $80,820 to conduct a mathematics institute for high school teachers, and $24,998 to develop an X-ray chemical crystallography project.[20] Fordham and institutions like it will nonetheless probably face continuingly great difficulties in establishing eligibility for the general governmental aid upon which survival may depend—unless in some respects they can change their characteristics.

ACADEMIC EXCELLENCE AND THE SECTARIAN UNIVERSITY

Quite apart from this economic problem is an educational question increasingly discussed by those concerned with Catholic universities. The question is, very bluntly, whether universities closely tied to particular Church institutions or committed to particular religious doctrines can achieve the highest levels of academic excellence.

Many of the major independent universities in America began as upholders of a particular faith or as trainers of future clergymen. Fordham's near neighbor, Columbia University, was once among those with a marked religious orientation. It originally required its president to be a practicing Anglican; its compulsory religious exercises were conducted according to the prescriptions of the Church of England.[21] Even after institutions such as Brown, Harvard, Princeton, Rutgers, William and Mary, and Yale had broken their links with particular churches, the religious atmosphere that continued to surround them might reasonably be supposed to have been obnoxious

---

[20] Fordham University Financial Report, June 30, 1967, p. 10.

[21] See J. W. Pratt, Religion, Politics and Diversity: the Church-State Theme in New York History 68-69 (Cornell, 1967). The advertisement that announced the opening of King's College (later, Columbia) in 1754 declared: "The chief thing that is aimed at in this College, is, to teach and engage the children to *know God in Jesus Christ*, and to love and serve him in all *Sobriety, Godliness*, and *Richness* of life, with a perfect Heart and a Willing Mind . . ." quoted in J. W. Donohue, Jesuit Education 98 (Fordham, 1963).

to Catholics. Hence one need not be surprised that in earlier times the adherents of the Catholic Church felt the need for institutions that were distinctively their own. Preserving and fortifying the faith, assuring that young people would not "go astray," were in themselves conceived to be among the important aims, if indeed not the most important aims, of Catholic institutions of learning.[22]

Those purposes seem less compelling today. Many influential Catholic educators have disavowed the notion that a university can be "merely the extension of the teaching function of the Episcopacy. . . . Its role is not merely to present safe doctrine as propounded by accepted commentators within an environment designed to protect young people from dangers."[23] A university atmosphere cannot readily be created, many of these educators fear, within the confines of the view that "the Catholic Church has the truth, that we know all the answers to the questions that really matter."[24] At a constantly accelerating pace in universities like Fordham, academic disciplines have freed themselves from external authority of a religious character. Faculty members have asserted the same sort of intellectual autonomy that marks the secular campus.[25] Although ecclesiastical control has not yet disappeared from Catholic academic institutions without a trace (as has occurred in many colleges and universities previously dominated by Protestant church organs), it has been strongly challenged.[26] And even those who do not decry it

---

[22] Compare the remark of a prominent Viennese cleric after touring America in 1842: "Since many Catholic youths want to obtain a higher education to become physicians, attorneys, or priests, it has long been the ambition of bishops to erect such higher institutions of learning and to supervise them in order that these young men, who otherwise would attend the public state schools, might not go astray." J. T. Ellis ed., Documents of American Catholic History 261 (Bruce, 1967).

[23] M. P. Walsh, "Shifting Priorities, Uncertain Future," Fordham Magazine, No. 1967, at 3, 5.

[24] P. Gleason, "American Catholic Higher Education: A Historical Perspective," in R. Hassenger ed., The Shape of Catholic Higher Education 49 (U. of Chicago, 1967).

[25] See P. J. Reiss, "The Catholic College: Some Built-In Tensions," in Hassenger, note 24 above, at 270-271; compare A. M. Greeley, The Changing Catholic College 139 (Aldine, 1967). But cf. J. W. Donohue, Jesuit Education 196-197 (Fordham, 1963).

[26] See, e.g., President Jacqueline Grennan of Webster College in an address delivered on March 5, 1968, before the American Association for Higher Education: "Should an institution of higher education necessarily committed to free inquiry and the frontiers of secular as well as theological knowledge be owned by a congregation which has freely subjected itself to hierarchical control?" Miss Grennan answered her own question negatively. She repeated her doubts on this score in an address at Fordham University on March 21, 1968, as reported in The Ram, vol. 50, no. 12, Mar. 26, 1968, p. 1, col. 2. Compare J. W. Trent,

tend to think that Church control is markedly slacker than it once was.[27]

Whatever may be the precise facts about their governance, their purpose, and their methods, numerous Catholic institutions of higher learning do seem to share the aspirations of avowedly secular colleges and universities. Today they ask whether traditional forms and emphases must be altered in order to reach the educational goals they now have in view.

Catholics in College 306 (U. of Chicago, 1967): "Two writers in particular have taken note of the innovations, of the upgrading of facilities, and curricula, and of the general educational development under way at Fordham University and the University of Notre Dame. These universities were observed to be making great strides toward educational excellence . . . But either directly or tacitly two questions were posed in the articles: Can these universities indeed become great universities? If they become great centers for intellectual inquiry, can they remain Catholic? Both questions were left unanswered."

[27] Compare, e.g., The Report of the President, Fordham University, 1965-1967, at 2-3: "There are outside pressures on every university—state university or private university, Catholic or without any religious affiliation. It is very hard to convince people who do not know, and just as hard to convince people who should know, that the pressures on a Catholic institution are not greater than the pressures from the state legislature or from major benefactors or from football coaches or from the athletic enthusiasts among the Alumni. In the popular mind (whatever that is), a visible or invisible cleric, located near or far, is thought to have more power than all these other pressures combined. And there are those who proclaim that a college can exist only if it is free of ecclesiastical control. And I am sure they mean it. I am not at all sure that they are right but I am certain that there have not been any pressures from ecclesiastics during the last two years."

CHAPTER 2

The Denominational University
Under The Law*

Will a previously Catholic institution of higher learning gain a greater measure of public assistance if it casts off religious ties? The answer to that question is surprisingly unclear. It must rest upon the somewhat shifting sands of both federal and state constitutional law. It may be affected by the precise kind of public assistance desired, as well as by the ingenuity of those who in future years seek to turn to the fullest social advantage the existence of educational pluralism in the United States.

Numerous statutes in the several states now differentiate between sectarian and nonsectarian institutions. This is not entirely a matter of legislative choice, subject to being changed by normal political processes. The differentiation is at least in part a recognition of constitutional limitations—limitations whose precise extent have yet to be determined, but which nevertheless dominate every discussion of aid to colleges and universities that are linked with religious organizations.

Federal constitutional law. Financial assistance from the federal government to private institutions must conform with the Constitution of the United States, whose First Amendment declares that "Congress shall make no law respecting an establishment of religion, or prohibiting the free exercise thereof." The same restriction rests upon state legislatures, wholly independently of the often more sweeping provisions found in state constitutions.

Only twice in all the years since 1791, when the First Amendment came into being, has the Supreme Court fully considered whether that amendment prevents expenditure of public funds in ways deemed

---

* The matters discussed in this section are considered in greater detail, with extensive documentation and with explanation of various analytical approaches, in Appendix A at pages 131-181.

9

beneficial to denominational educational institutions. In 1947, the Court upheld New Jersey's paying for school buses that carried children to Catholic parochial schools.[28] The legislative plan, the majority said, was for the benefit of children and their parents, and was not a hidden (and forbidden) aid to religion. Despite the permissive holding, the prevailing opinion stressed the necessity of maintaining an unbroken "wall of separation" between Church and State. To prevent any chipping away at that wall, the Justices added, taxes must never "be levied to support any religious activities or institutions."[29]

The Supreme Court's second encounter with public aid to sectarian schools occurred in 1968, when six of the nine judges held that publicly-purchased textbooks in secular subjects could be provided for use by New York's parochial school students.[30] The majority

---

[28] Everson v. Board of Education, 330 U.S. 1 (1947).

[29] 330 U.S., at 16. Throughout the many years since the Everson case, commentators have been busily suggesting how to apply the principles it announced. Absolutely contrary positions have been supported by reliance on rich passages culled from the Everson opinion. Some who believe that aid of any kind is constitutionally improper have argued that the actual decision was inconsistent with the opinion. In their view, transporting children to school is an assistance to the school, not merely to the child; it is not, they contend, a general public service provided indiscriminately for everybody (like police and fire protection), but is a means of facilitating education that has religious overtones, and this, they argue, is impermissible. Other lawyers in recent years have, however, adopted a less absolute position. They tend to conclude that payments for bus transportation and other fringe forms of assistance, like hot lunches and medical care, are constitutionally colorless. In their opinion, the Constitution would be a barrier only if governmental aid were directly related to the educational function as such, rather than to the children who are being educated. Some who espouse the "child benefit" or "pupil benefit" theory go somewhat farther; they say that money can freely be provided for avowedly educational needs (such as textbooks or scholarships) so long as no money is given to the schools themselves, but only to those who attend them. Going beyond even this generous reading of the Everson case, some authors maintain that aid can be given directly to a sectarian school, if the gift be earmarked for secular activities (such as. for example, physical education or instruction in German). Other writers have contended that public aid can, and perhaps must, be given sectarian education so that parents may freely exercise their religion by sending their children to parochial schools. They fear that exclusive assistance to public education might have the effect of establishing the religion of "secularism." One respected author has contended that the Free Exercise and Establishment Clauses preclude any and every statutory differentiation based on religion; this leads him to believe that parochial schools not only may be allowed, but must be allowed to share in whatever benefits may be conferred upon other kinds of private schools.

This summary of conflicting interpretations of and proposed additions to a supposedly authoritative exposition of constitutional doctrine perhaps adequately suggests that we are not here dealing with a "well settled field of law." For further development of contending theories, see Appendix A.

[30] Board of Education v. Allen, 392 U.S. 236 (1968).

opinion, couched in language more permissive than that used in the
New Jersey schoolbus case, emphasized that parochial schools perform
distinctly secular functions that can be disentangled from their religious activities. At the least, the opinion adopts a more expansive
version of the "child benefit" theory than had the New Jersey case,
two decades earlier. Its language, indeed, may be broad enough to
cover grants directly to sectarian schools, if restricted to well identified secular purposes.

Both of these important Supreme Court judgments related to
schools for children of tender years. Never has the Court considered
whether aid to denominational colleges or universities raises fresh
questions. Not long ago, it declined to do so when asked to review a
decision of the Maryland Court of Appeals, striking down grants to
sectarian colleges for secular purposes.[31]

Hence nobody as yet knows whether the Court would hold, as
some have predicted, that the Constitution may permit more extensive aid to religious colleges than to lower schools. The desirability
of maintaining pluralistic higher education, coupled with the supposedly greater maturity of college-age students, has bulked large in
the arguments of those who believe that the First Amendment will
not bar broad programs of aid to higher education.

Without pretending that the outcome can be foretold with great
confidence, we remain highly doubtful that unrestricted public grants
may be made to colleges closely identified with religion. We have,
however, concluded that the Supreme Court will probably find no
constitutional impediment to giving public moneys to sectarian colleges if their expenditure be limited to specific secular objectives. The
Court's refusal to review the Maryland case referred to above does
not, we think, connote acceptance of the Maryland judges' reasoning, which was formulated before the Supreme Court's most recent
utterance concerning expenditures for parochial students' school-
books. Nor, in our judgment, has the Court in any way precluded a
holding that, so far as the Constitution of the United States is concerned, public aid to colleges may possibly be more open-handed than
public aid to schools.

Federal statutory law. The as yet somewhat spotty federal legislation in aid of higher education has not drawn differentiations between sectarian and non-sectarian institutions. Many of the pertinent

31 Horace Mann League v. Board of Public Works, 242 Md. 645, 220 A. 2d. 51, appeal dismissed and cert. denied, 385 U.S. 97 (1966).

statutes do, however, declare theological schools to be ineligible for federal grants. They also exclude financial aid for programs designed to train teachers of religion. The grants contemplated by the present statutes may be made only for specific purposes, such as the construction of dormitories or science facilities.

Unless public support of church-related education suddenly becomes more politically palatable than it has been in the past, the present pattern of limited aid is likely to continue. If it be challenged on the ground that the federal constitution forbids public gifts to a church-related college, no matter what be the purpose of the gift, we think the challenge will fail. From this follows the conclusion that a college's religious ties will not block it from seeking a share of whatever funds Congress may in the near future choose to devote to strengthening American higher education. We stress again, however, our belief that these funds are unlikely to be made available for general institutional purposes, but only for specific objectives.

State constitutional law. The preceding discussion has dealt with the question of whether aid to religion-related colleges and universities is blocked by the vague words of the First Amendment of the federal constitution. As to that, we have expressed the optimistic belief that at least limited financial support can be given constitutionally. Our conclusion is strongly to the contrary as to the permissibility of *state* aid under *state* constitutional provisions, particularly under those which resemble the one now in force in New York:

> Neither the state nor any subdivision thereof shall use its property or credit or any public money, or authorize or permit either to be used, directly or indirectly, in aid or maintenance, other than for examination or inspection, of any school or institution of learning wholly or in part under the control or direction of any religious denomination, or in which any denominational tenet or doctrine is taught, but the legislature may provide for the transportation of children to and from any school or institution of learning.[32]

Like the Supreme Court of the United States, the New York Court of Appeals has upheld textbook aid to parochial school students.[33] The decision—which was concurred in by only four of the

---

[32] New York State Const., Article XI, §3.

[33] Allen v. Board of Education, 20 New York 2d 109, 228 N.E. 2d 791, 281 N.Y.S. 2d 799 (1967), aff'd, 392 U.S. 236 (1968).

seven judges—sustained the argument that aids to children were not direct or indirect aids to school, which themselves received no state funds. If grants were to be made directly to denominational colleges, to be expended by them for even an incontestably secular purpose, a similarly generous reading of the constitutional language would be impossible. We see no escape from the conclusion that institutional grants would be "used, directly or indirectly, in aid or maintenance" of the institutions to which they were given—and that this could not be constitutionally accomplished as to any institution of a denominational character.

This was plainly the opinion of New York's Attorney General when in 1967 he ruled that the state could not finance a distinguished professorship created at Fordham University as contemplated by the legislature. It was also the opinion of the Select Committee on the Future of Private and Independent Higher Education in New York, which in 1968 urged upon New York the desirability of subsidizing universities throughout the state, but foresaw that denominational institutions of higher education would remain unhelped unless a constitutional amendment were adopted. The legislature, acknowledging the desirability of aiding the private institutions in which so many young New Yorkers are educated, authorized a yearly subvention for degree-granting colleges and universities within the state, but specifically excluded all those ineligible under the state or federal constitution.[34] In administering the new law, the State Education Department will clearly not permit funds to flow to colleges and universities it considers sectarian, because they are barred by the Constitution of New York. Possibly, indeed, this kind of aid would be held inconsistent with the United States Constitution, even though, as we have said, sectarian institutions are probably eligible for other forms of assistance under the federal charter. Denominational institutions will, therefore, be unable to share in the benefits soon to be enjoyed by independent institutions, though all, whether independent or denominational, will share the same burdens of rising costs and expanding demands for service.

We do not, however, foresee a similar difficulty in respect of New York's extensive program of scholarship aid. Scholarship grants are made to students, not to institutions. If the program be challenged

---

[34] New York Laws 1968, Chap. 677, Education Law §6401. The amount of the subvention is to be determined by the number of degrees awarded—$400 for each bachelor's or master's degree, $2,400 for each doctorate.

because some of the scholarship recipients choose to expend their allotments, for tuition at a denominational college, we expect that the program's validity would be upheld.

Conclusion. Emerging from the preceding synopsis of legal materials presented more extensively in Appendix A, are these propositions:

1) An institution administratively or judicially determined to be "wholly or in part under the control or direction of any religious denomination, or in which any denominational tenet or doctrine is taught" will certainly be debarred from New York State or municipal subsides, which would be available to help meet the institution's general needs if the institution were regarded as independent;

2) A denominational institution's eligibility for grants under most of the now existing federal programs seems likely, though graver questions would arise if—as appears to be improbable in the immediate future—less restrictive programs of aid to higher education were enacted;

3) The constitutional issues sketched in these pages have not yet been clearly settled by the courts. They have historically aroused strong feelings among principled persons who hold opposed views. Considerable litigation, with its consequent distractions and possible legacy of bitterness, may therefore be forecast before authoritative decisions have removed all dispute.

Fordham University at the close of the academic year 1967-1968 was clearly one of the institutions affected by these propositions. If, however, it desired to do so, it could readily alter its status from that of denominationalism to that of independence. The means of accomplishing this result can be identified. Their palatability can be considered. Later pages summarize the measures that deserve attentive thought by an institution desirous of changing its personality, as it were.

Changes, if they be decided upon, must be more than nominal. The academic world as well as the officials who control public expenditures must be convinced of their reality. They deserve to be considered at all by an institution of Fordham's stature and pride only if they seem likely to make for educational advances. If Fordham were to change its identification, the motive would not be materialistic. Achieving eligibility for public subsidy is not in itself the end in view. It is simply one of the means that may conduce to the end of strengthening an already strong university. Achieving that desired goal will require not merely governmental decisions about institutional status. It will require also retaining the enthusiastic loyalty of those who, in the past, have contributed so greatly to Fordham's growth. To that loyalty must be added the enthusiastic approval of the community at large, and especially the academic community from which Fordham will draw many of its future scholars and teachers.

CHAPTER 3

The Identification of
Catholic Higher Education

The influence of Protestant churches upon institutions of higher learning has been almost infinitely varied in intensity and in manner of expression. It has ranged from rigidly imposed orthodoxy to vague benevolence. It has drawn force from many sources—at the one extreme, the simple power of example and personality; at the other, the formal instruments of governance. Often in the past and less often in the present, all or substantial numbers of the trustees who legally control an institution's affairs have been selected by a church body. This alone, one might suppose, might firmly fix the religious character of that institution. But the supposition does not always accord with the facts. The relationships between church and institution have sometimes become so perfunctory that the former's supposed dominance is a façade rather than a reality.[35] Although the situation may once have been different, a recent thorough study of church-sponsored colleges in this country concludes that in the generality of instances, national church agencies at present play "a relatively minor role" in shaping American higher education.[36] Religion and education have become increasingly differentiated in both public and Protestant church-related colleges.

This cannot be said equally about the academic institutions inspired by and under the continuing sponsorship of Catholic ec-

---

[35] This appears to be the case, for example, at Syracuse University, whose charter (New York Laws 1887, ch. 414) declares it to be "non-sectarian," but whose bylaws prescribe in Art. III (2) that eight of its trustees are to be elected as "organization trustees" upon the nomination of the Methodist Church. A similar arrangement exists at Northwestern University. But neither Syracuse nor Northwestern is generally thought now to be under church control or to have a specifically religious orientation.

[36] M. M. Pattillo, Jr. and D. M. MacKenzie, Church Sponsored Higher Education in the United States 276 (Am. Council on Educ., 1966).

18   THE SECTARIAN COLLEGE AND THE PUBLIC PURSE

clesiastical authorities. Professor Paul J. Reiss of Fordham University, fully cognizant of the general trend, observes that Catholic colleges have strongly sought to "maintain the integration of religion and education long abandoned by other private colleges." In his view, "Catholic colleges do not exist that are only nominally or partially Catholic colleges." In no college operated by Catholics, Professor Reiss says, does the Church have only that limited degree of authority it would be able to impose upon private enterprises (such as publishing houses) in which persons of the Catholic faith are active.[37] Whether this condition exists to the extent just suggested is doubted by some Catholic educators; and, even if it does now exist, its probable endurance may be, and often is, debated.[38] At the present moment of time, however, "*Catholic* higher education" remains an accepted concept among Catholics and non-Catholics alike.

An outsider finds considerable difficulty, nevertheless, in ascertaining the precise boundaries of the concept, chiefly because Catholic colleges utterly lack the homogeneity suggested by their common allegiance to the Church. Catholic educators themselves appear to have extremely unclear ideas about what makes a Catholic education distinctive, though most of them continue to speak of it as something unique.[39] The following pages comment upon some of the real or theoretical characteristics of Catholic higher education that supposedly set it apart from other educational endeavors.

---

[37] P. J. Reiss, "The Catholic College: Some Built-In Tensions," in R. Hassenger ed., The Shape of Catholic Higher Education 255 (U. of Chicago, 1967).

[38] In the work just cited, for example, Professor Reiss declares that despite the formal integration of religious and academic authority in Catholic colleges, many colleges in fact operate rather independently of the ecclesiastics who theoretically control them. "As a practical matter," he adds, "many of those in authority in the Church realize that they do not possess specialized competence in higher education, nor the time and energy needed to become directly involved in the operation of colleges within their jurisdictions. The typical pressures toward specialization in large organizations have permitted the development of an actual operating independence of the Catholic college from the dioceses and religious orders that own them. The tensions and conflicts—actual and potential—in this area are high, however, as the degree of independence is often a consequence of practical considerations rather than the product of a consensus of principles." Compare C. Jencks and D. Riesman, The Academic Revolution 375 (Doubleday, 1968), predicting "the eventual triumph of lay professionalism" over any special role of the religious in the Catholic college of the future. And cf. P. Gleason, "American Catholic Higher Education: A Historical Perspective," in the Hassenger volume cited in the preceding note, at p. 17: "The development of Catholic higher education has in fact followed the same general pattern as that of non-Catholic colleges and universities, but has lagged chronologically."

[39] For illustrative discussion, see J. W. Trent, Catholics in College 306 (U. of Chicago, 1967). For a more positive statement of purpose, see M. P. Walsh, The Role of the Catholic University, College Newsletter (National Catholic Educational Association), vol. XXIX, no. 2, p. 1 (Dec. 1966).

SOME SUPPOSED CHARACTERISTICS

Value orientation. Catholic educational institutions tend to regard themselves as conservators of human values to a degree unusual in secular colleges.[40] They say they are concerned, presumably unlike others, with the development of character and ideals, not merely with polishing the intellect and training for jobs.

In point of fact, most American academic institutions are concerned with character building.[41] They tend to declare that they educate students for living, not for making a living. They are concerned with "the whole man." Through their graduates, they mean to contribute to social improvement, an intention which presupposes values by which to gauge society's bettering or worsening. If the views of Catholic and most other academic institutions significantly differ in this regard, it is because the former may deem religious premises to be intimately related to and often determinative of human values, whereas the kind of "character" the latter try to build may not rest on any explicit theological foundations.

Probably neither the Catholic nor the non-Catholic institutions achieve their philosophical goals.[42] Most students, most of the time,

---

40 Compare A. M. Greeley and H. H. Rossi, The Education of Catholic Americans 6 (Aldine, 1966), ascribing to the proponents of education in religious schools the belief that "secular schools inculcate, at best, no values at all, and at worst, the wrong ones." This leads to the conclusion that "religion must be taught in school, preferably a school which will train its graduates in the usual academic subjects and prepare them for entry into American society and, in addition, develop in these graduates the proper value orientations and a strong sense of attachment to the Church."

41 A Jesuit writer has no doubt correctly asserted that "a zeal for the development of strong moral character is the single most common feature among philosophies of education from the primitive to the sophisticated and from the Christian to the Soviet"—though of course, as he adds, different systems may seek the desired end by different means. J. W. Donohue, Jesuit Education 160 (Fordham, 1963).

42 Compare Greeley and Rossi, note 40 above, at 54, commenting upon discussion of whether Catholic education has attained the philosophical goals laid down by popes or bishops. The authors conclude, realistically, that an educational system's philosophical goals "are just that: goals to be striven for, not objectives to be reasonably expected. The goals of Catholic education are anything but modest: they envision an adult who, if he were not a candidate for canonization, would surely be thought a rather remarkable human being. Christians who adequately reflect the model of behavior presented in the Gospels have been something of a rarity in the last two millenia, and to expect Catholic schools to accomplish on a large scale what the Church has not been able to during the first two thousand years of its history is somewhat naive." The authors also remark (at p. 7): "As social scientists, we maintain a skeptical view concerning the efficacy of formal schooling for the teaching of values . . . . The classrooms . . . . may contribute somewhat to the maintenance of a core culture or the creation of a cultural synthesis. But whether formal education really has much influence on either cultural values or social behavior is not evident. Most sociological inquiries

have in view objectives of their own, by which they are dominated far more than by the declared aims of their alma mater.[43]

Preservation of faith. Some, but not all, Catholic educators believe that they place greater stress on the centrality of man's relations to God than do teachers in nonsectarian institutions. This stress on transcendent values can of course emerge as stress upon particular doctrines or, in blunt terms, as indoctrination rather than as education.[44] The inculcation of piety and the reinforcement of Catholic theological convictions were undoubtedly among the main objectives of most Catholic institutions in times past, when public attitudes toward Catholicism were less benign than now. Moreover, room for debate and exploration tended to be narrow so long as Catholic educators were comfortably confident that correct answers had already been given to most questions worth asking. A sympathetic writer has pithily said that the earlier Catholic colleges "were not so much concerned with the pushing back of the frontier of truth as with passing on a given tradition of truth in which little in the way of addition or alteration was necessary."[45]

Even today many Catholic institutions exhibit a degree of intellectual quiescence that genuinely questing minds rarely achieve. Unlike their more sophisticated and better known contemporaries in Catholic academic circles, they speak and sometimes act as though preserving their students' faith were, for them, a far more compelling purpose than imparting an education in the arts and sciences. Thus, for example, a well established women's college declared in an institutional self-study that it "harmonizes" its entire "program with the

---

suggest that the more intimate settings of household, neighborhood, friendship, and workplace provide more effective modes of socialization than formal indoctrination."

43 Compare A. M. Greeley, Religion and Career: A Study of College Graduates 73-86 (Sheed & Ward, 1963): Denominational education through the high school and college years has seemingly created little difference in occupational values and career plans, moderate differences in church attendance, and moderate differences in expectations of life happiness between Catholics from the denominational colleges and Catholics from other schools.

44 Compare R. F. Drinan, The Constitution, Governmental Aid and Catholic Higher Education 9-10 (Nat. Cath. Educ. Assn., 1968): "Catholic colleges have in general remained the most value-oriented of all the church-related and private colleges in America. Such a status brings potential advantages and definite disadvantages. The potential advantages arise from the real diversity and true pluralism which Catholic colleges represent in American higher education. The disadvantages come from the possibility that Catholic colleges might be considered to be so denominational and sectarian that they would be deemed legally disqualified from receiving governmental assistance."

45 A. M. Greeley, The Changing Catholic College 26 (Aldine, 1967).

philosophy and theology of the Catholic Church;" the program is so organized that each student's "life and study and the atmosphere of the college are permeated, motivated, enlarged and integrated by the Catholic way of life as developed and expressed in the daily prayer, liturgy, sacraments and Holy Mass of the Church." According to a student handbook issued by the college, "Since the Christ-thought, the Christ-word and the Christ-deed are the norms of community living in a Catholic college for women, intimations of this presence should be found everywhere: In the chapel—[and] in the class room."[46]

Strongly stated religious purposes may be accompanied by distinctly doctrinal limitations upon academic freedom. The faculty handbook of the same women's college states: "We recognize that academic freedom must be exercised in a framework of academic discipline. Restrictions on human freedom are often necessary to insure greater human freedom. There is a body of objective truth made known to man by divine revelation which must be accepted for right living and a happy ultimate destiny. . . . When these truths are defied we must determine what is academic freedom and what is academic license. Absolute academic freedom cannot exist, nor is it desired in a Catholic college since the college imposes the restriction of religious orthodoxy."[47]

Although the quoted passages accord with uninformed impressions of Catholic education, many influential Catholics have flatly repudiated the underlying conceptions.[48] Nor does heavily emphasized

[46] Horace Mann League v. Board of Public Works, 242 Md. 645, 220 A. 2d. 51, appeal dismissed and cert. denied, 385 U.S. 97 (1966), Joint Record Extract at 90, 97, 465, 469; see also 310, 346, 354. And compare E. J. Power, History of Catholic Higher Education in the United States 34 (Bruce, 1958), discussing creation, at an archbishop's request, of a women's liberal arts college that would serve as "a center for missionary activities" and enable young ladies to "cultivate the moral virtues." But of course institutions may change, despite their founders' hopes and their present patrons' expectations. Compare R. Hassenger, "Portrait of a Catholic Women's College," in Hassenger, note 37 above, at 100, commenting on the attitudes of nuns who had pursued graduate studies in secular universities; the author concludes that in 1966 Catholic colleges for young women "can no longer be counted on to 'assure the parents of a safely hermetic, if not ascetically uncomfortable, education for their daughters.' "

[47] Horace Mann League v. Board of Public Works, note 46 above, Joint Record Extract. at 144. See also id., at 333. This policy may be less confining than appears at first glance, since teachers may allowably present views opposed to the Church's teachings, so long as they label them opinions and do not endorse their validity. See id., at 365-366, 369-381, 471, 479-488.

[48] See, e.g., Drinan, note 44 above, at 39, calling for recognition by Catholic colleges that "their primary and principal purpose is to impart an education in the arts and sciences as such—to Catholics, non-Catholics and non-Christians."

piety accord with the avowals or the behavior of Catholic colleges and universities as a whole. No single pattern of educational practice or philosophy can now be found in Catholic higher education. As is equally true of other religion-related institutions and also of those that are wholly state-controlled, "there is a vast diversity and pluralism within Catholic higher education, with some schools being very promising and exciting and others being very dull and discouraging."[49] They do apparently stress theological propositions more than do most other institutions of higher learning. Sometimes this is done by interstitial references to articles of the faith.[50] Sometimes (not always happily) it is done through course requirements.[51] The required courses may in some institutions be little more than exercises in memory; non-Catholics may be excused from the exercises, thus emphasizing their doctrinal as distinct from educational content.[52] In other institutions, by contrast, the specified courses may have a markedly intellectual focus, involving comparative studies in the field of religion, or searching scrutiny of theological concepts.

As to the remainder of the course offering, the curricular design of most church-related institutions is said to be "quite similar to that of other undergraduate colleges; specifically a balance among the broad fields of knowledge is usually provided through a plan of election within distribution requirements."[53]

---

[49] Greeley, note 45 above, at 17.

[50] Id. at 62, recording an interview with the president of a leading Catholic university, who summed up as follows: " 'How is this school different from any other American school? Well, I suppose we teach four or five themes here that you might not find at every school.' We asked him if this meant four or five courses and he said, 'Oh, no, it just meant four of five themes, like there is a God, there is a human soul, there is a life after death, that sort of thing.' " And compare the official catalog, 1966-1968, of Bellarmine College, Louisville, Kentucky, which says, "The truth which Bellarmine as a Catholic college strives to lead its students increasingly to love is not to be understood merely as coexistence with the truth which human intellect can discover by its unaided natural powers. It proclaims that there is a higher and more certain source of truth, namely, the divine revelation entrusted by God to His Church."

[51] Greeley, note 45 above, at 134-37, 179 discusses the frequently inadequate teaching skills devoted to courses in theology and remarks that the students in general "bitterly resent both the boredom and the compulsion of such courses." And see also Trent, note 39 above, at 272, reporting adversely on the value of most of the required courses in theology, as now presented in Catholic colleges.

[52] Compare J. Foster, "Some Effects of Jesuit Education: A Case Study," in R. Hassenger, note 37 above, at 165-166.

[53] Pattillo and MacKenzie, note 36 above, at 92. And see Horace Mann League v. Board of Public Works, note 46 above, Joint Record Extract at 77, 498-499, 507, 511-513, 521, 525-526, testimony of teachers that church doctrine has no effect on the content of their liberal arts courses.

Control over student conduct. To an extent now unusual (though not absolutely unknown) in other institutions of higher learning, Catholic colleges still prescribe their students' overt religious behavior. Many other—including, notably, Fordham—impose no ritual duties whatsoever, though they do offer generous opportunities for voluntary worship. Those who have observed Catholic institutions agree, in any event, that maintaining students' attendance at Mass and at the sacraments has been widely though not invariably accepted as an important institutional function.[54]

A recent critique of Catholic higher education declares that those who have fought against academic modernization have made control over students their "last desperate battleground." The old narrowly ecclesiastical approach to higher education, the critique concludes, "is slowly dying. However, its death is the slowest and most painful in the area of student life on Catholic campuses."[55] Even so, compulsory attendance at daily Mass or at Sunday worship is no longer commonplace in Catholic colleges.

A compulsory annual retreat does seem, however, to be usual in Catholic institutions of higher learning, including some of those under Jesuit control. Fordham is no longer among them in regarding the retreat as a student obligation. Continuation of this tradition is far from universally acclaimed by Catholic clerical educators.[56]

---

[54] Sociological studies tend to show that Catholics who have attended a Catholic college are more orthodox doctrinally and more diligent in worship than are their contemporaries who went to non-Catholic institutions. See, e.g., R. Hassenger, "The Impact of Catholic Colleges," in Hassenger, note 37 above, at 120; Greeley and Rossi, note 40 above, at 166-167. Whether this is because of the colleges or because those who chose to attend Catholic colleges were already somewhat determinedly religious in attitude, is difficult to ascertain. The family influence that pushed them toward a Catholic college may also have pushed them toward church attendance in post-college years. Compare Trent, note 39 above, at 312: "The data reveal a pervasive operation of self-selectivity among Catholic college students. Generally, the better, more intellectual students are not attending Catholic colleges. The colleges are recruiting students who in many cases are intellectually restricted products of an intellectually restricted Catholic education."

[55] Greeley, note 45 above, at 177.

[56] See. e.g., Greeley, note 45 above, at 178: "We were assured by otherwise intelligent and sensitive Jesuit educators that when the obligatory annual retreat was eliminated, the school would stop being a Jesuit institution. Despite this, some eight or nine Jesuit colleges have already eliminated the retreat and still seem to be securely in control of the Jesuit order. One Jesuit president remarked, 'St. Ignatius of Loyola would be scandalized to know that his Spiritual Exercises have been made a requirement for graduation.' Another Jesuit educator assured us that even though the retreat really didn't build up much in the way of good habits, it forced the young men and women to make at least 'one good confession' every year and that this was in itself enough justification for the obligatory retreat. It did not apparently occur to him that if only 'one good

Concern with student behavior does not stop, in Catholic institutions, with matters directly touching religion or religious observance. Of course not all institutions can be lumped together, but evidence does exist that student self-determination—as measured by such indicators as freedom of the press and ability to invite desired speakers to appear on campus—is significantly less cherished in Catholic colleges as a whole than elsewhere.[57] More dogged paternal (or maternal) supervision has continued in Catholic student residences than is now likely to be found in more sophisticated—or, perhaps, simply more abandoned—institutions elsewhere. At least until recently every dormitory in a western Jesuit university "had one or more priests living in it, and rooms were inspected for infractions of the rules. Discovery of a copy of *Playboy*, for example, could involve certain penalties."[58]

Choice of faculty members. Very few church-related colleges, a survey has established, "restrict faculty appointments to members of their own churches. People who think that rigid sectarianism is the principal defect of church-related higher education are fifty years behind the times."[59] This statement can no doubt be made truly as to both Protestant and Catholic institutions. Neither group *restricts* appointments to co-religionists.[60] Neither has as its principal defect a *rigid* sectarianism.

---

confession' a year was all the young people would make, there might be something drastically wrong either with American Catholicism or with Jesuit higher education. Nor did it occur to him that this one compulsory confession might be obtained at the price of turning the young people against retreats, against Catholic higher education, and against the Church itself. Finally, it has apparently not occurred to some Catholic educators (or, for that matter, students or parents) that to expel a young person because he has not attended a religious service which is not required by the general law of the Church might be an atrocious and intolerable infringement of the student's human freedom."

[57] E. G. Williamson and J. L. Cowan, The American Student's Freedom of Expression 159-162 (U. of Minn., 1966). And compare R. F. Weiss, "The Environment for Learning on the Catholic College Campus," in Hassenger, note 37 above, at 81: "Probably the most noteworthy over-all finding to emerge from this study is the confirmation that Catholic institutions do vary widely among themselves, particularly in such sensitive areas as the encouragement of student freedom and of individual responsibility, and participation in the development of policy. There is a definite tendency, however, for Catholic colleges and universities to rate somewhat lower in this regard than most other institutions."

[58] Foster, note 52 above, at 164.

[59] Patillo and MacKenzie, note 36 above, at 88. But cf. the authors' remark (at 87) that "Institutions commonly seek some evidence of religious affiliation in prospective teachers, but too often nominal church membership is regarded as sufficient."

[60] A significant number, however, do appear so to restrict appointments to the theology department, and, especially among Catholic colleges, the philosophy department. See Horace Mann League v. Board of Public Works, note 46 above, Joint Record Extract, 736-737.

The probability remains, however, that religion has often been a consciously dominant factor in choosing faculty members of Catholic colleges and, to the extent that members of a sponsoring religious body of priests or nuns may have been available, has been decisive.[61]

This is partly explicable on purely economic grounds. Survival of many institutions, whose treasuries could not have met a normal academic payroll, has been made possible by the dedicated members of religious orders who have contributed their services as faculty members. In many of the smaller and financially weaker colleges religious personnel have provided the great bulk of teaching.

But even this characteristic of Catholic educational institutions has undergone great change in late years. The percentage of the faculty drawn from a teaching order has declined as courses have proliferated. The numbers of the religious have simply been unable to keep pace with the enlarged demand.[62]

Although Catholic universities and colleges have not insisted that all lay faculty members be committed Catholics, appointees have nevertheless been preponderantly of the Catholic faith. This is not primarily a consequence of intentional discrimination. Institutions with a strong religious identification are simply more likely to attract faculty members from that religion than from others. This tendency is particularly pronounced when, as some Catholic colleges have done, the employing institution informs prospective teachers that particular religious attitudes are intended to be reflected in all phases of instruction. In some instances Catholic colleges have explicitly declared their expectation that all faculty members will understand and sympathize with the principles of Catholic philosophy.[63] Although that expectation may in fact rarely or never cause a denial or termination of employment, its expression in itself probably lessens the willingness of non-Catholics to seek appointment. Moreover, altogether apart from any desire to give preference to members of the Church, Catholic

61 Compare Foster, note 52 above, at 32, asserting that in the university then under study, "Hiring was strictly an administrative prerogative . . . When the introduction of anthropology into the curriculum was proposed, the dean made the unwelcome judgment that we must certainly get a good Catholic to teach that."

62 Compare J. P. Leary, "The Layman in Catholic Higher Education," America, Feb. 18, 1967, at 251, 253.

63 Horace Mann League v. Board of Public Works, note 46 above, Joint Record Extract, at 44, taken from the faculty handbook of a Maryland college. Another Maryland institution stated in its self-evaluation that it needed a faculty "living in accordance with Catholic teaching and tradition or well disposed toward them." Id. at 312.

institutions have as a practical matter been likely to be acquainted with teachers and students at other Catholic colleges; since personnel recruitment often involves reliance on convenient sources of information, this may result in employing a high percentage of Catholics. This relative insularity is, however, now diminishing. The better Catholic institutions today range far in their search for well qualified instructors; like non-Catholic colleges and universities, they find recruitment of lay faculty to be increasingly difficult in an era when good teachers are in especially short supply. This difficulty, experienced most keenly just when the ecumenical spirit has been blooming vigorously in Catholic and non-Catholic institutions alike, has stimulated Catholic colleges' readiness to employ non-Catholic academic personnel.

The power-wielders. In the early days in this country, bishops seem to have had a major part in shaping, if not altogether controlling, institutions of learning. Manpower needs, far more than ideological conviction, squeezed them out of the academic picture. They could not find enough priests to care for diocesan pastoral duties, let alone to staff a growing number of colleges and universities. So they turned for help to religious communities that were eagerly willing to assume responsibility for educational management. The possibility of transferring academic administration to laymen, as had been done increasingly by Protestant institutions once under clerical control, seems not to have been seriously considered. Education was too interwoven with religion to be removed from ecclesiastical hands.

Furthermore, the religious teaching orders themselves became the promoters of new Catholic colleges in this country. Having no passion for self-minimization, they were not hasty about surrendering power to control the institutions they had founded. A religious community that has borne the burdens of creating a new college believes, according to Father Greeley, that it " 'owns' the school and the administrators merely 'run' it. If the administrators were independent of the religious order, then those who 'run' the school would presumably be independent of those who 'own' it and could make decisions that would be unacceptable to the religious order or to the controlling groups within the order."[64]

Virtually every institution of higher learning, whatever be its religious affiliation and even if it has no religious tie at all, is at least nominally subject to control by external authority. This external

---

[64] Greeley, note 45 above, at 141.

authority may be, as is common among "independent" colleges, a board of trustees, who hold legal title to the institution's assets and who have been given by law "full power to manage the institution."[65] Or it may be, as is common among tax-supported colleges, an elected or appointed board of regents. In many non-Catholic institutions, the external power to make decisions tends to be vestigial, formal, and little noticed, at least in regard to normal university matters.[66] In many Catholic institutions, however, extra-mural control is likely to be a matter of readily perceptible practice rather than mere theory.

This is not to say that academic judgments are constantly subject to revision by shadowy figures in Rome, by the local bishop's bureaucracy, or by higher officers in the religious order that "owns" the institution. Nonetheless, Church authorities in years past have formally or informally reversed decisions that had been made on educational grounds alone.[67] The possibility of their doing so again is perhaps less hypothetical in some of the Catholic colleges than is the possibility that the trustees of, say, New York University or the University of Pennsylvania will impose their judgment on academic matters upon the institutions they supposedly own and govern.

At least some Catholic faculty members are in fact subject to direct religious discipline that can unequivocally restrict scholarly work in ways no longer deemed tolerable in non-Catholic institutions. Some religious orders exercise extremely broad censorial powers; their censors can and sometimes do decide not merely whether a

[65] M. A. Rauh, College and University Trusteeship 13 (Antioch, 1959).

[66] Compare J. J. Corson, Governance of Colleges and Universities 98 (McGraw-Hill, 1960: ". . . since the early eighteenth century, the faculty at Harvard has formed what has been described as 'the immediate government'; since the early 1800s the faculty has constituted a body authorized to exercise substantial powers granted it by the corporation . . . . Thomas Jefferson, when he established the University of Virginia (opened in 1825), stipulated that members of the faculty would have substantial freedom in determining courses of study and maintaining discipline, and as a group broad authority to make decisions about educational program and membership on the faculty. These and other precedents set a tradition that has influenced the governance of American colleges and universities since those early days."

[67] Prof. Gleason has noted, for example, that when Georgetown sought to stress its own character as a university, "the Jesuit authorities in Rome were fearful of seeming to compete with the papally approved Catholic University, and they deliberately curbed the development of graduate work at Georgetown." See Gleason, note 38 above, at 41. Father Greeley reports that a nun "was exiled for several years from a college at the request of a local chancery office which objected to Salinger's 'Catcher in the Rye' being on the reading list." Greeley, note 45 above, at 131.

religious faculty member's writing is consonant with faith and morals, but also whether its publication would be wise.[68]

Yet, if the matter be considered both historically and operationally, the exercise of control by external authorities or persons does not really set Catholic education apart from any other. Although the trustees of prestigious non-Catholic institutions have, in the main, now been tamed to a state of academic innocuity, this was certainly not always the case.[69] Nor, indeed, have all trustees of non-Catholic colleges and universities, whether public or private, been content even in the present day to be less assertive than those who exert pressure on Catholic schools. The reports underlying the American Association of University Professors' list of Censured Administrations provide eloquent evidence to the contrary.[70] "Imprudent" publications have been discouraged in secular as well as in Catholic universities, as could be testified to by the professor in Wisconsin (where dairy products are the backbone of the economy) who had reached the locally unpalatable conclusion that oleomargarine is as nutritious as freshly churned butter. Orthodoxy of opinion has been enforced on non-Catholic as well as on Catholic campuses, sometimes by compulsory expurgations or by fresh affirmations of faith.[71]

---

[68] Greeley, note 45 above, at 132, speaks of a social scientist's five volume work that was banned from publication because the order's censor believed that its appearing in print would be "imprudent." Obviously, only a few decisions about imprudence can go far to discourage future scholarly initiative.

[69] See R. Hofstadter and W. P. Metzger, The Development of Academic Freedom in the United States 156-163, 202-203, 258, 269-274, 420-436 (Columbia, 1955), for illustrations of intrusion by trustees into educational issues of considerable moment. Indeed, during the seventeenth and eighteenth centuries close control by the trustees of educational policy was taken for granted, and in the early nineteenth century "the system of control by a non-resident board, carried over from the colonial colleges, evolved into an instrument of academic government that was officious, meddlesome, and often tyrannical. One finds the trustees of colleges prescribing the work of the classroom, writing the laws of student government, shaping the curriculum, subjecting the private lives of teachers to scrutiny and espionage." Id., at 304. As late as the turn of the century a trustee of Northwestern University could write: "As to what should be taught in political science and social science, they (the professors) should promptly and gracefully submit to the determination of the trustees when the latter find it necessary to act." Id., at 459.

[70] See, e.g., "Academic Freedom and Tenure: Wayne State College (Nebraska)," A.A.U.P. Bulletin, Winter, 1964, at 347-354.

[71] See, e.g., Wieman v. Updegraff, 344 U.S. 183 (1952); Slochower v. Board of Higher Education, 350 U.S. 551 (1956); Baggett v. Bullitt, 377 U.S. 360 (1964); R. M. MacIver, Academic Freedom in Our Time 150-152, 158-201 (Columbia, 1955); G. R. Stewart, The Year of the Oath 82-90 (Doubleday, 1950). And see W. Gellhorn, The States and Subversion 375-382 (Cornell, 1952). See also Patillo and MacKenzie, note 36 above, at 161.

Moreover, just as some non-Catholic institutions resemble their Catholic contemporaries in being subject to external dictation by non-educational power-wielders, some Catholic institutions resemble the better non-Catholic colleges in being essentially autonomous. Our conclusion in this respect is not based on objectively verifiable data, but on numerous conversations with educators who seemed sensitively proud of their academic independence. In neither Catholic nor non-Catholic colleges, we believe, is autonomy so much a matter of law as a matter of mounting tradition. The chief discouragement of "outside interference" in academic affairs is the purely functional discovery that institutions of higher learning cannot be managed by directors whose main interests are non-educational. As Catholic colleges involve themselves ever more vigorously in educational activities going far beyond the communication of established doctrines, they come increasingly to resemble their contemporaries in the realities of governance as well as in the discharge of academic responsibilities.

The distinctiveness of Catholic higher education. The preceding discussion has sought to identify characteristics that might successfully differentiate Catholic higher education from all other. The search has not been fully successful. No doubt significant differences do still exist. By and large, however, Catholic colleges in America—and particularly the leading Catholic universities—have tended to become more and more identifiably American and less and less identifiably Catholic. They no longer offer courses of instruction inspired chiefly, as once they often were, by the academic traditions of Catholic Europe. They desire to be "accredited" by agencies in this country whose measurements of acceptability apply to church-related and secular institutions alike. Students at Catholic colleges plan in ever larger numbers to go on to graduate and professional schools, and this pushes the colleges toward educational programs that will impress those under whom Catholic graduates will subsequently seek to study. The Catholic population from which college students are drawn is not now a disadvantaged socio-economic group, outside the American main stream or marked by distinctive needs or aspirations.[72] Almost without conscious volition Catholic colleges, taken as a whole, have in late years moved from being a cultural resource of the Church to being a cultural resource of the Nation.

[72] A. M. Greeley, Religion and Career: A Study of College Graduates 25-42 (Sheed and Ward, 1963). Findings concerning students' backgrounds are also summarized in A. M. Greeley, The Changing Catholic College 33 (Aldine, 1967).

Yet, despite everything that lessens the isolation of Catholic institutions as a group, belief persists widely among Catholics (and assuredly also among non-Catholics) that the adjective "Catholic" does have distinctive meaning when linked with higher education. Catholic boys and girls comprise the overwhelming bulk of those who attend Catholic colleges; they—or perhaps their parents—were drawn to these schools because they were presumed to be different from others. Catholic colleges themselves sometimes seem somewhat schizophrenic, in one breath proclaiming themselves to be just like everyone else and in the next declaring themselves to be a separate educational species. When individually interviewed in the course of the present study, Catholic educators were hard put to isolate the qualities that made their respective institutions different from others; they tended to fall back upon intangibles—"It's just the atmosphere" or "The presence on campus of the religious members of the faculty serves as a constant reminder to students that you can be an intellectual without becoming an unbeliever" or "Well, you see, it's all a matter of emphasizing the moral ingredients of what we teach" or "We aren't afraid, as a secular institution might be, to pass judgment on moral issues." Even though apparently unable to define more precisely the distinction between Catholic and non-Catholic colleges, few of those interviewed were ready to deem the two groups indistinguishable other than in historical terms.

All of this makes difficult a contention that institutions of higher learning linked with the Catholic Church should be regarded by the public at large as though they were essentially the same as, say, Ohio State University or Vassar College. In any case, it discourages belief that some simple operation—snipping off a small piece here or adding a small piece there—might eliminate lingering doubts about the true catholicity of Catholic colleges and universities.

In the following sections we shall eschew the impossible task of attempting to find one or a few generalizing principles that distinguish Catholic from independent institutions. We shall instead consider the multiplicity of factors that are relevant, focusing particularly on one institution, Fordham University. We shall try to assess which of the characteristics that identify Fordham as Catholic may possibly block its being treated by the law as though it were nonsectarian. We shall also offer suggestions about changes that might broaden still further Fordham's already wide acceptance in the academic community as an outstanding institution judged by criteria applied to non-Catholic universities.

THE MOSAIC THEORY OF SECTARIANISM

If, as has been suggested, no standarized litmus paper test will determine whether an institution should be regarded as basically and independently educational or as basically and dependently an adjunct of denominational activity, how shall the determination be made? Unless and until official views of eligibility change drastically, it must be made somehow if a church-related college or university hopes for general financial assistance out of the public treasury. A determination of status is especially necessary whenever an institution of higher learning in a state with a constitution like New York's seeks municipal or state support that officials must withhold if the institution is "wholly or in part under the control or direction of any religious denomination" or is teaching "any denominational tenet or doctrine."[73]

This branch of the discussion can be commenced by a flatly negative proposition: Assuredly an institution need not expunge every trace of religion or become actively anti-religious in order to prove its freedom from religious domination. Religion has importantly influenced most phases of American life. Ours is a society, an official document has well said, "in which aspects of religion are inextricably entwined with knowledge and culture."[74] Courses in theology and religion can be and are presented in incontestably public institutions of higher learning without successful objection, so long, at least, as their purpose is not to inculcate belief, but to achieve understanding.[75]

---

[73] New York State Const. Art. XI, Sec. 3.

[74] Memorandum of Department of Health, Education, and Welfare, in "Constitutionality of Federal Aid to Education in Its Various Aspects," Senate Doc. No. 29, 87th Cong., 1st Sess. (1961), at 10.

[75] See D. W. Louisell and J. W. Jackson, "Religion, Theology, and Higher Education," 50 California Law Rev. 751 (1962); D. A. Giannella, "Religious Liberty, Nonestablishment, and Doctrinal Development," Part II, 81 Harvard Law Rev. 513, 582 (1968); L. Pfeffer, "Constitutional Aspects of Religion in State Universities," in H. Allen ed., Religion in the State University 44, 48 (Burgess, 1950); Calvary Bible Presbyterian Church v. Board of Regents, 436 P. 2d 189 (Wash., 1967); Note, "Church-State: A Legal Survey," 43 Notre Dame Lawyer 684, 726-734 (1968). And compare the following strong dictum in Abington School District v. Shempp, 374 U.S. 203, 225 (1963): ". . . it might well be said that one's education is not complete without a study of comparative religion and its relationship to the advancement of civilization. It certainly may be said that the Bible is worthy of study for its literary and historic qualities. Nothing we have said here indicates that such study of the Bible or of religion, when presented objectively as part of a secular program of education, may not be effected consistent with the First Amendment."

Nor need those courses be taught by instructors who are themselves unsympathetic with religion.[76] Awareness of mankind's spiritual beliefs and their reflections in human affairs, knowledge of and feeling for the religious documents which have so powerfully molded thought and conduct, sensitive grasp of the conceptions that underlie religious commitment may well be deemed among the fruits of a truly liberal education.[77] Nothing in constitutional theory or in common sense requires that they be altogether withheld from persons educated in institutions desirous of establishing a non-religious character.

Studies of man's religious thought and action are in fact commonplace in private institutions acknowledged by everyone to be "secularized" despite a denominational or, at any rate, distinctly pious past. Wesleyan University and Columbia University serve to illustrate how an educational institution can continue to be mindful of religion without, in the process, becoming regarded as something more (or less) than purely educational.

Wesleyan was founded by Methodists in 1831. Its original charter specified, however, that no institutional rule could "make the religious tenets of any person a condition of admission to any privilege in said University;" specifically, neither the president nor faculty members could be made "ineligible for or by reason of any religious tenets that he may profess, nor be compelled . . . to subscribe to any religious test whatever." Nonetheless, the specific religious orientation of the new university was not left in doubt. Its trustees were to "hold and manage" the University's property in trust for branches of the Methodist Episcopal Church, which continued to be represented on the Board of Trustees until 1937. From its earliest days Wesleyan encouraged religious studies that were Methodist in their flavor. Its 1871-1872 catalogue, for example, spoke of the opportunity then

---

[76] See P. G. Kauper, Religion and the Constitution 109 et seq. (Louisiana St. Univ., 1964).

[77] Compare the views of Reverend Leo McLaughlin, the then President of Fordham University, as reported in the Fiftieth Anniversary Issue of The Ram, vol. 50, no. 3, p. 1, Feb. 7, 1968: "On the purely academic level, it is a fact that religion has influenced the lives of men in all ages and in all places. This fact of man's history can be studied as a purely academic discipline. In fact, if it is excluded from the academic discipline, the university has excluded a very large portion of man's history and culture from its curriculum and one can wonder whether it is truly catholic with a small 'c'.

"On another level, there is the supernatural order. This plays a part in the life of every man. The university is Catholic with a large 'C' if somehow a man completes his program in that university with a greater appreciation of the role of the supernatural in his own life. This may be academic, but it has to go beyond the academic."

afforded for "the study of Theology, the Greek Testament, and Bib-
lical Exegesis," and added that those "who pursue the full course,
including Hebrew, can, with comparatively little extra labor, complete
an extended Theological course." When Wesleyan celebrated its
semicentennial in 1881, the main speaker reminded his audience
that though "no offensive sectarianism" was to be introduced into
instruction or administration, the "guardians of the Wesleyan University . . . always intended that Christianity should be distinctly
recognized in it, and that the general spirit and manner of Methodism
should pervade its philosophy and its worship."[78] Not until 1961
did the Methodist Church act formally "to recognize that Wesleyan
University is no longer related to The Methodist Church and . . . to
so notify the administration of Wesleyan University"—a recognition
that had been sought repeatedly by Wesleyan's president.[79]

For present purposes, the important fact to note is that Wesleyan's separation from the Methodist Church—or, to put it differently,
its secularization—did not cause it to blot out every manifestation
of religion on the campus. In the very year when its independence
was finally acknowledged by the Methodists, Wesleyan's catalog
declared that the Methodist Church had profoundly influenced the
development of the institution, which "remains a small Christian
college placing marked emphasis on religious and ethical values. . . .
Wesleyan, her roots deep in Christian tradition and in liberal and
scientific truth, remains committed to her primary responsibility,
the education of men 'whose labor is in wisdom, and in knowledge,
and in equity.' "[80] An appreciation of religious thought, an awareness
of religious activity that has shaped history, an understanding of
religious organization, past and present, have plainly been deemed
by Wesleyan's faculty to be related to this "primary responsibility."

---

[78] Semi-Centennial of Wesleyan University, June 29, 1881, at 13-14. A revision
of the Wesleyan charter in 1870 had in fact introduced an element of "offensive
sectarianism." It provided in Sec. 5 that "at all times the majority of the trustees,
the president, and a majority of the faculty shall be members of the Methodist
Episcopal Church." This restrictive provision was expunged in 1907, when the
charter was again revised; Sec. 2 specified that "no denominational test shall be
imposed in the choice of trustees, officers, or teachers, or in the admission of
students." For discussion, see W. N. Rice, "The History and Work of Wesleyan
University," in Celebration of the Seventy-Fifth Anniversary of the Founding of
Wesleyan University, Middletown, Conn., 1907, at 49.

[79] Letter Jan. 26, 1961, from Ralph W. Decker, Director, Department of
Educational Institutions, The Methodist Church, to Victor A. Butterfield, President,
Wesleyan University.

[80] Wesleyan College Catalog, 1960-61, at 9, 10.

A recent catalog reveals five history courses and five philosophy courses that heavily stress religion, in addition to twenty-three courses in the Department of Religion itself.[81]

At Columbia College, which is the undergraduate branch of indisputably independent Columbia University, religion enters a great range of course offerings in the departments of Art History, Contemporary Civilization, History, Humanities, and Philosophy among others, in addition to the twenty courses offered by the Department of Religion itself.[82] In Columbia's Graduate Faculty of Philosophy, fifty-two courses are listed under the auspices of the Department of Religion.[83] The content of these numerous offerings need not now be described. Their very existence sufficiently demostrates that in order to be secular, an institution is not compelled to close its eyes (or its students' minds) to religion's significance.

This proposition is perhaps even more strongly supported by the presence in America of great "secular" universities that maintain divinity schools or schools of religion on a parity with other academic units in which advanced degrees are awarded. Harvard and Yale are illustrative.[84] Although these university departments may be ineligible for grants of federal funds under existing programs of aid to higher education, nobody has yet argued that the parent universities are religious institutions in academic garb.

Still, despite these illustrations that secularity in education need not be marked by irreligion, careful note must be taken that all the institutions of learning here mentioned strongly proclaim and conscientiously practice non-denominationalism—or, at the very least, a readily observable multi-denominationalism. Although each is or was historically Christian in emphasis or explicit purpose, all are respectful toward religions generically, and in none is the offered training aimed at demonstrating the validity of a single true faith. By hypothesis each student has retained full power to choose among competing faiths or to construct his own or to have none at all.

[81] Wesleyan University Catalog 1967-1968, at 132-134, 140-142, 143-146.

[82] Columbia College Catalog 1967-1968, at 159-163.

[83] Columbia University Bulletin, The Graduate Faculties, 1967-1968, at 314-323.

[84] See G. H. Williams ed., The Harvard Divinity School (Harvard, 1954); Harvard University Catalogue 1966-1967; Bulletin of Yale University, series 63, no. 22, at 241 (1967).

Neither the faculty nor any other authority has already made the choice, wholly or in large part, in his behalf.[85]

If, then, secularism in education is not merely the antonym of religion in education, and if, nevertheless, significant consequences flow from classifying educational institutions as secular or religious, as the case may be, the would-be classifier must search for other guidelines. Nobody has yet authoritatively identified them. Nobody has said that any one factor, isolated from everything else, will force a conclusion concerning an institution's true nature. The best that can be offered at this point is the approach taken by members of Maryland's Court of Appeals when adjudging various colleges' eligibility for state educational grants.[86] The judges asserted, in essence, that an institutional portrait emerges as does a pattern in a mosaic. A mosaic design is created by putting together fragments insignificant or featureless in themselves, which gain meaning through relationship to other fragments. So, too, the judges thought, could they arrive at a finding about an institution's basic character, by harvesting impressions that acquired persuasive force only when pieced together. The prevailing opinion by Chief Justice Prescott of Maryland suggests that at least the following are matters about which inquiry might be fruitful if a total impression were desired:

1. What the college says about itself; its self-description;

2. The composition of the governing board and the manner of its selection;

3. The nature of the college's administrative staff, faculty, and student body;

4. The college's ties with organizations of co-religionists;

---

85 Compare Gene Currivan's account of the 65th Annual Convention of the National Catholic Educational Association, reporting that organization's conclusion concerning a "new phase" in Catholic education as follows: "The spirit of religion will continue to prevail but in a much more subtle form, designed, especially at the upper levels, to have a much wider and less parochial appeal. It will include, as it does now at many universities such as Fordham and Notre Dame, the discussion of all faiths by men of those faiths." New York Times, Apr. 21, 1968, Sec. 4, p. 52, col. 1.

86 Horace Mann League v. Board of Public Works, 242 Md. 645, 220 A. 2d 51, appeal dismissed and cert. denied, 385 U.S. 97 (1966). The validity of the Court's test of sectarianism does not depend on whether the court was correct in deciding that such a test was needed in that particular instance. Nor does a judgment that an institution is sectarian absolutely foreclose grants to it in furtherance of some specifically defined public objective. This matter is further examined in Appendix A.

5. The extent to which the college is owned by or economically dependent upon a church or its affiliated organs;

6. The nature of the academic and other associations in which the college holds membership;

7. The degree of emphasis upon religious symbols in the college's surroundings;

8. The type of religious observance or activity the college demands, facilitates, or suggests;

9. The college's readiness to present, allow, or encourage on-campus religious activity by groups other than the one with which it has historically been linked;

10. Religion in the curriculum;

11. Extra-curricular programs with a religious flavor;

12. The professional appraisal of the college's program by academic accreditation agencies and other evaluators;

13. The fruits of the college's labors, as reflected in the careers of its graduates;

14. The community's view of the college and what it does.

A listing like that of the Maryland Court asks questions without ever suggesting precisely how much weight may be accorded the answers. Nor does it say which indicators should be accepted as guides when the indicators point in several different directions.[87]

---

[87] In the Horace Mann case itself, Hood College was held to be secular although seven of its trustees were chosen by church bodies, which also contributed slightly to the college's treasury. Moreover, the college professed a religious orientation, required its students to attend chapel, and prescribed a course in Old and New Testament history. On the other hand, its students and teachers were heterogeneous; faculty members were selected without regard to religious beliefs and without restriction upon their freedom to teach as they might wish; and, all in all, the college's sectarian fervor had abated until it had now become a mere recollection rather than a genuine force. Contrarily, Western Maryland College was held to be sectarian. One more than one-third of its trustees were required to be Methodist clergymen; almost all of its teachers were Protestants and about half of them were Methodists; atheists were unwelcome; and affirmative efforts were made to preserve a religious atmosphere on the campus. Two other colleges—Notre Dame of Maryland and St. Joseph—were identified as Catholic (and, thus, sectarian) because virtually all their students professed themselves to be Catholic, as did most of their faculty; members of religious orders comprised a large part of the teaching staff; all students were required to complete courses in theology and philosophy with a Catholic emphasis; and religious observances were frequent. Id at 672-684, 220 A. 2d at 66-73.

Many state constitutions, however, are somewhat more specific in suggesting how and where to draw the line between sectarian and secular universities. New York's basic charter, for example, forbids the granting of public support to any educational institution which is "wholly or in part under the control or direction of any religious denomination" or in which "any denominational tenet or doctrine is taught."[88] These phrases, despite their seeming specificity, do not preclude consideration of the many other ways in which a religious denomination may become intertwined with a university. The constitutional language does nevertheless focus attention on structures of institutional governance more than on institutional atmosphere or image; it also emphasizes that compelled religious observances and course offerings in the religion department count for more than the predominant faith of students or teachers in determining whether a school is sectarian.

Recent New York legislation authorizing direct grants to colleges and universities has left to the State Education Department the task of ascertaining whether an applicant for public funds is eligible to receive them.[89] The Commissioner of Education has instructed each private institution of higher learning in New York that, if it hopes for State aid, it must inform him "concerning the purposes, policies and governance of the institution, and concerning its faculty, student body, curricula and programs."[90] Among the matters he has identified as relevant to the discharge of his responsibility are most of the factors that, as shown on a preceding page, were considered to be significant in the *Horace Mann* case. The Commissioner has especially emphasized denominational connections that might affect selection of students and faculty, and he has also attached heavy importance to the place of religion in the curriculum and college life.

The Commissioner has manifested no desire to place high hurdles in the path of those who seek to establish their eligibility for support. He is no doubt mindful of weighty advice concerning the social desirability of general aid to higher education.[91] Nevertheless New

---

[88] Article XI, § 3.

[89] New York Laws 1968, ch. 677, Education Law Sec. 6401.

[90] Memorandum on Constitutional Eligibility of Certain Non-Public Institutions of Higher Education for State Aid Pursuant to Chapter 677 of the Laws of 1968, August 5, 1968, circulated to Chief Executive Officers attached to a memorandum of August 12, 1968, from Commissioner of Education James E. Allen.

[91] See Report of Select (Bundy) Committee on the Future of Private and Independent Higher Education in New York State, at 47-52 (1968).

York's constitutional restrictions forbid inattentiveness to sectarianism if it does exist, and the Commissioner has now served notice that he, like the Maryland court, will utilize a "mosaic theory" when making determinations of educational status.

This may not give much solace to those who wish for certitude. It does, however, provide justification for a close look at the tiles of Fordham, in order to evaluate the mosaic they form in the aggregate.

CHAPTER 4

Fordham University
As It Is and As It Might Be

The discussion we are about to commence will inevitably have a substantial ingredient of subjectivity. We shall state as conscientiously as we can what we know or think about various facets of Fordham University, but our perceptions rest on months, not years of observation. We shall hazard judgments concerning the significance of things that are being done or left undone at Fordham, but our judgments are, at bottom, mere predictions about how the facts will be appraised by others. For neither our perceptions nor our judgments do we claim verifiable accuracy. What we do claim for them is disinterestedness. We have not sought to support a thesis, formulated in advance by us or by anyone else; and we have not sought to give comfort or offense to holders of any particular opinion concerning the desirable path of Fordham's future.

As noted in the preface, the following pages speak as of the end of the 1967-68 academic year. By means of footnotes and an epilogue, we have attempted to indicate the more important changes at Fordham between this time and late February 1969.

1. FORDHAM'S SELF-DESCRIPTION

An institution, like an individual, is not invariably the most reliable reporter concerning its personality. Nevertheless, self-description is a reasonable starting point for an examination of Fordham's qualities. A difficulty arises here, however, because Fordham's self-description lacks stability. At times Fordham makes itself sound committedly Catholic in the traditional sense, at other times it makes itself sound committedly educational without reference to Catholicism, and at yet other times it makes itself sound simply uncertain. An impression emerges that the primary desire in recent years has been to stress the institution's devotion to educational purposes unin-

39

fluenced by religious predilections; but cultural lag or editorial inattentiveness has made for continuing unclarity in this respect.

Catalogs and bulletins. The undergraduate departments of Fordham are its numerically largest element as well as its emotional center. "An Introduction to the Undergraduate Colleges of Fordham University," a handsomely printed brochure of sixty pages, was made available in 1967 to prospective applicants, school guidance counsellors, and other interested persons. It asserts Fordham's "oldest tradition" to be "its commitment to educate talented young men and women in the liberal arts and basic sciences. This commitment emphasizes a rigorous intellectual formation, which stresses humanistic and cultural values, which is open to students of differing religious faiths and backgrounds, and which provides an opportunity not only for the mastery of secular intellectual disciplines but the possibility of studying them in an environment where religious values have a coordinate presence on the Campus." The brochure then touches upon the resources of the metropolis in which Fordham is located. An historical allusion is made to Fordham's having been "founded under Catholic auspices" and having been "under the guidance of the members of the Society of Jesus." But, the publication declares, the University is "governed by a self-perpetuating independent Board of Trustees, under a charter granted by the New York Board of Regents," and it "is not Church-related in the sense that it receives financial support from a Church body, or that it requires religious practices of its students." The University does express its belief that "the rich intellectual and moral heritage of Catholicism has relevance to a humanistic education and therefore has a place on any campus where the varieties of human experience are studied." The "heritage of Catholicism," however, "should be approached academically, and in comparison with other traditions of present and past societies. The University seeks to attract professors and students from both Catholic and other traditions, in order to provide a more stimulating intellectual environment, and to increase together valuable insight into problems of common interest and concern."

The characterization just quoted seems consonant with generally accepted notions concerning independence.* An institution need not

---

* For more recent self-descriptions that place less emphasis on the University's religious ties, see Student Handbook 1968-1969; An Introduction to the Undergraduate Colleges of Fordham University—1969; Fordham College Bulletin 1968-1969.

forswear or execrate the denominational motivation of its past in order to establish the educational motivation of its present. Nor need it ignore the important part Catholicism has played in shaping world history and culture; it need not pretend an unawareness of "the rich intellectual and moral heritage of Catholicism." A special interest in matters related to particular ethnic or religious groupings is not inconsistent with education that is detached from denominationalism in purpose or in control.[92]

The catalogs of most of the branches of the University are congruous with the paragraphs extracted above from the introductory brochure. Polite bows, to be sure, are frequently made by the catalog-writers toward those who for so many years devoted themselves to Fordham's progress; nobody who reads the catalogs is likely to overlook the institution's Jesuit ties.[93]

In a few instances, however, the official language goes much farther, pointedly suggesting a religious or philosophical framework within which intellectual activity must fit.[94] The 1967-1968 catalog

---

[92] Compare here the following characterization of Brandeis University (which is often popularly referred to as a "Jewish university" or as a "university under Jewish auspices") in C. Jencks and D. Riesman, The Academic Revolution 319 (Doubleday, 1968): "A by-product of the wave of ethnic self-consciousness provoked by the Hitler massacres and the founding of Israel, Brandeis nevertheless chose a name that stressed its commitment to 'American' rather than narrowly 'Jewish' standards of greatness. Avowedly non-sectarian, it placed no special emphasis on either Jewish religion or the Jewish secular radical tradition. It aimed for precisely the same kind of academic and professional distinction as the leading Gentile universities.

"The relationship between Brandeis and the Jews was thus rather like the relationship between the University of Tennessee and Tennesseans . . . It was not that Brandeis was thought to be different from rival institutions, or that its boosters were attracted by unique programs tailored to their specific needs. For both donors and applicants, Brandeis' appeal was simply that it was 'theirs.' The donors were . . . likely to be second or third generation East European immigrants, whose millions would otherwise have built hospitals, bought Israeli bonds, or contributed to Jewish 'civil defense.' Yet it no more occurred to these donors that the Brandeis curriculum or pattern of student life should deviate from nationwide academic norms than that Mount Sinai Hospital should deviate from national medical standards. Brandeis was meant to be 'separate but identical,' a monument to Jewish ability to compete successfully in the non-Jewish world on 'American' rather than distinctively 'Jewish' terms."

[93] See, e.g., Fordham University School of Law, Catalog 1967-1968, at 12: "The School of Law is a community of scholars within the University, enjoying and perpetuating the heritage of Jesuit interest in the law and legal education." This same phrasing appeared in The Self-Study of Fordham University, a report prepared in 1963 for consideration by the Middle States Association of Colleges and Secondary Schools.

[94] In the Self-Study, note 93 above, at 72, the sentence quoted in the preceding footnote was followed by this: "The faculty of the School of Law manifests in its teaching its belief in God as a source of all law. It recognizes and believes in the Natural Law, and adheres in its teaching to the principles of the Natural Law."

of the School of Social Service is illustrative. It states (page 24) that the School "stresses ideals and objectives in line with the social teaching of the Church [including] the supernatural destiny of man [and] the primacy of spiritual values." Nothing in this characterization is inherently objectionable, but all of it is inherently inconsistent with religious neutrality. Our own recent impressions of the School of Social Service lead us to think that the catalog verbiage has become misdescriptive. It is inaccurate not in the sense that the School's teaching in any sense flatly conflicts with the social teaching of the Church, but simply in the sense that what the School actually does is determined without conscious effort to conform with, fortify, or subvert religious doctrines. Later editions of the catalog will no doubt harmonize the School's words with its present practices.

We advise, in any event, that every institutional publication intended to give information about Fordham be subjected now to careful editorial scrutiny. The purpose should of course not be to misrepresent reality by substituting noncommittal blandness for religious declarations. The editing should merely eliminate anachronistic language that may have survived changes in educational philosophy.[95]

In one collateral respect, going beyond phraseology to practice, the University might usefully review the academic calendars disclosed by its scattered units' catalogs. Fordham College has in recent years greatly reduced its observance of religious holidays. In the earlier decades of the twentieth century Fordham suspended classes in order to mark a considerable number or religious occasions (exclusive of the Christmas and Easter vacations—sometimes now called "spring vacations"—that have become commonplace in American educational institutions of every description). In 1966-1967 the number of specifically Catholic observances had shrunk to four—Feast of All Saints, Feast of the Immaculate Conception, St. Patrick's Day, and Ascension Thursday. Not one of these four remained as a college holiday in 1967-1968. Away from the main campus, however, the practice varied. The Law School, for example, suspended its classes in 1967-1968 on the dates of Feast of All Saints, Feast of the Immaculate Conception, and Ascension Thursday; St. Patrick's Day happened to fall on a

---

95 The bulletin of the School of Education, for example, asserts (p. 10) that the School shares "the University's deep commitment to Catholic liberal education" and accordingly "seeks to provide curricula in professional education in which the broad concepts of Christian humanism...have a persistent and enduring role." Thought should be given to whether the true meaning of the quoted phrases cannot be conveyed adequately without suggesting that somehow peculiarly Catholic principles animate this professional school.

Sunday, so that no conflict with classes occurred in 1968. If, as seems to be the case, the changed holiday schedule on the University's main campus is intended to reflect a religious de-escalation, all branches of the University should be brought into conformity with the change.

Faculty Handbook. The Fordham University Faculty Handbook appeared in a revised edition in 1965, at the very time that the University's presidency was changing hands and a new institutional philosophy was becoming manifest. The Handbook (page 9) tells the Faculty, in terms similar to those used in publications addressed to students, that Fordham is not Church-related in the sense of receiving material support from any church body. Fordham is said to be, nevertheless, "a Catholic university in its philosophy and commitments." These are then described in the following general language: "The objectives of Fordham University are . . . the preservation, the interpretation, the transmission and the extension by research of the human patrimony of knowledge, ideals, and values"— which are also, one might add, the declared objectives of virtually all non-Catholic institutions of higher learning. The Handbook continues somewhat more specifically: "As a Catholic university in the Jesuit tradition of personal interest in the individual, Fordham seeks to stimulate its students' growth toward scholarship, informed intelligence, appreciation of spiritual values, and a fuller realization of their personal responsibility to society and to their fellow men. It seeks to strengthen the Catholic student's understanding, appreciation, and practice of his Faith, while making no religious demands upon the non-Catholic. At all times it attempts to demonstrate to the community at large the value of the truths and ideals it cherishes and teaches.

"The University seeks to offer to the members of the faculty a truly Catholic environment and those essential academic facilities whereby scholars, informed with the spirit of the Judeo-Christian tradition, may be enabled through enlightened intelligence and co-operative effort to form a true center of Catholic culture, and to share in that unity of purpose which makes a university out of a collection of schools or departments."

The quoted sentences suggest a rather specific religious focus and a somewhat clearer expectation about faculty members' Catholic orientation than would be anticipated in a non-denominational university. The initial declaration that Fordham is "a Catholic university in its philosophy and commitments" may be merely a flash of rhetoric, but to those who may seek evidence of religious bias, the wording will no doubt prove to be telling. The assertion that the University feels an obligation to strengthen Catholic students' religious practice tends to confirm the view that institutions of higher learning under Catholic auspices are importantly (though not necessarily dominantly) inspired by zeal for Catholicism rather than for education as such. Stress upon creating "a truly Catholic environment" in which scholars may work together "to form a true center of Catholic culture" may connote different things to different readers, but the wording undoubtedly does intimate the unidentified writer's belief that Fordham's intellectual atmosphere is meant to be different from that found in independent universities—and that all faculty members, Catholic and non-Catholic alike, are to join in preserving this special institutional air.

We observe that the Handbook from which the above material has been quoted was published in 1965. A considerable portion of the language now under discussion had been approved by the President and Trustees and initially promulgated by the Academic Vice-President during the summer of 1961.[96] Later pronouncements by the University indicate, we think, that a significantly changed outlook now obtains. The Fordham University Undergraduate Student Handbook 1967-1968 embodies in its introductory description of the University some wording that also appears in the Faculty Handbook, but none of the passages we have just examined. The comparable material in the Student Handbook has been markedly changed, as follows (page 3):

Fordham University, although 126 years old, is a university in transition. Much of the change has been shaped either by changing social conditions or changes in the Church after Vatican II. It has been said that it is up to the universities to play a leading role in furthering the ecumenical movement—and Fordham is determined to be among the leaders in this vital area.

Unchanged, however, is Fordham's determination to provide an enriching opportunity for students to study the various arts and sciences and to prepare for service in certain professions. . . .
In view of modern social, cultural, economic, political and

---

[96] See Self-Study of Fordham University, note 93 above, at 51-64.

religious needs, Fordham seeks to broaden the outlook of its students by bringing the members of its scholarly community into contact with colleagues of every race and religion from all parts of the world.

Even as it adapts to meet modern day needs Fordham wishes to retain its tradition of personal interest in the individual. Fordham seeks to stimulate its students' growth toward scholarship, informed intelligence, appreciation of spiritual values, and a fuller realization of their personal responsibility to society and their fellow man.

This declaration of institutional purpose has a markedly different flavor from the expressions published only two years earlier in the Faculty Handbook, which might now advantageously be harmonized with the Student Handbook.

In this connection we take note also of a proposed new Constitution of Fordham University, the third draft of which, dated April 9, 1968, we have had opportunity to study. The Constitution declares the purposes of the University to be these:

Fordham University exists for the promotion of education in the broadest sense of the term. In pursuance of this objective it seeks to develop an appreciation of man's cultural heritage and to discover and disseminate truth through the orderly pursuit of new knowledge, utilizing in the search for truth all the techniques, new and old, of the various academic disciplines. The University seeks further to provide for persons of all ages organized, objective, and highly competent instruction. As part of the total American and world communities, the University recognizes its obligation to further the general good of society. In pursuit of this social mission the University is prepared to assume such active responsibilities as will further the search for truth and the academic interests of its students and faculty, and as will contribute to the general good. Committed to the belief that the recognition and observance of moral and ethical standards are essential to social harmony and public order, Fordham University seeks to explore and expound the value systems which mankind has found helpful in the never-ending search for peace and harmony. The University considers the transcendental dimensions of man's existence factors in human conduct deserving research and explication. In conducting such investi-

gations and instruction the University spurns indoctrination and
places its reliance upon the methodology of rigorous scholarship.

Although no one word or set of words in a constitution can
conclusively determine a university's nature, adoption by Fordham
of this proposed statement of purpose would more than offset the
doubts the present Faculty Handbook may arouse.

Advertisements. We have reviewed numerous examples of past
and current advertising by Fordham. In advertisements that appear
in periodicals read chiefly by Catholics, we discern a tendency to
stress Fordham's Catholic ties. In *America* and *Commonweal* during
1966 and 1967, for example, Fordham prominently described itself
as "A Catholic university dedicated to the mind and spirit of man,"
stated its determination "to make clear its faith in man and God to
a world which is sometimes frightened of God and despairing of
man," and referred to its sharing in "400 years of Jesuit educational
heritage." In advertisements that have appeared during the past
several years in the metropolitan daily press and in newspapers of
local circulation, Fordham has avoided identifying itself with Catholicism or with religion in the abstract, but has spoken instead
about innovative programs, new facilities and resources, and educational aspirations.

We do not naively suppose that every writer of advertisements
is wholly committed to telling the truth, the whole truth, and nothing but the truth. Nevertheless an institution's published statements
that are calculated to attract new students or financial support can
fairly be regarded as a self-characterization to which weight attaches.
In this context we suggest that Fordham should carefully guide the
advertisement-writers who seek to create its "image".[97] The picture

---

[97] Compare P. J. Reiss, "The Catholic College: Some Built-In Tensions," in
R. Hassenger ed., The Shape of Catholic Higher Education 258, 259 (U. of
Chicago, 1967) : Many institutions face "the basic issue of the relative priority
of religious *vis-à-vis* educational goals . . . At times it appears that schizophrenia
develops over this dilemma, with the college anxious to polish up its secular
image when it comes to seeking government or foundation grants or support
from the general community. At such times recognition is duly made of the
fact that there are non-Catholics on the faculty; that the college accepts students
of all faiths; that the whole range of secular subjects is taught; that large
numbers of professional and business men have been educated for the nation
and the community; that the board of lay trustees includes prominent citizens,
including non-Catholics, and so on. . . . At other times, however—as, for example,
when recruiting students—the Catholic character of the college is played up,
emphasizing that the college provides a 'Catholic education,' that the religious
needs of the students are fully met..."

that may emerge from advertisements should be the same in any event, regardless of where the advertisements have been placed.

Certification under New York Education Law. Fordham University formulated its most unequivocal self-description in a document executed in 1948.

In 1948 New York enacted a prohibition of discrimination in admission of applicants to educational institutions. All New York institutions were directed to accept qualified students "without regard to race, color, religion, creed or national origin." The state legislature acknowledged, however, "a fundamental American right for members of various religious faiths to establish and maintain educational institutions exclusively or primarily for students of their own religious faiths or to effectuate the religious principles in furtherance of which they are maintained." Hence the new statute permitted a limited degree of discrimination on the basis of religion. All that an institution need do in order to be exempt from the law in this respect is to certify in writing to the Commissioner of Education that it is "operated, supervised or controlled by a religious or denominational organization" and that it "elects to be considered a religious or denominational institution."[98]

On October 6, 1948, Fordham University did certify, through its then president, that it was controlled by the "Society of Jesus (Roman Catholic)," thus remaining free to apply religious tests in selecting its students.[99]

Fordham's admissions policies, as we shall have occasion to show in later pages, have by now become non-discriminatory, whatever they may have been in 1948. Since Fordham's own desires and actions are now in fact harmonious with New York's anti-discrimination law, no reason exists for seeking an exemption from the statutory requirements. The certifications of earlier years therefore give Fordham nothing of value to it. So long as they might remain in effect, however, the governmental authorities of New York could scarcely ignore Fordham's own assertion that it is under denominational supervision or control.

---

[98] Education Law Sec. 313 (4) (1953).

[99] Two complaints against Fordham filed with the State Commission Against Discrimination have been dismissed because of its certification. McFarland v. Fordham University School of Social Service, Case No. CE-7277-61, August 21, 1961; Waxman v. Fordham University School of Education, Case No. CE-15416-68, April 30, 1968. Both involved charges of racial discrimination. The two investigating commissioners assumed that the exemption from the prohibition on religious discrimination removes the Commission's jurisdiction in regard to racial discrimination as well, a conclusion not compelled by the statute's language.

Perceiving the desirability of disavowing certifications that had become obsolete, Fordham's president addressed the following communication to the New York State Department of Education on July 19, 1968:

> Fordham University now wishes to withdraw this certificate and elects to be considered as [sic] nondenominational institution for the purposes of Section 313 of the Education Law. The University admits students without regard to questions of religion, race or nationality. No preference in admissions practice is given to any student because of his religious affiliation or lack of religious orientation.

We have no reason to suppose that the Commissioner of Education, who accepted Fordham's self-description in 1948 without independently inquiring into the facts, will hesitate to accept Fordham's revised self-description in 1968.* The only direct consequence of decertification will be Fordham's becoming amenable to a state law from which it has been exempt. The indirect consequence will be erasure of a characterization that, as matters previously stood, might have blocked a fresh and fair examination of what Fordham has truly become.

Contractual characterizations. We have been informed that some of Fordham University's contracts, especially with goverment agencies, characterize it as, specifically, a Catholic institution. We have not ourselves reviewed these documents and are uninformed concerning the reasons they include a religious identification. They should now be reexamined, in our opinion, to ascertain whether their descriptive provisions accord with present facts.

The official seal. Fordham's official seal was designed in 1914. The following description and explanation of it may be found on the inside back cover of the Student Handbook:

> The seal is molded about the coat of arms of the Society of Jesus to demonstrate the fact that the school is under the control and guidance of the Society. Around this appears the name of the University, the date it was founded, its motto, and the various schools. . . . The coat of arms of the Jesuit Order has the Greek letters in the lapidary form of the name of Jesus

---

* Fordham was notified on November 21, 1968 by the State Education Department that its certificate filed under Section 313 was withdrawn.

—IHS—with a cross resting on the bar of the H and three nails beneath. . . . The motto of the University, 'Sapientia et Doctrina,' is situated on a blue scroll below the central shield and rests on a gold field emblematic of learning (Doctrina). Scattered over the field are fiery tongues symbolic of the Holy Spirit of Wisdom (Sapientia). . . .

If Fordham does in fact choose to detach itself from religious governance, it must be watchful about even such small indicators as its traditional symbolism. This does not mean that seals must be smashed and history be rewritten. It does mean, however, that history must be brought up to date. Fordham can continue to acknowledge its having been "under the control and guidance" of the Society of Jesus; but if in fact the nature of the relationship between the University and the Society were in the future to be different from what it formerly was, then the explanation of the traditional symbols should be changed correspondingly by speaking in the past tense.

Believing that seals and other symbols have little more than antiquarian interest for most Americans, we see no reason why Fordham need abandon its present seal in order to help demonstrate its newly developed independence. Coats of arms and other bits of heraldry, including seals and symbols of office, nowadays more often look backward than forward. At Columbia University an important element of the official symbols is a king's crown, harking back to Columbia's pre-Revolutionary existence as King's College. Retaining the crown has not in itself led to Columbia's being denounced as pro-royalist, un-American, or anti-democratic; retaining a remembrance of St. Ignatius should not in itself lead to Fordham's being denounced as denominational. The question that really needs to be explored is whether the Society of Jesus would object to Fordham's continuing to use the Jesuit coat of arms purely decoratively and sentimentally rather than, as formerly, for purposes of identification.

2. THE COMPONENT PARTS OF THE UNIVERSITY

Fordham University, like most great American universities, in many respects resembles a federation of principalities more closely than a monolith. On its two main campuses are located four liberal arts colleges: Fordham College (for men), Thomas More College (for women), Bensalem, The Experimental College (highly unconventional, residential, co-educational), and the Liberal Arts College at

Lincoln Center (opening in 1968). Other preponderantly undergraduate elements are the College of Pharmacy, the College of Business Administration (a graduate school of business will commence operations in 1969), the School of Education (which has a graduate division), and the School of General Studies, which provides non-credit courses for adults and also evening programs that lead to bachelor degrees in business administration, education, and the liberal arts. The Graduate School of Arts and Sciences, on the main Rose Hill campus, has become an increasingly important element of Fordham's claim to recognition as a true university. The School of Law, the first unit to arise at Fordham's midtown campus in Lincoln Center, will soon be joined there by the School of Social Service and the School of Education.

None of these is likely to suggest questions about Fordham's status as a collectivity. Their counterparts—except for the still evolving experiment in Bensalem—are found in many universities. Some of the less prominent elements of the University do, however, differentiate it from the generality of academic institutions. They deserve special attention.

College of Philosophy and Letters. Located at Shrub Oak in northern Westchester County, the College of Philosophy and Letters provides an education for some one hundred and seventy members of the Society of Jesus. Its specific purpose is to equip Jesuits for teaching, educational administration, or postgraduate work and to prepare them broadly for their later theological studies.

The physical facilities, which were newly created at Shrub Oak in 1955, are owned by Loyola Seminary. By a contract entered into by Loyola and Fordham on November 30, 1955, Fordham undertook to "establish an institutional branch" on Loyola property and to assume full responsibility for planning and executing the academic programs that had formerly been Loyola's. Only members of the Society of Jesus could become students at Shrub Oak. Fordham's degrees would be conferred "in accordance with the curricula to be described in the catalogue of the College of Philosophy and Letters, as approved by the academic authorities of the University." Linking Fordham and Loyola was declared by the contracting parties "to be to the mutual advantage of the University and Loyola in their efforts to provide academic training for young men studying as members of the Society of Jesus."

Until 1966 the College of Philosophy and Letters functioned as a three-year college, comprising the junior and senior years of undergraduate work and a year of graduate study. Emphasis was laid on classical languages and philosophy, according to the curriculum that was registered with the New York State Department of Education in 1956. During the years between 1956 and 1966, Jesuit youth completed their freshman and sophomore collegiate studies at "juniorates" elsewhere. In June 1966 one of these—the Collegiate Department at St. Andrew-on-Hudson, in Poughkeepsie[100]—was transplanted to Shrub Oak, which then took the form of a four-year liberal arts college. "The College of Philosophy and Letters thus took the lead," Fordham's president wrote in 1967, "in establishing a new kind of Jesuit house of studies. The graduate program was dropped and the conventional elements of juniorate and philosophate were combined into a unified undergraduate college."[101]

Assuredly Fordham's accepting the burden of conducting a "Jesuit house of studies" has no element of unworthiness about it. It does, however, point strongly in the direction of denominational purpose. The Shrub Oak program is designed solely for Jesuit scholastics; the faculty is composed primarily of Jesuits,[102] and all of the faculty who reside at Shrub Oak are Jesuit. If Fordham were to decide forthrightly to cease being an organizational element of the Society of Jesus, it should by all means consider terminating its responsibility for the College of Philosophy and Letters at Shrub Oak.

We understand that for reasons apart from this institutional matter the University plans such a step. Considerable opinion has

---

[100] St. Andrew-on-Hudson had been affiliated with Fordham University for many years. Although administered by the New York Province of the Society of Jesus and functioning as a religious community in itself, St. Andrew Seminary was theoretically a part of Fordham University by reason of an inter-institutional agreement approved and registered by the New York State Department of Education in 1936. A report by the Middle States Association of Colleges and Secondary Schools in 1950 declared that St. Andrew was in fact "an entirely independent institution" not "in any way an integral part of Fordham University." Academically, St. Andrew "leads its own life under the direction of officers appointed by the provincial authorities and actually in no way is responsible to the Dean of Fordham College." The report urged that St. Andrew-on-Hudson "seek authority from the New York State Board of Regents to operate independently" and that Fordham discontinue "an artificially established control and relationship," created apparently for the purpose of obtaining "a privilege for an institution which this institution deserves on its own merit." The report from which the above material is drawn is set forth in The Self-Study of Fordham University 1963, at 42-43.

[101] Report of the President, Fordham University, 1965-1967, at 20.

[102] At present, the teaching staff includes nineteen Jesuits and only five laymen (most of whom are part-time instructors).

developed in favor of moving Jesuit scholastics from the small world of the isolated seminary to the larger world of the university campus. Father Paul Reinert, the president of St. Louis University, has urged that seminarians, along with other Catholic students, should "study in an atmosphere that is ecumenical and pluralistic. They must learn the give and take of ideas and beliefs because this is the kind of world they are going into."[103] And Rev. R. J. McNamara, S.J., of Fordham's Sociology Department, has similarly advocated that persons preparing for the priesthood should attend an ordinary college instead of a detached academy of their own. Bringing the seminarians to the college campus is already an accepted reality in some areas, and Father McNamara has forcefully outlined the educational benefits achieved by this move.[104]

We have been advised that, responding to considerations like those just outlined, the Jesuit Order—with Fordham's ready assent —now anticipates disbanding the present Shrub Oak establishment.[105] If the plans mature, those who would otherwise have been insolated on the Loyola Seminary campus will be distributed among Jesuit colleges, including Fordham. Those who are destined to be full-fledged Fordham students will be subject to the same admission requirements as others. They will reside apart from other students in an off-campus hall owned and maintained by the Society of Jesus, not by the University.

The absorption of these young Jesuits in Fordham's undergraduate program presents no problem of denominationalism. New York has declared its public policy to be that educational institutions should in no wise "discriminate against any person or persons seeking admission as students . . . because of · · · religion . . ."[106] Fordham need not discriminate against Jesuits, thus violating the law, in order to prove that it is not an instrument of the Society of Jesus.*

[103] Quoted in J. W. Trent, Catholics in College 265 (U. of Chicago, 1967).

[104] R. J. McNamara, "The Priest-Scholar," in R. Hassenger ed., The Shape of Catholic Higher Education 207-209 (U. of Chicago, 1967).

[105] No legal complexities are involved, from Fordham's point of view. A transfer of property rights is not involved because, as already remarked, Fordham does not own Shrub Oak. The 1955 contract with Loyola Seminary permits either party to terminate the institutional relationship by giving twelve months' notice of desire to do so on July 1 of any year.

[106] New York Education Law Sec. 313 (3) (a) (1953). See discussion at p. 79 above. Whatever problems might be caused by Fordham's decertification under this section were a non-Jesuit to apply for admission to Shrub Oak, will be eliminated when and if Shrub Oak ceases to be a Fordham campus.

* For more recent developments, see the Epilogue.

Fordham Preparatory School. Fordham Prep is a secondary school of high repute and distinct promise. It is an integral part of Fordham University.[107] Its presence within the University is in keeping with ancient tradition, for when St. Ignatius laid the foundations of Jesuit education, he contemplated a continuum of instruction beginning at the age of seven or eight and extending into manhood.[108] Economic realities have prevent Fordham Prep's realizing the Jesuit ideal of gratuitous schooling for those worthy to receive it, but the school has undoubtedly provided an excellent educational experience for many eminently promising boys.

The school is located in the very center of the Rose Hill campus. A current campaign to raise funds for a new school building was launched by a gift of $500,000 from the University's none too ample cash resources.[109] Many of the School's graduates have in the past gone on to Fordham College; and today Fordham Prep and Fordham College share in a significant educational experiment—the "3-3 Program"—aimed at completing preparatory and baccalaureate work in six years instead of eight. Sentiment, warm personal associations among Prep School and University staffs, and sheer propinquity combine to give Fordham Prep an important place on Rose Hill. For this reason one hesitates to suggest that the School now be amputated.

Nevertheless amputation must be undertaken if Fordham University is to achieve a new identity. The Preparatory School is unqualifiedly committed to impressing Catholicism upon its youthful pupils. That commitment prevents its fitting effortlessly into a larger institution devoted to educating a diversified group of somewhat older men and women. Until very recently the Prep School said that it "limits its student body so far as possible to Catholic boys who by their native ability, their demonstrated achievement or their families' station in life give promise of future leadership . . . It hopes to produce a Catholic gentleman and leader."[110] Subsequently it softened this by describing itself in its 1967-1968 Bulletin of Information as Catholic in orientation and as conducting a four year

107 The original "college" from which Fordham grew included education at what is now both the high school and the college levels. Not until the early years of this century were the two levels separately identified by name.

108 For general background, see J. W. Donohue, Jesuit Education 3-31 (Fordham, 1963).

109 Report of the President, Fordham University, 1965-1967, at 27.

110 The Self-Study of Fordham University 1963, at 76.

course in Catholic theology, which "non-Catholic students are most welcome to attend." At the same time, the Prep School said that no applicant would be considered unless he had taken "the Cooperative Entrance Examination sponsored by the Archdiocese of New York and the Dioceses of Brooklyn and Rockville Center"—all in all, not a hearty welcome to the public at large. A recent plea by the Prep School for a building construction fund is headed "To Make a Boy into a Man of Christ." It stresses the School's heritage of "Jesuit training and educational excellence." It describes the 'beautiful chapel" with adjoining rooms for instruction in theology. From the roof of the proposed building a skylight "will illuminate the chapel by day, reminding the Prep student of the centrality of Christ in his life as a boy and man, and centering his curriculum and training on Him." The line that divides the inspirational from the indoctrinational seems to be too finely drawn at Fordham Prep to permit the continued inclusion of this excellent boys' school in a non-religious university.

Separating the one from the other may perhaps not be as traumatic as might at first be feared. As long ago as 1931 the then Father Provincial of the New York Province of the Society of Jesus had remarked that in this province only at Fordham had the high school department not been severed from the higher levels; he added that "separation of these departments, at least locally and if possible also in their administrative and financial elements, has been the accepted policy for many years and the complete and entire separation has been effected in most places."[111] Efforts to separate and relocate Fordham Prep followed, but were abandoned in early 1934 when Cardinal Hayes blocked (for wholly non-canonical reasons) a proposal by the Jesuit Fathers to purchase a suitable new site for the school.[112] This bit of Church history gives one reason to believe that no doctrinal objection prevents the proposed institutional surgery, which would simply parallel the operation that separated St. Peter's College (a Jesuit institution) from St. Peter's Preparatory School in nearby Jersey City not many years ago.

Allowing Fordham Prep to retain its present location in the very heart of the University's campus would inevitably generate doubts concerning the finality of the separation of the two educational enterprises on Rose Hill. If Fordham's present contract with

111 Quoted in R. I. Gannon, Up to the Present: The Story of Fordham 189 (Doubleday, 1967).
112 Id., at 191.

Loyola Seminary is terminated as some now anticipate, the vacated Shrub Oak campus might perhaps advantageously be considered as a home for Fordham Preparatory School. Possibly the Society of Jesus might be willing to accept direct responsibility for the Prep School. Donors who generously provided funds for Loyola Seminary's work might not feel that their gifts had been misused if Shrub Oak were utilized during term time as a base for converting Catholic boys into Catholic gentlemen and leaders, while during the summer months it became once again a seminary in which Jesuit scholastics, dispersed during the academic year, resumed their preparation for a priestly life.

As for the "3-3 Program," the removal of Fordham Prep from Rose Hill would in no sense prevent continuation of what appears to be a promising educational experiment. Fordham University's announced readiness to accept suitably recommended students after three instead of four years of preparatory schooling might well become one of Fordham Prep's attractions for especially promising youngsters. At the same time the University might make efforts to institute a similar program with one or more nonsectarian schools.*

Mother Celine House of Studies and Mount Saint Florence. Located in Harrison, New York, some fifteen miles from the Rose Hill campus, the Mother Celine House of Studies is the teacher training school of the Sisters of the Resurrection. In 1953 it was registered by the State Department of Education as an institutional branch of Fordham University, under the special jurisdiction of the School of Education.

In 1956 the Sisters of the Good Shepherd persuaded the University to establish an extension branch of the School of Education at Mount Saint Florence, their training center in Peekskill, New York, about thirty miles from Rose Hill.

Obviously neither of these two establishments, both of them wholly under religious control, has ever been truly an element of Fordham University. Rather, Fordham through them has rendered an off-campus service. Should this service have been regarded as extending the educational reach beyond the conventional academic boundaries or as, at least in large part, a kindness to co-religionists? These questions are suggested by the closed nature of the two institutions for which Fordham has provided instructors and organizational advantages (notably the possibility that novice teachers can

---

* For more recent developments, see the Epilogue.

satisfy state educational requirements without leaving the religious community). A multiplication and variegation of off-campus programs for academic credit might be persuasive that Fordham's interest is truly educational. The contrary impression is strengthened when off-campus work occurs only in religious communities.[113]

The particular arrangements described above are no longer in effect. Revival of these or similar activities should probably be discouraged, if proposed in the future. Operation of essentially religious extension centers is somewhat inconsistent with the University's increasing detachment from the Church's concerns.[114]

Institutes, Centers, and Special Programs. Every university prides itself nowadays on specialized adjunct bodies which manifest the richness of the institution's intellectual life and the range of its current scholarly productivity. Like others, Fordham maintains academic appendages of which it may justly be proud.

One of these, the Cardinal Bea Institute, founded in 1965, undertakes to study the relevance of religion to contemporary life. We have not been given to understand that study in the Institute is confined to the present day significance of only one religion, Catholicism. Its declared general purpose is "to provide a forum on the university level where representatives of the Christian churches and the various academic disciplines can discuss the future of religious values in American life."[115] An institute with that purpose would not be out of place in even the most determinedly secular university.[116]

---

[113] Until recently, moreover, the tuition charge for a nun has been only two-thirds of the standard fee for a layman. Fordham University School of Education, Catalog 1967-1968, at 19, shows the undergraduate fee to be $44 per credit; but a nun or brother was charged only $29.50 per credit. The catalog notes that "this special rate will no longer be in effect" after September 1968. If Fordham is to be considered nonsectarian, any differentials of this sort should be eliminated.

[114] In 1938, Fordham had extension centers at five Motherhouses. R. I. Gannon, Up to the Present: The Story of Fordham 217 (Doubleday, 1967). None of these remains.

[115] Fordham University Graduate School of Arts and Sciences Catalog 1967-1969, at 142. In 1967 a distinctively Catholic program occurred under the Institute's auspices, when it presented a seminar for the American hierarchy on the implications of Vatican II for Catholicism in the United States. See This Is Fordham Today 10 (1968).

[116] This type of academic activity can readily be differentiated from, say, the Fordham Institute of Mission Studies, from which Fordham withdrew its sponsorship in 1966. That Institute was devoted specifically to preparing Catholic missionaries for work in Latin America. This was no doubt a worthy educational activity, but one having so strong a religious flavor that it could not pass muster as proper work for an independent university. Compare R. I. Gannon, note 114 above, at 289: The interest of The Very Reverend Monsignor John (Ivan) Illich

We nevertheless sound a cautionary note. This offshoot of the University in fact touches mainly upon matters of interest to the Catholic Church. We do not recommend abandoning what now exists, but we do recommend a steady broadening of interests as opportunities may occur.

What has been said about the Cardinal Bea Institute is pertinent also to the intellectual pursuits of the John XXIII Center for Eastern Christian Studies. This center was founded in 1952 to concentrate on research in Byzantine-Slavic culture, history, and theology, particularly to shed light on the past and future relations between the Roman Catholic and the Eastern Orthodox branches of Christianity. This impresses us as a thoroughly suitable area of scholarly research. No reason suggests itself why Fordham should eschew having an acute interest in these phases of human experience. But participation in the Center is apparently limited to Jesuits. Many, perhaps even a majority, of those attached to the Center are involved virtually exclusively in pastoral work and liturgical presentations. However valuable these activities may be, they are not characteristic of a neutral university. We therefore recommend Fordham's disengagement from the Center unless, as seems improbable, it be reconstituted as a non-exclusive research establishment.

The Center is now separately incorporated, paying its own salaries and doing its own fund raising. It is housed, without charge, in a University-owned building adjacent to the Rose Hill campus. Most of the Jesuits attached to the John XXIII Center have no University connection that obligates Fordham to satisfy their wants. Perhaps a simple lease, creating a landlord-tenant relationship in place of the present gratuitous hospitality, would sufficiently mark the fact that Fordham's resources are considered unavailable for application to non-University needs.* The lease itself could take account of the

---

"had shifted to the preparation of volunteers who would work for Christ in the clergy-starved dioceses south of the Rio Grande. For this work he planned to acquire a former hotel in Cuernavaca, Mexico, and assemble a faculty for what he called 'The Center of Intercultural Formation.' All he needed now was an American university on the letterhead as a sponsor and a university president as chairman of the board of directors. In 1961 Monsignor Illich was released by Cardinal Spellman to become a member of the Fordham Institute of Mission Studies, and after the formalities of incorporation, worked out the details of the center in conjunction with its trustees . . . . (For reports on the subsequent history of the Center and Monsignor Illich's difficulties with Church officials, see New York Times, Jan 23, 1969, p. 1, col. 1; Feb. 2, 1969, Section E, p. 5, col. 1; Feb. 4, 1969, p. 2, col. 3; Feb. 5, 1969, p. 3, col. 2.)

* On November 1, 1968 such a relationship was formally established, although it is questionable whether the yearly rent of $12 is sufficient to dispel the appearance of gratuitous hospitality.

fact that a few Fordham faculty members reside in the Center and use its library and other facilities.

Even more than the two scholarly institutes just described, Fordham's summer institutes raise a fairly sharp issue about the University's participation in Church work as such instead of confining itself to distinctly academic tasks. These programs may be isolated for mention here.

(a) The Vocation Institute is conducted annually under the nominal auspices of the Graduate Division of Educational Psychology, Measurements, and Guidance, but under the actual direction of Reverend John F. Gilson, S. J., who has been its planner since 1951. In that year an Institute on Religious and Sacerdotal Vocations was formed by Father Gilson "in response to an urgent plea sent out to the Church from the Vatican."[117] An attendance of more than a thousand at the first session and a "vocation exhibit" which drew 75,000 visitors to booths in the gymnasium showed the existence of widespread interest in what the Institute offered.[118] By 1968 the Institute had evolved into two days of discussing "ways and means of stimulating vocations to the religious life," followed by two week-long workshops: The Thirteenth Annual Workshop for Directors of Novices, Postulants, and Junior Professed and the Twelfth Annual Workshop for Local Superiors and Administrators of Religious Communities of Women.[119]

(b) The Confraternity of Christian Doctrine Conference occurs during five summer evenings, known as "C.C.D. Summer Catechetical Week." It is planned as a conference among nuns, clergy, and laymen concerning methods of teaching Catholic doctrine.[120] We may add at this point that a related program occurs during the academic year in the School of General Studies, which in 1967 began presenting a non-credit "Saturday School of Theology" for the benefit of Confraternity of Christian Doctrine teachers and others, both religious and laymen, who might be interested.[121]

---

[117] Gannon, note 114 above, at 289.

[118] Id. at 290.

[119] Fordham University Summer Session Catalog 1968, at 81.

[120] Ibid.

[121] See Report of the President, Fordham University, 1965-1967, at 26: "A limit of 500 students was set and quickly reached, and nearly 200 applicants had to be refused. It is planned to continue this program in subsequent semesters since there seems to be a great demand for these types of theological courses."

(c) The Institute for Teachers of High School Religion is a week-long program of all-day sessions offered by the Department of Religious Education. It carries no academic credit, but it intended to "complement the Master's Programs in Religious Education." The announcement of the Institute notes succinctly: "Program includes Mass."[122]

Quasi-educational offerings like the three just described apparently meet a lively demand and should no doubt be continued. Their sponsorship by Fordham University is another matter. We perceive no strong argument against their remaining on the Fordham campus if Fordham were to enter into a contract for the use of its facilities by a new sponsor, independent of the University as such.

The preceding comment suggests a more general observation concerning the employment of the University's physical resources in furtherance of interests extrinsic to Fordham itself. Like most universities, Fordham through its various academic units and departments is the host to programs, conferences, congresses, colloquia, seminars, and workshops that have scholarly dimensions or public service implications tangentially related to the University's main academic concerns.[123] Although these may make heavy temporary demands on manpower or space, they are nevertheless generally accepted within university circles because they adorn campus life, contribute to institutional prestige, facilitate professional and personal relationships, and, perhaps exceptionally, stimulate fresh intellectual activity. In addition, many universities at times, usually during summer recesses, rent space for use by external organizations that need dormitory and meeting room accommodations; they also contract to present programs that have special interest for a narrowly confined group, such as the executives of a large corporation. Fordham like others engages in these semi-business activities, as landlord or program producer. Its "customers" have been, preponderantly, linked with the Catholic Church. We do not recommend any chilling of Fordham's now cordial business relationships with those who may wish to use the campus during what would otherwise be idle periods. We do believe that a conscious effort should be made, however, to add to and diversify the present clientele.

---

[122] Fordham University Summer Session Catalog 1968, at 83.
[123] See Gannon, note 114 above, at 289-290.

No change in principle is involved. Fordham has already been the scene of Red Cross, inter-church, and other conferences that were clearly not Catholic. A greater infusion of similarly secular and non-denominational activities on the summer-time campus would help build awareness that Fordham is a great community center, rather than, more narrowly, a center of Church affairs.

Mitchell Farm. One of Fordham's detached properties, in the pleasant countryside near Lake Mahopac, is an estate know as Mitchell Farm. The Farm has two chief uses. It is occasionally the scene of conferences, when continuous conversation among participants is likely to be more productive than attendance at a series of formal sessions; thus Mitchell Farm serves for Fordham somewhat the same purpose as Arden House and Ainslie House do for Columbia and New York University, respectively. Secondly, Mitchell Farm functions as a summer house for members of the Society of Jesus throughout the New York Province, for whom it is a low-cost vacation resort.

The latter utilization is Mitchell Farm's true reason for being. We think it appropriate that ownership of and control over Mitchell Farm should be unequivocally in the hands of the Jesuit Order, rather than even nominally in Fordham's* To the extent that Fordham desires in future to use it as an off-campus conference center during non-vacation periods, we recommend that the University arrange to do so by suitable rental contract with the new legal owner.[124]

3. THE GOVERNANCE OF THE UNIVERSITY

Archdiocesan relations. Fordham University is clearly not a dependency of the Archdiocese of New York, from which it receives no financial support and to which it owes no legal obligation. Over the course of many earlier years a considerable amount of reporting, conferring, and negotiating does seem to have linked Fordham's administration with archdiocesan officialdom and with the archbishop then in office. In the recent past the late Cardinal Spellman, himself a Fordham alumnus, showed an active interest in the University both as an old grad and as a prelate. His influence within the University was not lessened by his "steering" wealthy benefactors in its direc-

---

* For more recent developments, see the Epilogue.

[124] The Lewis Calder Center for ecological studies, located in Armonk, is used for normal university purposes and its retention as university property raises no issue of denominationalism.

tion.[125] *De facto* though possibly not *de jure,* the Archdiocese at times seemingly exercised a sort of veto power over University decisions.[126]

At present, as best we can ascertain, a correctly courteous relation exists between the University and the Archdiocese, but without any implication of the subordination that apparently existed in the not distant past. Important decisions at Fordham appear now to be communicated to archdiocesan officials for their information rather than for their approbation. Action is not held in abeyance until clearance has been obtained. The known sentiments of the Archdiocese are not lightly ignored; an honorary degree, for example, would probably not be conferred upon a person whose accomplishments or associations were appraised unenthusiastically by the Archdiocese. As to some things every university makes educated guesses about the probable reactions of those whose good will it desires to retain. Hence Fordham can be and sometimes no doubt is influenced by archdiocesan opinions that have never been directly voiced. Looking at the relationship as a whole, however, we are satisfied that Fordham is genuinely independent of the Archdiocese and that no structural change is needed in this respect in order to evidence the University's freedom to act in accord with its own best judgment.

The Jesuit "owners." The linkages between the University and the Society of Jesus are of a different nature. For many years the Society asserted flatly that it "owned" Fordham. Acceptance of this notion of ownership has been widespread. It is reflected, indeed, in the 1967 by-laws of the Board of Lay Trustees of Fordham University (a body to which added reference will be made presently). These by-laws explicitly state that "legal ownership of the University is vested in the Society of Jesus and the legal control of the policy and management of the University is exercised in accordance with the

---

125 Compare C. Jencks and D. Riesman, The Academic Revolution 345 (Doubleday, 1968): "...a teaching order that does not want to depend wholly on tuition to cover cost must raise money from local Catholic businessmen, competing with Catholic hospitals, charities, schools, and the Church itself. An order that is at odds with the local bishop is unlikely to fare well in such competition."

126 See, e.g., discussion concerning medical school in Gannon, note 114 above, at 157-158; transfer of preparatory school to new location, id. at 190-191, 243. A Jesuit scholar, commenting on the somewhat prickly contacts between a Catholic university and the local chancery office, believes that the "problem is complicated by the fact that the precise nature of the relationship between the local bishop and the university—at least in the United States—is a matter of considerable canonical obscurity." A. M. Greeley, The Changing Catholic College 163 (Aldine, 1967).

prescriptions of the Order and Canon Law, through the Jesuit Board of Trustees . . ."[127]

With all respect, we believe that the available historical and legal materials do not support the claim of ownership, though unquestionably the Jesuits do have a significant equitable interest in Fordham's physical property and institutional good will that should not be expunged without the Society's acquiescense.

What is now Fordham University was incorporated by a New York statute of 1846.[128] Nine named persons were then constituted "a body corporate, by the name of St. John's College, Fordham, the said corporation to be in all respects an university, and its object the promotion of education." The original incorporators—none of whom was a Jesuit and one of whom was a Protestant[129]—were "appointed trustees of said corporation," with power to name their successors and to carry on the new institution's affairs.

By agreement with Archbishop John J. Hughes, to whom a substantial consideration was paid at the time, the Jesuits assumed responsibility for conducting St. John's College as an educational enterprise. At the outset the Archbishop and the Society of Jesus had corresponded and had had "understandings" bearing the earmarks of transfers of title; but these were not legally significant (in part because the Archbishop did not himself have title to the property the Jesuits may have thought they were buying) and were never formally recorded. From 1846 until 1860 the Jesuits and the Archbishop continued a peppery debate about who was responsible for what; but nothing they said or did during this period could alter the fact that then as now Fordham's properties were firmly held by nine corporate trustees—of whom, incidentally, four were non-Jesuit at least until 1855, nine years after the Jesuits seemingly believed they had become Fordham's owners.[130] If for some unforeseeable reason Fordham were now altogether to cease existence and the corporation created in 1846 were to dissolve, the University's properties would not, in our opinion, simply pass to the Society of

---

[127] By-Laws of the Board of Trustees, Effective as of May 17, 1967, Art. III (1).

[128] New York Laws 1846, ch. 61.

[129] The other incorporators were a bishop, four priests, and three Catholic laymen. Two trustees resigned toward the end of 1846 and were replaced by Jesuits. Gannon, note 114 above, at 138.

[130] The above condensation of history is based on an admirably detailed study by F. X. Curran, "Archbishop Hughes and the Jesuits: Fordham's Prologue," appearing in Woodstock Letters, no. 97, 5-56 (1968). Compare Gannon, note 114 above, at 34, 37, 49.

Jesus as the 'real owners," but would be conveyed, pursuant to judicial decree, to some other corporation empowered to continue their educational use.[131]

The Jesuit Trustees. Whether or not the Society of Jesus owned Fordham, it indubitably "owned" the trustees during a century or more.[132] Until very recently the trustees have been Jesuits resident in the University community. Some have been superannuated members of the Society for whom honorific posts have been sought. Others have been subordinate administrators, accustomed to following the leadership of their president rather than passing judgment upon his acts. Significant decisions were rarely (if at all) made in meetings of the board of trustees. Sometimes they were the product of discussion within the "President's Special Council," which included "the members of the advisory group required by the Rule of the Society of Jesus."[133] Sometimes they grew out of private consultations between the president and his religious superiors in the Province or in Rome, which were followed by *pro forma* actions of the trustees.

At Fordham this organizational pattern has now been broken by an extraordinarily speedy succession of events.

Instead of continuing to be a major shaper of the University's plans for construction, new course offerings, and faculty selection, the Provincial of the Jesuit Order has during the past decade progressively withdrawn, leaving in academic administrators' hands the autonomy that, as a high-ranking Jesuit recently said conversationally, "one associates with a *bona fide* university." During 1965, one of the Jesuit trustees died and the eight others successively resigned, after first voting to fill each existing vacancy with a trustee suggested by the president. The trustees as of July 1, 1968, were (except for the president himself) persons not directly connected with Fordham and therefore not in a subordinate position. All, however, were Jesuit priests. One was the Provincial of the New York Province, Society of Jesus. One was the Editor of *America*. Two others were, respectively, the president and executive vice-president of a nearby Jesuit uni-

---

[131] For fuller development of the thesis that the property owned by a corporation created by civil law is not to be regarded as church property, even though the corporation is largely under the influence or auspices of a church body, see J. J. McGrath, Catholic Institutions in the United States: Canonical and Civil Law Status 2, 8-10, 23-26 (Catholic Univ. of America, 1968). And compare Bradfield v. Roberts, 175 U.S. 291 (1899).

[132] For a succinct and highly critical description of Jesuit boards of trustees in general, see Greeley, note 126 above, at 7-9.

[133] The Self-Study of Fordham University 1963, at 80.

versity. The remaining four were educators from other Provinces. "The change in board composition," explained President McLaughlin "brings it closer to the structure of secular universities."[134]

This is no doubt true in the sense that Fordham's trustees are no longer its administrators, sitting as appraisers of what they themselves have done. The Fordham board as now constituted indeed does have elements of detachment and independence that were previously lacking. It nevertheless continues to be drawn from a single brotherhood, with extremely close ties of internal allegiance and with obligations (whose precise limits have never been put to the test) to be guided by external authority.[135] The changed composition of the Fordham board of trustees should bring to the University the benefit of an occasional critical judgment by educators not themselves involved in Fordham's daily affairs, but it does not loosen or lessen the Jesuits' control of the University.

The lay trustees. More significant by far is the extra-legal development of a "Board of Lay Trustees" alongside the legal "Board of Jesuit Trustees."*

Created in 1958, the Board of Lay Trustees now consists of thirty-three members (two of whom are women) whose by-laws limit them to advising and cooperating with the president and other administrators.[136] The body nominates its own members, "subject to the approval and appointment by the President of the University."[137] The Lay Board cannot meet in the absence of the University president or his delegate.[138] Its purely advisory nature and its historical connection with money raising and community relations have been stressed in an official description given to faculty members.[139]

---

[134] Quoted in Gannon, note 114 above, at 301.

[135] A former Fordham president has written of the trustees that they possess wide authority granted by the State, extending in theory to changing the president and, even, to selling the University. He adds: "They are limited however in the exercise of this civil authority by canon law and the constitutions of the Society of Jesus." Gannon, note 114 above, at 301-302. In this connection one may again recall that, as has been pointed out in previous pages, the New York Constitution forbids the use of public funds in aid of any institution that is "wholly *or in part* under the control or direction of any religious denomination."

* The creation of a new Board of Trustees with a majority of laymen is described in the Epilogue.

[136] By-Laws of the Board of Lay Trustees of Fordham University, Art. III (2) (1967).

[137] Id., Art. IV (2).

[138] Id., Art. V (2).

[139] Fordham University Faculty Handbook 11 (1965).

In fact, however, the Lay Board has evolved into something very different from what the formal documents suggest. It is a great deal more than a paper tiger. It meets jointly with the Jesuit Trustees—under the chairmanship, incidentally, of the chairman of the Lay Trustees rather than of a Jesuit—and all the trustees, lay and clerical alike, vote on matters requiring decision. An executive committee, headed by the Lay Trustees' chairman, is composed of two Jesuits and eight laymen. Other committees are similarly drawn from the memberships of both boards.

Fordham has thus achieved in practice though not in law an amalgamation of clerical and lay trustees, the former retaining full legal power, however, to disregard the laymen if a basic conflict were to develop. Formally, Fordham has not gone so far as St. Louis University, which in January 1967 vested legal ownership and control in a self-perpetuating board composed of eighteen laymen and ten Jesuits, under a layman's chairmanship. Actually, the two institutions are in approximately the same posture because fundamental decisions within the St. Louis board require approval by a two-thirds vote, which could not be obtained if the Jesuit members were unitedly resistant.[140]

The move toward an enlarged role for laymen in Fordham's governing body accords with a 1966 resolve of the Society of Jesus.[141] The combination in a single assemblage of what were formerly two entirely separate bodies, one lay and one clerical, very probably reflects a changing mood in American Catholic institutions. Today non-Catholics as well as Catholics are among the estimable laymen

---

[140] By-laws of St. Louis University, Art. VI (1967). The by-laws provide, among other things, that the University's president must be a Jesuit, that the "University will be publicly identified as a Catholic university and as a Jesuit university," and that the University "will be guided by the spiritual and intellectual ideals of the Society of Jesus." Presumably no change in these provisions would gain the assent of the Jesuit trustees.

[141] A brochure published by St. Louis University in 1967 entitled "An Innovation in Higher Education," describing the then newly constituted board of trustees, contains the following information (at 2): "The Very Rev. Peter Arrupe, S. J., superior general of the Society of Jesus, gave his approval of the move in a letter to Father Reinert. 'I am very happy with the proposed greater collaboration of laymen in the direction of the University,' he said, pointing out that it was in line with a decree on education which was approved in October, 1966, by the Thirty-First General Congregation of the Jesuit Order meeting in Rome. The decree recommends 'close collaboration with the laity' in Jesuit education and suggests for study by Jesuit institutions 'the advisability of establishing boards of trustees composed both of Jesuits and Laymen.'"

committed to furthering the welfare of Fordham, St. Louis, and Georgetown Universities.[142]

The significance of lay participation. The "laicizing" of governing boards that were previously composed exclusively of a religious order's representatives may have a considerable impact on Catholic institutions. Enthusiastic lay trustees may perhaps be able to tap financial resources that might otherwise not have been reached, and may perhaps also help in recruiting able lay faculty members and good students.[143] They may perhaps, as a prominent Jesuit has suggested, be able to influence political decisions favorable to the institutions for whom they speak.[144] They may perhaps add a new dimension to the wisdom and judgment of those whose lives have been devoted exclusively to academic rather than "practical" affairs[145] —though, equally, they may perhaps blunder into error as have the the trustees of other universities.[146] They may through their own

[142] In 1967 and again in 1968 Georgetown University, this nation's first Catholic university, added laymen to its board of directors, along with Jesuits not otherwise connected with Georgetown.

[143] J. W. Trent, Catholics in College 309 (U. of Chicago, 1967), expresses belief that, in these respects, lay participation in administration "may be essential for most Catholic colleges in the future."

[144] See R. F. Drinan, The Constitution, Governmental Aid and Catholic Higher Education 33 (Nat. Cath Educ. Assn. 1968), in which the author urges united action to "blunt the movement towards a monopoly on higher education by the officials of the public university establishment," and adds: "These efforts, however, probably cannot be successful, or even initiated, without a board of trustees made up of a broadly-based group of community leaders. If a board of trustees, all known leaders, speaks for a private college of which they are the governing body, their voice is far more likely to be heard than the voice of a lay or clerical faculty group from this college . . . . The creation, therefore, of real decision-making boards of trustees for Catholic colleges is not only desirable but probably absolutely necessary if Catholic and other private colleges are to organize themselves and present a successful plea to legislatures and to the court of public opinion on behalf of private colleges."

[145] E. J. McGrath and G. E. DuPont, The Future of Catholic Higher Education in the United States 26 (Columbia Institute of Higher Educ., 1967). suggest that "if the Catholic institutions were to include on their boards of control up to 25 percent religious and 75 percent laymen, they would establish bodies which may be more capable of meeting the emerging complex problems of the establishment of higher education in the United States than boards composed either entirely of religious or entirely of laymen." The authors add (at 27) that appointing laymen to governing boards should help Catholic colleges "move toward the growing ideal of a 'free Christian college' . . . and away from their tradition aimed largely at defending the Catholic faith."

[146] A particularly sharp doubt about the utility of lay trustees has been expressed by Jencks and Riesman, note 125 above, who believe that Catholic liberals, both clerical and lay, have mistakenly thought that lay trustees will be progressive. Catholic lay trustees, they argue, are no more likely to be intellectual or forward looking than their non-Catholic counterparts. "Most lay advisory boards'" they contend, "are today made up of wealthy real-estate

religious diversity, if in no other manner, further the ecumenical spirit which today has taken on new meaning and force in many Catholic circles.

Laicization as it has thus far occurred, with all the possibly advantageous consequences just outlined, nevertheless does not eliminate the issue of denominational control over Fordham. To end debate on that score the Jesuit Board's present monopoly of legal power would have to end.

A possible legal change. In our opinion this change in legal relationships could be achieved very simply, if indeed it were desired.* Fordham's present charter probably needs amendment to permit enlarging the board of trustees.[147] The guiding document now seemingly contemplates nine trustees, no more and no less.[148] An amendment having been made, the present legal trustees—that is, the Jesuit Board of Trustees—could then plan to select and elect the persons who would fill the vacancies in the newly enlarged board; or, if this seemed desirable in Fordham's circumstances, it could provide for election of some of them by the University's alumni, as is done in many other prominent institutions of higher learning.

Before adding to their ranks, the present legal trustees could adopt fresh by-laws that would accurately reflect the authority and manner of functioning of the about-to-be changed board. Restrictions like those placed upon the St. Louis University trustees would not be consonant with an independent status. No clear necessity exists for asking present Jesuit board members to resign from the governing body, to be instantly supplanted by laymen; clergymen of all faiths serve on university boards of trustees without demur. Nor need the future election of Jesuits or other religious persons be precluded.

tycoons, hopefully influential political figures, loyal football promoters, and the like. The laymen appointed to governing boards during 1967 were for the most part of this same stripe. These men are in many cases quite literally more Catholic than the Pope." The clerical members of the college governing boards, the authors add by way of contrast, have usually served previously on college faculties and some have been trained in secular graduate schools.

* The actual change of these relationships is described in the Epilogue.

147 Under New York law, the Board of Regents has the power to alter university charters. See Education Law § 219 (1953).

148 In this respect Fordham's charter differs from that of St. Louis University. Fordham's charter, New York Laws 1846, ch. 61, sec. I, constituted nine named persons "and their successors" a body corporate; Sec. 2 appointed those nine to be trustees and stipulated that six members should constitute a quorum for transaction of corporate business. The St. Louis charter, Missouri Laws 1832, ch. 228, Sec. 2, empowered the five named incorporators to fill vacancies in their number and also to "appoint an additional number of trustees, whenever in their judgments the exigencies of the institution may require such increase."

Mandating their election should, however, be avoided. So also should election of Jesuits in such proportions that they would have predominance in fact if not in absolute numbers. A court might well decide that an institution where decisive power is effectively in the hands of Jesuit trustees is under the control of the Society, even in the absence of proof that the Society tells the individual trustees how to cast their votes.

The choice of the University's future president should be committed to the new board in the same unconditional manner as exists under the present charter, which gives the trustees unrestricted authority to appoint and dismiss.* If future trustees were to select a Jesuit as Fordham's president, his religious affiliation would not decisively signify the University's status so long as neither the by-laws nor external control over the trustees' actions had forced the selection to be made on a religious basis.

In some quarters fear has been expressed that a truly independent board of trustees might at some future time vote to liquidate Fordham altogether or might supinely allow it to be absorbed by another educational body. If this fear be genuine, it could perhaps be set at rest by an addition to Fordham's charter, though in all candor we deem the addition to be an unnecessary, if not a positively undesirable expression of suspicion concerning a presumably honorable and competent board of trustees. The amendment we have in mind would create a small body separate from the board of trustees and to be named by the Jesuit Order, with power to veto trustees' decisions to sell or dispose of the corporation's assets "not in the usual and regular course of the affairs of the corporation."[149]

---

* For the process of election of Fordham's new president in 1968, see the Epilogue.

[149] The proposal here made bears superficial resemblance to a feature of the 1968 corporate reorganization of Alverno College, founded in Milwaukee, Wisconsin, by the Congregation of the School Sisters of St. Francis. The board of trustees had consisted of nine nuns. Its membership was expanded to fifteen, including four "Guarantors," chosen by the General Council of the Congregation, with the President becoming an additional Guarantor ex officio. The five Guarantors, all of whom also function as trustees, have these added powers: a) they can deny approval to sales of corporate assets outside the regular course of business; b) they can disapprove any future proposed amendments of the by-laws or articles of incorporation; and c) they appoint the nominating committee when a new president is to be named. Although the trustees as a group have legal responsibility for Alverno College and are to determine its general policies, the Guarantors have the real power "to guarantee perpetuity of the original commitment of the Congregation of the School Sisters." Rather plainly, the grasp of the religious hand has been only somewhat loosened, rather than wholly released, in respect of the control over Alverno College's future development. The proposal made in the text differs from the Alverno arrangement in

Because the likelihood of any such transactions is remote, the nominal existence of the Jesuit appendage would probably not be regarded as subjecting the University to denominational supervision or control. Although the creation of the appendage would never be contemplated at all were there no desire to retain at least a modicum of supervisory authority, the Jesuit nominees' authority would pertain not to the conduct of educational affairs, but solely to the possible liquidation of property in an unusual and irregular manner. This measure of residual control would not, we believe, itself be deemed dispositive; it might well, however, be considered significant if a court had been struck by other indications of the Order's continuing involvement in the University.

Before leaving this topic we must note a further argument against seeking to retain even this much of a safeguard against suppositious profligacy or faithlessness on the part of future trustees. If Fordham were to be sold today, either piecemeal or lock, stock, and barrel, one could readily understand that the Jesuit Order which had brought Fordham's property into being would have a lively curiosity about the transaction. As time passes, however, Fordham may acquire new property with which the Society of Jesus will have had no connection whatsover. A dormitory complex, for example, might be constructed in some future era upon the initiative of the reconstituted board of trustees, using only funds from public sources. If at a time in the still more distant future the trustees then in office were to decide, for some reason they deemed adequate, to sell the dormitories, can justification be found for requiring that the sale be approved by Jesuit overseers? We believe not.[150]

---

that the Jesuit guarantors (if that were their name) would not be board members, nor would they have power to pass on amendments or to influence the choice of a president. (The above information is derived from "Restatement of Articles of Incorporation of Alverno College" and "By-laws of Alverno College of Milwaukee, Wisconsin," published February 17, 1968.)

150 This belief has led us also to reject the possibility of adding to the articles a simple reversionary paragraph providing that were the corporation ever to dissolve or become extinct, all its property should then vest in the Society of Jesus, to be used by it for educational purposes related as closely as may be feasible to those of the dissolved corporation. A reverter might be defensible as to specific existing property that could be traced back to the Society. But as time passes, Fordham may acquire more and more property independently of the Society. The Atomic Energy Commission might conceivably, for example, give Fordham a cyclotron and the Department of Health, Education, and Welfare might give it funds for a new language laboratory or library building. No sustainable argument can be made in favor of vesting title to these properties in the Society as a substitute for the University, were the latter for some reason to go out of existence. Indeed, the legality of doing so is highly doubtful.

Our recommendation is that Fordham consider carefully whether it truly desires to create a board of trustees free from denominational control and in whose independence the public will have confidence. If it does wish this kind of board, its decision should be straight-forwardly effectuated without formalistic protections against experienced trustees' developing a taste for mass imprudence or institutional suicide.[151]

4. THE UNIVERSITY'S ADMINISTRATION

In the opinion of a retired Fordham president, "still more striking" than the infusion of laymen into the board of trustees has been "the replacement by laymen of Jesuits who formerly held the key positions on the faculty."[152] The change has indeed been pronounced. As recently as 1963 all major posts in the University save the deanships of the College of Pharmacy and the School of Law and the Acting Deanship of the School of Education were held by Jesuit priests. Jesuit "regents" (who have since been withdrawn) served in some of the branches not headed by a Jesuit dean, presumably to assure regularity.[153] When a layman became the Executive Vice-President in charge of the Intown Division (that is, the Lincoln Center campus,* he was described as "the highest ranking layman in Fordham's history."[154] Other laymen serve as Vice-President for Academic Affairs and Dean of the Graduate School, Vice-President for University Relations, Vice-President for Student Personnel and Dean of Students, Director of University Libraries, Director of Undergraduate

---

[151] Precisely this forthright step was taken by Webster College, now a co-educational liberal arts college near St. Louis, whose corporate charter until November 15, 1967, stated flatly that it was "owned and operated by the Sisters of Loretto." On that date the Sisters, upon their own initiative, secured an amendment to the previous articles of incorporation, by which the college came wholly under the governance of a self-perpetuating board of directors. No religious restrictions appear in the amended articles or in the board's by-laws. The present eighteen-member board (whose chairman is a Jewish business man) includes two Sisters of Loretto, three Protestant educational administrators of national prominence, and a number of other persons well known in business and community affairs. For further information concerning Webster College developments, see "Community of Learning—Webster College, Saint Louis, Missouri," a brochure sent to prospective students in 1968.

[152] Gannon, note 114 above, at 301.

[153] Compare Fordham University Faculty Handbook 15 (1965) : "The Regent of a School or College is the liaison officer between the President and the Dean and Faculty of the School or College concerned."

* The officer in question was subsequently named to be Executive Vice-President of the entire University; the vice presidency limited to the Intown Division was abolished.

[154] Report of the President, Fordham University, 1965-1967, at 4.

Admissions, Dean of Thomas More College, Dean of the College of Business Administration, Dean of the School of Education, Dean of the School of Social Service, Dean of the School of Law, Dean of the College of Pharmacy, Chairman of Bensalem (the Experimental College), Dean of the Evening College (Lincoln Center), and Dean of the Summer Session.

In many large American universities one must search, as through a maze, in order to discover the true seats of power. In probably no other modern social organism has authority become so dispersed as in the academy. This has not been true in the past, however, on Fordham's Rose Hill campus, where nobody has been disposed to doubt the might of the president. "All administrative authority," a Fordham Self-Study stated in 1963 (at p. 80), "is held by the President . . . who is appointed by the Father General of the Society of Jesus after consideration of recommendations from local officials, and is then elected for purposes of the civil law by the Board of Trustees. All administrative authority . . . for the University . . . is held by him, and is either exercised directly or delegated by him to others, as is customary in Jesuit institutions."[155] Yet it is true today that actual power is becoming more and more decentralized. The enlarged engagement of lay administrators, some of whom have lengthy experience in secular institutions or in public affairs and all of whom seek long-term professional fulfillment through commitment to an academic institution rather than to a religious order, has in itself rendered top level authoritarianism unfeasible even if, as is plainly not now the case, it were still desired.[156]

---

[155] Compare, however, J. W. Donohue, Jesuit Education 191 (Fordham, 1963): Some Jesuit administrative practices "will provoke criticism from modern theorists of school management. Control of organization is, for one thing, highly centralized and the power to make and implement policies is largely in the hands of the top overseers at the head of the line . . . . Yet we can judge empirically that there is more to the picture than this. For the Jesuit school over four centuries has shown the vitality that is only preserved when there is a readiness to reappraise policies, entertain criticism and then innovate. Without this readiness, the organization would have declined and passed from rigidity to fossilization. In its administrative practice, then, one may presume a quality which may not have been reduced to a specific rule but which is more important than any single regulation."

[156] Compare Greeley, note 126 above, at 75-76, reporting an interview with two "medium-level" administrators at a university other than Fordham, as follows: "It was perfectly clear to the two of them that their president (who was also their religious superior) made it impossible for them to do their jobs by what they would have considered to be even the most minimal professional standards. If they had been laymen working under such circumstances, they would almost certainly have quit, but their religious vows made it impossible for them either to leave or to engage in open revolt against the president."

In an earlier branch of this discussion we have suggested that the trustees must have freedom in future presidential selections if Fordham is to gain recognition as an independent university.* We repeat that suggestion in the present context. Continued appointment of the president by the Father General, with nominal ratification by the trustees, would import a heavy element of control, counterbalancing many other significant developments in Fordham's academic organization.[157]

We note in passing, chiefly because the matter has been raised by others, that most but by no means all of the laymen whom Fordham has thus far appointed to major administrative positions are Catholics. This we deem to be of little relevance for present purposes. The ethnic and religious diversity of those selected as senior administrators in recent years is sufficient to show that Fordham has not adopted a covertly discriminatory policy. Unless the University were suddenly to reverse its course, the number of non-Catholic appointees will no doubt increase as academic circles become persuaded that one need not be of the Catholic faith in order to find congenial intellectual and professional relationships at Fordham. Meanwhile the preponderance of Catholic laymen in responsible posts, in and of itself, does not fix the institution's status any more than the probable preponderance of Protestant laymen in corresponding posts at, say, the Ivy League universities classifies those institutions in religious terms.

---

* For the process of election of Fordham's new president in 1968, see the Epilogue.

[157] The importance of the point just made is underscored by the organizational principles of the Jesuit Order. Its statutes describe the Father General as the authoritative leader of the Society's educational institutions; their heads are merely subdelegates of his power. Even when the institutional chiefs are assisted by non-Jesuit deans, a Jesuit author has declared, it remains true that "Jesuit schools and colleges are not managed wholly from within since the repositories of highest authority are elsewhere." He adds comfortingly, "Still, the administration is no more external than it is in a public educational system and the top board is no more apart than are the trustees of any non-public American college or university. All the Jesuit administrators, moreover, are from the ranks of the Society; all have had the basic cultural and spiritual formation provided by the Order; all have had actual classroom experience. Except for the General, all these principal administrators, the provincials and rector, have limited tenure in office and they are required to listen, at least, to the advice of a panel of consultors. These qualifications preserve the organization from many of the irritations experienced by schools subject to trustees, who often lack professional educational competence even when they are not actually capricious, or to bureaucrats in municipal and state departments or to political legislatures in control of school finances." J. W. Donohue, Jesuit Education 194 (Fordham, 1963).

As for the still prominent number of Jesuits in Fordham's administration, we are inclined to think that neither an immediate reorganization nor a special rule for the future is indicated. Normal attrition—death, retirement, and departure for other posts—will of course affect the incumbents. No policy now exists, so far as we have ascertained, of requiring that particular positions be filled by none other than Jesuits. Hence, when new appointments must be made to fill the vacancies that will inevitably occur as time passes, the Fordham president then in office will not be restricted in searching for suitable personnel. We know of no reason in law or policy for denying future appointments to qualified members of the Society of Jesus if they are chosen on their merits and are not simply obediently absorbed.[158]

Important Jesuits have predicted in our presence that Fordham (and other educational institutions) in years to come will experience increasing difficulty in locating Jesuit priests who are willing to serve as academic administrators. In the circumstances that now exist and that can be foreseen, Fordham would be ill advised to place limitations upon its future recruitment. The University should avoid active favoritism in choosing administrative personnel, but it need not develop special intolerances in order to demonstrate its having ended its past dependence upon the Jesuit manpower pool.

5. THE FACULTY

Fordham's present appointment policies and procedures (we do not speak of the past) are consonant with those of independent institutions of learning. Persons under consideration for academic positions need not be Catholic.[159] Nor need they be "sympathetic"

---

158 Compare Greeley, note 126 above, at 126, reporting low faculty morale on many Catholic campuses because the professors "have precious little confidence in the administrative competence or leadership ability of the administrators. They often feel—and in our judgment quite correctly—that those who have been appointed to administrative positions have received their posts either because of the internal politics of the religious order or because they are considered 'safe' by their religious superiors and not because they understand in the slightest what a university is or how academic excellence is achieved."

159 Fordham University Faculty Handbook 36 (1965): "Although Fordham University is operated under Catholic auspices, it is not required that all members of the faculty be Catholic. Moreover the University Administration fully respects the religious beliefs of all the men and women who share in the work of the University." The Handbook adds, at 40: "The University Church and the other University Chapels are open to the faculty at all times. Masses are offered at convenient hours for faculty members when school is in session."

with Catholic principles or committed to the "Christian philosophy of life."[160] Recent appointments (not only of junior staff, but also of division and department heads) include Protestants, Jews, and persons whose religious commitments are not known. Jesuits are no longer simply assigned to departments regardless of departmental wishes, but must pass through the same selection process as other candidates.[161] Members (both male and female) of Catholic orders other than the Society of Jesus, as well as Jesuits unconnected with the New York Province, have been appointed in substantial numbers, and to our knowledge at least one carefully trained candidate of the New York Province has recently been rejected. The University's ordinances and policies concerning promotion, acquiring tenure, retirement privileges, collateral benefits, and duties do not differentiate at all between the lay and the religious faculty.[162]

We find nothing on the face of the record, so far as it relates to the faculty, that would require change in order to qualify Fordham as an uncontrolled university. Nor do we believe that current experience is at variance with external form, in the special situation of the Jesuit faculty members. Nominally their religious superiors can transfer them to duties elsewhere despite their having acquired professorial tenure at Fordham. In practice, the present Provincial for Higher Education—who was himself a long-time Fordham faculty member before assuming his post, and who seems to have retained a faculty outlook—consults the wishes of the individual, instead of simply shifting him summarily from institution to institution in order to meet an organizational need of the moment. The actualities of educational and personnel administration in the New York

---

160 Compare Horace Mann League v. Board of Public Works, 242 Md. 645, 220 A. 2d 51, appeal dismissed and cert. denied, 385 U.S. 97 (1966), Joint Record Extract 144, 246, 263-264.

161 Faculty Handbook 18-19. Jencks and Riesman, note 125 above, at 400, voice skepticism about faculty selection in self-styled Catholic colleges. "Academic professionals," they say, "want their colleagues chosen on the basis of professional accomplishments, and they want them chosen by fellow professionals. An institution that refuses to follow these rules is unlikely to attract appreciable numbers of distinguished scholars over the years, for they will not regard it as a 'real university.' Yet we find it very hard to see how an institution that accepts these rules can long remain Catholic in any important sense. Surely the idea of a Catholic college or university implies some deviation from this narrowly professional and secular standard for choosing the membership of the community. . . ."

162 Faculty Handbook 21-23, 25-26, 27-36.

Province today do not leave Fordham faculty members utterly de-
fenceless, as teachers in some Catholic colleges are said to be.[163]

This is not to say that Fordham experiences no special problems
attributable perhaps to past emphasis on clerical leadership at all
levels. Of the seventeeen academic departments in Fordham College
in 1967-1968, for example, nine were headed by laymen and eight
by Jesuits, though of the 231 teachers in professorial ranks listed in
the 1967-1968 college catalog, only about a third were Jesuits*—of
whom more than half (43 out of a total of 78) were concentrated
in only two of the seventeen departments.[164] One possible explanation
for the disproportionate number of priests among departmental
chairmen is that the average Jesuit, living on campus and free of
the distractions of family life, is able to devote more time to university affairs than the average layman. But a former Fordham
department head believes that lay faculty members in a Catholic
college often feel themselves to be outsiders because their clerical
colleagues have continuingly close relations and, thus, considerable
influence with their fellow clericals who are principal members of
the administration.[165] Of course this situation will change when, as

163 Compare Greeley, note 126 above, at 132: Even though a religious faculty
member "may be promoted, he certainly has no tenure in his department and
can be removed or sent to a high school half-way across the country without
ever being consulted. Of course he can also be appointed to a department
without the chairman of the department being consulted. Thus, a lay chairman
of an academic department can never be sure when the provincial of the
religious order that administers the school is going to remove one of the members
of the department or indeed assign another man to the department without the
chairman of the department being given any right to examine the man's
credentials."

* More recent figures are contained in the Epilogue.

164 The percentage of Jesuits among Fordham's teachers and administrators
in recent decades has been: 1946—27 per cent; 1956—24 per cent; 1966—20
per cent. This is in keeping with experience elsewhere. Between 1956 and 1966
the number of lay teachers in Catholic colleges and universities increased by
190 per cent; the number of religious increased by only 14.3 per cent during
the same decade. McGrath and DuPont, note 145 above, at 24. J. D. Donovan,
The Academic Man in the Catholic College 23-24 (Sheed & Ward, 1964), gives
the percentage of laymen in the faculties of Catholic men's colleges as follows:
1872—27 per cent; 1924—56 per cent; 1934—62 per cent; 1964—70 per cent.

165 P. J. Reiss, "The Catholic College: Some Built-In Tensions," in R.
Hassenger ed., The Shape of Catholic Higher Education 265-266 (U. of Chicago,
1967): "The religious faculty, since they normally constitute a religious community in addition to their faculty roles, form an informal subgroup who have
closer contact with each other, and who also have greater contact with the
principal administrators who are part of the same residential community. Thus
while officially religious faculty are not distinguished from other faculty, there
is an informal association of religious faculty and administrators that functions
as an 'in-group.' It is for this reason that lay faculty, although in the majority,
can still think of themselves as part of the 'out-group.' They are brought into

we have remarked has already been occurring at Fordham, members of the religious community are replaced as academic administrators more and more often by laymen.

Another development that will presumably reinforce faculty unity at Fordham is the Academic Senate. The Senate came into being in 1964, with no very clear understanding of its nature, but with a sense that a "significant green light had been turned on."[166] At one of its early meetings the Senate President reported to his colleagues that the present president of the University had stated his desire to have "a strong Faculty Senate to help administer the University" and to share in his plans for "streamlining and up-dating the Fordham structure."[167] Since then the Senate has occupied itself with matters of considerable moment (such as the procedure for selecting department chairmen) and also with the academic trivia (such as faculty parking lot privileges) that arouse perhaps more vigorous debate than do matters of real substance. Although its constitution recognizes that the Faculty Senate has no dispositive power,[168] it does seem to have a voice to which attention is paid. The president and his chief aides, moreover, have been sharply reminded on several occasions that decisions of interest to faculty members

---

full consultation on a particular policy question as members of committees or as administrators, but they may often find that an issue has already been extensively discussed and shaped by the 'in-group.' The operation of the 'in-group' thus creates certain problems of integration, although it clearly presents certain advantages in the operation of a college not to be found at the non-Catholic college." And see also M. M. Pattillo, Jr. and D. M. MacKenzie, Church Sponsored Higher Education in the United States 159 (Am. Council on Educ., 1966). But cf. Greeley, note 126 above, at 67, reporting that at three well-regarded universities "the younger and more liberal of religious faculty members contended that there was better communication between the administration and the lay faculty than between the administration and the religious faculty."

166 Gannon, note 114 above, at 295. A study committee had recommended that "The effective exercise of its responsibilities by a body as large as the Faculty of the University requires that it be organized in a manner that will permit it to ascertain its collective view and express its opinions." Subsequently, on May 14, 1964, the then president of the University established an interim Faculty Council to carry this recommendation into effect. The academic year 1964-1965 was devoted to drafting a "Constitution of the Fordham University Faculty Senate," which was approved by referendum vote in May 1965. Later that month the Faculty Senate, composed of twenty-four elected faculty representatives, met for the first time under the new constitution. Fordham University Faculty Senate, Biennial Report May 1956-April 1967, at 1-3.

167 Biennial Report, note 75 above, at 5.

168 Const. Art. I-B declares the Senate's "right and duty to advise the President of the University and to initiate recommendations on policy in all areas of University activity." The Senate is to "deal directly with the President of the University," and its own president "shall have the right to confer with the President of the University within a reasonable time after a request for such a meeting."

had been made without consulting the Senate. Presumably these expressions of dissatisfaction will lead to keener future awareness that the entire faculty, through elected representatives, expects to share in decisions formerly made after discussions in a much narrower circle. Whatever may be one's estimate of the value of faculty members' corporate judgment, about which considerable skepticism exists in some quarters,[169] the Fordham Faculty Senate should at the very least diminish lay professors' fears that their opinions will be overlooked.

Concern about the sensibilities of lay faculty members should not obscure the fact that the religious professors may have discontents, too. At Fordham on several occasions we heard the opinion that a richly deserving Jesuit's promotion to a higher rank may sometimes have been postponed because his department head then needed the vacancy in order to retain the services of a layman who might go elsewhere if dissatisfied. High-ranking administrators in whose veracity we have complete confidence have assured us that this has been altogether untrue in recent years. It has nevertheless been strongly believed by some of the religious.[170] On the other hand, we have not gained the impression that Fordham's religious faculty members feel themselves overburdened by pastoral work either on or off the campus. Assumption of priestly responsibilities is voluntary, not simply an obligation assumed along with a professorial teaching load and other academic duties. Hence, so far as we are informed, Fordham's

---

169 See, e.g., Greeley, note 126 above, at 119: "It does not seem to us that greater faculty democracy is the answer to academic improvement in the Catholic colleges. On the contrary, faculty democracy and citizenship are much more likely to be a consequence of rather than an antecedent to academic improvement. Those writers who feel that greater faculty control is a solution to the present dilemmas of Catholic higher education would do well to examine the impact of powerful faculty influence at other American universities, where the faculty acts as a major veto group on educational reform and innovation. Some friendly critics outside the Catholic system have suggested that, while there certainly must be more democracy and faculty citizenship in Catholic colleges, it would be a mistake for the Catholic schools to blindly imitate the procedures at non-Catholic schools." But cf. Biennial Report, note 166 above, at 39: "There exists abundant historical evidence showing a direct relationship between academic excellence and prestige of certain universities and the application of academic policies. See Charles P. Dennison, 'Faculty Rights and Obligations in Eight Independent Liberal Arts Colleges,' Columbia University, 1955; see also, 'Manual of Academic Senate,' University of California, November, 1966; 'University Senate By-Laws,' University of Michigan, April 1966."

170 But cf. Greeley, note 126 above, at 123-124: "Many of the lay faculty contend that there is a double standard for promotion, with one existing for the religious faculty and another for the lay faculty."

religious do not have the same sort of "publish or parish" problem that is said to be widespread on Catholic campuses.[171].

One problem of significantly large dimensions does affect the entire Fordham faculty and may color the University's future. We refer to the issue of academic freedom. Even some who favor public generosity toward denominational institutions believe that it should withheld from those in which academic freedom is inhibited, lest public aid be used to constrict rather than expand the growth of ideas through free inquiry.[172] In some quarters the view has been expressed that denominationalism (or ecclesiastical control) must inescapably come into conflict with academic freedom as now generally understood.[173] We think it unnecessary to reach so generalized a conclusion, especially since both ecclesiastical and academic attitudes are today evolving with extraordinary rapidity.[174] We limit our discussion to academic freedom as defined at Fordham alone.

The Fordham Faculty Handbook declares the University's position concerning academic freedom to be as follows: "The primary purpose of education is the free and unhampered discovery and communication of truth. To the extent of his ability every man, and above all every university professor, has not only the right but also the duty to participate freely in this work of searching after and communicating truth. In so doing every faculty member must be free to adopt those methods and to use those techniques which he finds most helpful in his work, and to communicate his findings openly to the academic community." This broad statement is then immediately qualified by a cautionary observation that academic freedom "is not and cannot be absolute. It must be exercised within the framework of academic discipline and with respect for the moral

---

171 Compare Greeley, note 126 above, at 130-131.

172 See D. A. Giannella, "Religious Liberty, Nonestablishment, and Doctrinal Development," Part II, 81 Harvard Law Rev. 513, 587 (1968).

173 See, e.g., R. M. MacIver, Academic Freedom in Our Time 285-289 (Columbia, 1955). See also E. Manier, "Introduction," in Manier and J. Houck ed., Academic Freedom and the Catholic University 9-22 (Fides, 1967), comparing the secular concept of academic freedom with one advanced as appropriate for a Catholic university.

174 Note, for example, the norm for Catholic colleges and universities enunciated by the recent Vatican Council: "...individual branches of knowledge [are to be] studied according to their own proper principles and methods, and with due freedom of scientific investigation." The Documents of Vatican II 648 (W. Abbott ed., 1966), quoted in Giannella, note 172 above, at 587n. Of course the norm does contain fluid words such as "proper" and "due," but the dominant intent seems to be to stress professionalism of outlook in matters of a purportedly scholarly character. See generally Manier and Houck, note 173 above.

law, good manners, good taste, and a respectful consideration of the non-academic world." With these thoughts in mind, Fordham announces its commitment to the following propositions:

1)   The teacher is entitled to full freedom, in research and in the publication of the results . . .

2)   The teacher is entiled to freedom in the classroom in discussing his subject, but he should be careful not to introduce into his teaching controversial matter which has no relation to his subject or that which is contrary to the religious or other aims of the institution.[175]

To this is added a reminder of the University's expectation that "all faculty members, whatever their religious beliefs, will maintain standards of conduct consistent with their professional status and the basic aims and spirit of the University."[176]

The quoted provisions have not been in conflict with academic freedom principles supported in the past by the American Association of University Professors. Until recently this influential professional body has been tolerant of "limitations of academic freedom because

---

[175] Fordham University Faculty Handbook 26 (1965).

[176] Id. at 36-37. A Jesuit author who believes that professors in Catholic institutions enjoy virtually unlimited academic freedom adds that a problem might conceivably arise if a faculty member were divorced and then remarried. This would cause perturbation, he believes, not so much among academic administrators as among religious superiors "who were defending this rampart as one of the last that remained to their notion of what a Catholic university ought to be . . . . Some of those in key positions in the religious order still consider the lay faculty to be, in some fashion or another, members of the order, and they are terrible concerned about the impact on the order's reputation of behavior of faculty members that someone outside the university community might judge to be immoral." Greeley, note 126 above, at 111-112.

Note must be taken, also, of the possible vulnerability of religious faculty members to ecclesiastical pressures not applicable to lay professors. See, e.g., J. W. Trent, Catholics in College 268-269 (U. of Chicago, 1967): "Siena College students and faculty members clamored for clarification when Bishop William Scully of Albany, New York, suddenly curtailed the civil rights and social work of Father Bonaventure. This Franciscan priest, a faculty member of Siena College, had been an active worker in Albany's inner city and a frequent critic of the city's administration. The Siena College administration upheld the bishop's action . . . . The bishop's statement, published Thursday in The Evangelist, the diocesan weekly newspaper, said that the decision to curtail the Franciscan priest's work was 'an administrative decision, not one of policy' and added that 'such decisions are the responsibility of the bishop alone and the reasons for such decisions must be left to God and the conscience of the bishop.'" See also New York Times, Aug. 28, 1968, p. 6, col. 1, reporting that Bishop James A. McNulty had abruptly dismissed seven priests from the faculty of St. John Vianney Seminary because they objected publicly to Pope Paul's encyclical on birth control.

of religious or other aims of the institution" so long as the limitations were "clearly stated in writing at the time of the appointment."[177] Mounting concern about restrictive policies in some church-related institutions, however, led in 1967 to a more carefully designed formulation of the relationship between religious doctrine and educational responsibility.[178]

Regardless, however, of whether Fordham's position as formulated in 1965 has or has not been acceptable to the American Association of University Professors, it does plainly label the University as one whose specific religious aims set limits upon academic permissibility. We are uninformed about any positive applications of doctrinal restrictions upon the teacher's work in the classroom, but the mere assertion of an expectation that the teacher will be guided by religious rather than professional considerations would cast a shadow on Fordham's claims of freedom.[179]

In this circumstance the proposed new Constitution of Fordham (Third Draft, April 9, 1968) takes on especially large significance. Article IX (3) (c) provides that instructional and administrative personnel may be suspended or removed for "conduct inconsistent with accepted professional and moral standards. This shall not be so interpreted as to constitute interference with academic freedom." Article X then spells out what "academic freedom" means. The pertinent portions of that Article are as follows:

> 1. All members of the instructional staff of the University shall be entitled to full freedom in classroom teaching and related activities while discussing their proper subjects of instruction. They shall be entitled to full freedom in research and in publication of the results of their research. No University censorship shall be imposed on their publications or utterances as members of the larger society outside the University community. No faculty employment shall be terminated, nor shall tenure be denied because of considerations violating academic freedom.

---

[177] See, in this connection, L. Joughin ed., Academic Freedom and Tenure—Handbook of the AAUP 139 (U. of Wisconsin, 1967).

[178] See "Report of the Special Committee on Academic Freedom in Church-Related Colleges and Universities," 53 AAUP Bull. 369 (1967).

[179] As to the chilling effect of a similar pronouncement by a Jesuit university other than Fordham, see J. Foster, "Some Effects of Jesuit Education," in R. Hassenger ed., The Shape of Catholic Education 165 (U. of Chicago, 1967).

2. The following obligations shall be respected by all members of the instructional staff as essential corollaries of academic freedom:

a) Controversial matter which has no relation to the subject of instruction shall not be introduced into classroom teaching. . . .

b) . . . .

c) Public expression, orally or in writing, of opinions or beliefs shall be accompanied by a clear indication that the individual responsible for them is not a University spokesman, since the public may judge his profession and his institution by his utterances. Accuracy, appropriate restraint, and respect for the opinions of others shall characterize all public utterances.

Adoption of these or similar propositions that eliminate the previous reservations concerning religious conformity will greatly strengthen the chances of Fordham's gaining academic and public approbation.* Since New York's Constitution forbids aid to universities "in which any denominational tenet or doctrine is taught," establishing that Fordham does not seek to indoctrinate its students is particularly important, and a policy of unrestricted academic freedom is one of the more effective ways of doing that. In all probability the new formulation involves a changing of words much more than a changing of behavior; at any rate, we know of no administrative behavior under the 1965 pronouncement that would have to be altered if the proposed constitution were adopted. But, perhaps especially in the area under discussion, mere words do have a vitality of their own, and restrictive words cannot be ignored even if they have not in the past been accompanied by deeds. We therefore strongly recommend approval of the unrestricted policy proposed by the constitutional draftsmen.

6. THE JESUIT COMMUNITY AND RESIDENCES

The existence of Fordham as a university is both complicated and enriched by the presence on its campus of a Jesuit residence,

---

* In the autumn of 1968 Fordham adopted a new Code of Academic Due Process which was apparently intended, in part, to eliminate these reservations, though the Code itself is procedural in nature.

Loyola-Faber Halls.[180] The residence is occupied by the Jesuit Community, that is, Jesuits who now serve as Fordham's faculty or administrators, who have retired after past services to the University, or who perform religious duties related directly to the spiritual well-being of Fordham students, faculty, or fellow Jesuits. Some 170 members of the Society of Jesus, of whom about 20 teach in the Preparatory School and 120 are active University personnel, share in the amenities and fellowship of the Community.

The president of the University is also its Rector,* in which capacity he is responsible for promoting the spiritual welfare of all Fordham Jesuits (in whatever capacity they may serve) and for providing for their material wants as well.[181] To help the Rector in what would otherwise no doubt be an overwhelming burden, a Superior has been appointed by the Society of Jesus to serve as the Rector's delegate.[182] The Superior, not the Rector, advises the resident Jesuits concerning their problems, weighs their requests, grants leaves of absence to engage in activities away from Fordham, and, in general, sees to community needs.

The Fordham Jesuit Community as such has no income of its own, nor do its members. All the expenses of maintaining Loyola and Faber Halls (which are in fact contiguous and interconnected), including provision of sustenance and an allowance for the personal wants of those who reside there, are borne by the University as a cost of operation. The amount budgeted for these purposes is far less than the amount earned by (but not in fact paid to) the individual Jesuits who serve the University in various capacities. The difference—amounting in 1967-1968 to $485,000—is the net value of the "contributed services" that constitute so large a share of Fordham's economic resources. Financially pressed as it has been year after year,

---

[180] In the past, Spellman Hall was similarly used. It is now a dormitory for girls and contains administrative offices for Thomas More College.

* For a subsequent separation of functions, see the Epilogue.

[181] The Self-Study of Fordham University 1963, at 80.

[182] A former Fordham president has written that "in addition to all the incongruous things any American university president is expected to do, . . . the incumbent at Fordham was expected, as Rector, to be the Religious Superior of 120 Jesuits; always in his place at table, always in his pew in the chapel, always in his room for conference, ready to make each one's personal problem his own." For a decade ending in 1949 the president was entirely relieved of the responsibilities of being Rector, but the division of responsibility for the University and for the Jesuit Community proved unsatisfactory to those involved at the time; so the presidency and the rectorship were again combined in the same person. Gannon, note 114 above, at 229-230.

Fordham might well have found itself insolvent had it been forced
to pay, in hard cash, salaries appropriately related to the administrative and teaching posts filled by Jesuits.

Yet it is precisely this symbiosis between the University and the
Community, each dependent on the other for nutriment and vitality,
that creates one of the most difficult of all problems for Fordham in
quest of a new identity. So long as the University explicitly and entirely supports the Jesuit Community, Fordham can scarcely establish
itself as nondenominational. Nor, for that matter, can the University
readily dispel the notion that its destinies are under the control of
those whose massive gift of service enables Fordham to maintain
fiscal equilibrium. Moreover, the dual role of the president of the
University as academic and religious chieftain serves further to tighten
the intertwining of Fordham and the Jesuit Community. If Fordham
is to be widely accepted as educationally independent, disentangle-
ment must somehow be achieved despite the obvious difficulties.*

Faced by a somewhat similar situation, St. Louis University in
1967 proceeded by use of conventional legal devices to "spin off" the
Jesuit Community that had previously been an element of the University. A civil corporation known as "The Jesuit Community Corporation at Saint Louis University" was newly formed, apart from
the university corporation itself. To it was leased the Community
residence, to be used until the Community completed plans to construct or purchase a new home. At the Community's head is a Rector
appointed by and serving at the pleasure of the General of the
Society. He has no power whatsoever over the University; nor does
the president of the University have power over the Jesuit Community, in which he lives and where, like all other members of the
Community, he is subject to the Rector.

The Jesuit Community Corporation gains its income chiefly
from the earnings of Jesuits in salaried positions at St. Louis University.[183] From its own income the Community Corporation then
meets expenses, as budgeted by those responsible for the Jesuit Com-

---

* For changes along these lines, see the Epilogue.

[183] "The salary of the individual Jesuit," the University has agreed, "is to be
determined at the same rate as for the layman of comparable experience,
competence, and position in the University," and he is also to receive all "fringe
benefits for which he may qualify."

Other Community Corporation income derives from Mass stipends, personal
gifts and donations, honoraria for lectures, and per diem charges to Jesuits who
have been assigned to live within the Community, but are not employed by or
retired from St. Louis University.

munity's affairs. The difference between income and outgo leaves a substantial sum at the Community's disposal. Since the Community acknowledges that its "primary apostolic work" is the support of St. Louis University, the Community has stated its intent to remit all its surplus funds to the University as, in effect, an equivalent of "contributed services." The Rector of the Community and the University's president have agreed to confer about the amount available for contribution, but if they disagree about what should be donated, "the decision of the Rector of the Jesuit Community shall prevail according to all justice and equity." In 1967-1968 the Community Corporation agreed to "pay, by way of alms in contributed services, monthly sixty per cent of the Jesuits' collective salaries," retaining the other forty per cent "to support the Jesuits and the Community.[184]

Precise emulation of this pattern may not be feasible at Fordham if the past dominance of the Society of Jesus is henceforth to be muted instead of reemphasized as it was during the St. Louis reorganization. Jesuits have during a century and a quarter made substantial sacrifices for Fordham, through the contributed services whose money value might have been expended for other Jesuit purposes had not the Society and the University been so closely identified with one another that they seemed almost a unity. If the unity be broken, the generous Jesuit giving that has sustained the University could not be taken wholly for granted in the future as it has been in the past.

The St. Louis structural changes do nevertheless have great suggestive value for Fordham. Separating the Community and the University is not only central in terms of the University's legal status;

---

[184] All the above descriptive material concerning the St. Louis situation is drawn from documents generously made available to the authors by St. Louis University. "The Jesuit Community Corporation at Saint Louis University" was incorporated on September 1, 1967. In contemplation of that civil formality the Provincial of the Missouri Province of the Society of Jesus, the Rector of the Jesuit Community, and the President of St. Louis University had framed a series of agreements concerning the Community, the status of Jesuits attached to the teaching or administrative staffs of the University, and continued involvement of the Society in the University's affairs. These, embodied in "Foundation Statements and Articles Relevant to the Jesuit Community at Saint Louis University," became effective on September 1, 1967. The agreements can be revised only by concurrent action of "the official representatives of all three parties," but "In case of disagreement among the Provincial, the Rector, and the President, the Provincial shall have the final say in the wording of any provisions."

it may be affirmatively desirable on other grounds.[185] The affairs of the one should be made distinguishable from the other's simply to allow for clarity of planning. For this purpose the corporate device utilized in St. Louis can readily be adopted in New York as well.

If a Fordham Community Corporation (governed by its own officers, not by the University's) were to be newly created, the University could sell it Loyola Hall and the plot of land on which it stands, which is now wholly owned by Fordham. Either in the form of a restrictive covenant in the deed of sale or as as option to repurchase, Fordham could and should protect itself against the possibility that the resulting enclave within its campus would ever be used for purposes incompatible with the University's interests. Faber Hall, whose construction was financed in part by federal funds, presents a different problem. Because of the public's involvement in this structure, we think no effort should be made to transfer its ownership. Its continued utilization by the University as a residence for Fordham teachers and administrators should present no difficulty.

The agreed upon purchase price of Loyola Hall (with the underlying land) and the dormitory rent for Faber Hall should be paid to the University, we suggest, in monthly installments that will roughly equal the net value of contributed services. At Fordham as at St. Louis University, the salaries earned by New York Province Jesuit staff members should, we believe, be placed at their disposal in fact, just as salaries are paid to laymen and to other religious staff members (including even Jesuits if not attached to the New York Province). What the recipients do with their earnings is for them to decide in accord with their religious vows, but without prescription by the University. Presumably the Jesuits who constitute the Fordham Community will pay over their salaries to it and will look to it, as now they look to the University, for their sustenance. The Community will thus have funds with which to meet the financial obligations arising from its use of Loyola and Faber Halls.

In the course of time the purchase price of Loyola Hall will have been fully paid, so that the amount of contractual payments will diminish. Until then, however, the Community Corporation

---

[185] See J. J. McGrath, Catholic Institutions in the United States 36, 37 (Catholic Univ., 1968).

would be legally bound to continue paying to the University in the form of purchase price a sum that would supplant the loss of "contributed services."

When the University could no longer rely on this contractual assurance of continuing help from the Fordham Jesuit Community, the Community would of course remain free to donate additional monies, prompted by sentimental attachment to the University, its members' involvement in Fordham's work and their concern for its success, and the Jesuit Order's present readiness to support experimentalism in educational organization. So long as Fordham's emergence as an independent university comes about not by revolution against the Jesuit Order's control, but, instead, by evolutionary development which the Order itself endorses, no reason exists why Jesuit interest in Fordham's well-being should abruptly cease. Prudence dictates the expectation, nevertheless, that the extent of Jesuit financial support may decline over the years if the present Fordham inter-relationships are significantly altered. Still, if the decline is only gradual, the University should be able to find means of offsetting the loss and, in the end, even more adequately supplying its fiscal wants.

A further word must be said about Faber Hall. If (as has been suggested in an earlier passage) Fordham Preparatory School were to move away from the Rose Hill campus, twenty Jesuit teachers who now reside in the Community would probably no longer be attached to it. Moreover, Jesuit administrators and teachers at Fordham will probably be fewer in the future than now, regardless of any changes in institutional design; half of all Jesuits now active in colleges and universities will have retired within the next fifteen years, the number of those entering the Order has been dropping, and the percentage of Jesuit recruits who are interested in higher education has been dropping even more markedly. The present demand for faculty living quarters in Faber Hall may therefore diminish markedly. No long term commitment of that space seems desirable at present. If Faber Hall should cease to be required for faculty housing, it could no doubt be quickly transformed into a student dormitory, for which Fordham has an urgent need.[186]

---

[186] Another building in which Jesuits reside is the John XXIII Center, next to the Rose Hill campus. Our recommendations regarding it are discussed above at pp. 57-58.

7. THE STUDENTS

Selection. Apart from the College of Philosophy and Letters,[187] Fordham has no religious restriction that affects its choice of undergraduate students. Its bulletins of information and also its application forms prominently state: "Information regarding religious preference, racial characteristics, and ethnic origin is neither requested nor taken into consideration by the Faculty Committee on Admissions." Our own examination of admissions procedures confirms the accuracy of the statement just quoted. The staff in the Admissions Office is diversified. College scholarships are not awarded on the basis of the applicant's religion.[188] No preference is given to applicants who have clerical sponsors, nor do application forms call for recommendations by clergymen. Especially in recent years aggressive efforts have been made to recruit students who attend public high schools in the New York metropolitan area.

In actual fact, nevertheless, over 95 per cent of the freshmen who enrolled on the Rose Hill campus in the autumn of 1967 described themselves as Catholics, and only 16 per cent came from public schools. The Fordham professional schools apart from Rose Hill have somewhat more heterogeneous student bodies, but still with a heavy preponderance of Catholics—more than 70 per cent in the School of Social Service, more than 50 per cent in the School of Education, more than 60 per cent in the School of Law. In the entering class that will launch the new liberal arts college on the Lincoln Center campus in the autumn of 1968, approximately 70 per cent of the students are likely to be Catholic.

Fordham's policy affirmatively favors a diversified student body. Its faculty and chief administrators are impressed by studies of the Admissions Office and the National Merit Scholarship Corporation, which concur in finding that highly qualified high school boys and girls tend to seek out colleges with mixed student bodies. Furthermore, many at Fordham are keenly interested in recruiting substantial numbers of entrants from "inner city" high schools, where many youngsters not of the Catholic faith are enrolled. When Admissions Office personnel visit schools of whatever nature, they stress Ford-

---

187 Discussed at pp. 50-52 above.

188 A regional scholarship plan, offered to the outstanding leader of each Jesuit high school in the country, see Gannon, note 114 above, at 246, has been abandoned. The University is well advised to avoid any policy, no matter how mild, that involves preferential treatment based on religion.

ham's academic features; as one official put the matter, "We make a secular university pitch, never a religious one. We don't sell Fordham as a place where you can save your soul. The kids to whom we are talking want to know whether they can get a good education at Fordham—and a good job afterward."

The present concentration of Catholic students is, then, a product of factors other than any current institutional policy. Fordham's former and present students, themselves preponderantly Catholic, naturally tend to "steer" their relatives and friends to their own alma mater. The University's past insistence that it was peculiarly Catholic and therefore, by hypothesis, safe for Catholic children gave it an identification which will not speedily disappear, no matter what steps Fordham may now take toward religious independence. We can only conclude that the University must continue—indeed, if possible, should increase—the efforts it is already making to develop a diverse student population.

This should not, in our view, be done primarily in order to establish Fordham's freedom from denominational bias; what has been done already is probably sufficient for that limited purpose. It should be done—as it has in fact been done—as a step toward Fordham's achieving the academic excellence it vigorously seeks. As a recent confidential Admissions Office report has pointed out, bringing together an undergraduate class composed entirely of outstanding students "does not necessarily create the most desirable educational community. Homogeneity can breed sterility. Nature loves diversity and so too with education. 'It is a basic principle of evolution, as well as human affairs, that diversity is a chief source of progress.' " We believe, as does the Fordham administration, that this is as true of religious diversity as of other kinds.

Control over student activities. Unlike a number of other institutions under Catholic influence or control, Fordham today seems not to constrain students' thought and action in accord with religious doctrine.[189] Compulsory attendance at religious devotions ended in 1961. A code of student conduct has been undergoing revision at the hands of an evenly balanced student-faculty committee, under the chairmanship of the Vice-President for Student Personnel, a layman. The present code is completely secular in tone and moderate in

---

[189] Cf. Carr v. St. John's University, 17 A.D. 2d 632, 231 N.Y.S. 2d 410, aff'd, 12 N.Y. 2d 802, 235 N.Y.S. 2d 834, 187 N.E. 2d 18 (1962); upholding the power of St. John's University, Brooklyn, to oust students who had wed in a civil marriage ceremony rather than according to religious prescription.

terms.[190] Nor is an indirect effort made to influence students toward religious enthusiasms by bestowing awards or distinctions on those whose behavior the Church might especially applaud.[191]

Fordham gives more than lip service to the notion that students should be free to challenge traditional attitudes and to formulate their own answers to questions others may believe have already been resolved. During 1968, for example, a prominent student group presented a lecture series on "Man and Woman in Contemporary Society." Among the topics discussed was "Love, Sex and Values," with talks by Albert Ellis, psychotherapist and executive director of the Institute for Rational Living, author of *Sex Without Guilt,* whose "attitude toward sex," according to the sponsoring committee's spokesman, 'is similar to that of Hugh Heffner," publisher of *Playboy* magazine; Richard Hettinger of Kenyon College, "noted for his lecture series 'Sex and the Single Student,' " author of *Living With Sex: The Student's Dilemma,* who reportedly believes that students' sexual problems are caused by "society's failure to come to grips with the realities and complexities of sex;" and Rev. Quentin Lauer, S.J., the then chairman of Fordham's Philosophy Department.[192] Lectures on marriage problems, contraception, and related topics have been presented without insistence that Church doctrine be respected. The Philosophy Club sponsors lectures not on Thomism, but on scientific revolutions, Karl Marx, and cybernetics.[193] The campus newspaper is published without censorship, with results that sometimes displease faculty members.[194] Currently contentious groups such

---

[190] See Fordham University Student Handbook 1967-1968, at 26.

[191] This comment is based upon our detailed examination of "Awards and Honors, Fordhan College, June 1967," a 30-page recording of institutional honors and recognitions.

[192] Fordham Ram, Vol. 50, No. 12, March 26, 1968, p. 2, col. 1. The University, far from seeking to hide news of the students' initiative, included a report of it in its official weekly news bulletin, Inside Fordham, March 26, 1968. The sponsors of the series also prepared an excellent annotated bibliography, which was apparently duplicated and distributed among students at the University's expense.

[193] Fordham University Student Handbook 1967-1968, at 112.

[194] Compare Fordham University Faculty Senate, Biennial Report May 1965-April 1967, at 13-14: "February 21, 1967. Dr. Martin J. Meade, Vice President for Student Personnel and Dean of Students, appeared as a guest . . . . The issue of student publications was discussed at length, specifically *The Ram,* which apparently received no direction from the faculty or the administration. Although it was recognized that censorship was to be avoided, there was some question as to why the University should subsidize this publication to the extent of $17,000 per year, in view of some alleged objectionable articles which have appeared in *The Ram.* Dr. Meade pointed out that the Administration had been unable to find a person willing to accept the responsibility of moderator for this publication. The Senate took no positive action with respect to the appointment of a supervisor over the student publications."

as Students for a Democratic Society (on the left) and Young Americans for Freedom (on the right) function on campus, and Thomas More College girls have set up an information table in the lobby of the Campus Center to inform male students about emigrating to Canada to escape military service.

Clearly, Fordham does not impose its institutional weight on the individual student in order to press him into an approved mold shaped by authority of the Church or the University.

Religious activism within the student body. In a later section we shall deal with religious activity under University auspices. Our present discussion has to do with activities and attitudes of students themselves, individually or in groups. It is directed to the question of whether a species of denominational zeal has grown out of or is otherwise related to the homogeneity of the Fordham student body. If this has occurred even without the University's conscious choice, the nature of the institution might be affected.

A survey of the career plans declared by entering freshmen in Fordham College and Thomas More College during each of the past several years indicates that approximately twenty-five freshmen boys (out of 625) but no freshmen girls (out of 225) believe they are preparing for religious vocations. During the same period four to six students have left Fordham annually in order to take religious vows. Neither the expectations nor the actions of Fordham students force upon the University the role of supplier of future priests or nuns.

As for religiously-oriented student organizations on campus, only two have been noted. The Fordham College Sodality has existed, apparently, from Fordham's earliest days. Once upon a time it devoted itself to such activities as organizing living rosaries in honor of Mary. Now it is composed of about thirty young men and women who desire to devote energy to religious living, but who do so by probing into moral and social issues as well as worshipping. An organizer of stimulating lectures and symposia, a strong believer in ecumenical development, Sodality has become in some campus eyes a nest of Catholic radicals and pacifists.[195] The other campus group

<hr>

[195] A branch of the Sodality has existed in the downtown School of Education and will presumably continue with a broadened membership drawn from Fordham units located on the Lincoln Center Campus. The Intown Sodality has stressed tutoring projects in underprivileged areas in New York City and elsewhere in the country. Since 1965 its "Poverty Apostolate" has given material assistance to needy families in Tennessee and Kentucky. Fordham University Student Handbook 1967-1968, at 115.

is the Confraternity of Christian Doctrine, with a membership of about a hundred. C.C.D., as it is familiarly known, has become a social work organization much more than a spreader of the gospel; but its Catholic orientation is clearly shown by its clients if not by the nature of its deeds. C.C.D. members engage in parish teaching, tutoring of underprivileged and emotionally disturbed children, and counseling in Church-related centers.[196]

Obviously the existence of these religiously motivated student groups, with their rather small memberships, does not transform Fordham's campus into a denominational center. No University regulation, practice, or unspoken policy prevents the creation of additional groups having different religious orientations. If students of the Jewish, Protestant, or other religions ever decide to organize a club, they will be unhampered in forming counterparts of the Newman Clubs that Catholic students have established at many universities.[197] Meanwhile, the involvement of perhaps 150 students in activities related to their Catholic faith does not, for better or for worse, tincture the University as an entirety.

The special case of the School of Education. Despite the generally observed non-denominationalism of the University's student admissions policies discussed earlier, a special problem does perhaps exist in the School of Education. In 1953 Fordham became the official archdiocesan training agency for the religious of New York, for whom the Archdiocese helped defray costs and whom the University until 1968 aided by a favorable differential in tuition fees.[198] Such a differential would be out of line with a claim to be a nonsectarian institution. We have been informed that the School no longer enjoys a special status in the Archdiocese. Any formal designation as an arch-

---

196 Id. at 97-98. With C.C.D. may be compared another social welfare organization of Fordham students, FUSE. FUSE (Fordham University Social Effort), a university-wide group, does not, like C.C.D., have a Jesuit faculty adviser; in fact, it has none at all. It seeks to focus "the body of experience, knowledge, and personnel that is Fordham on the massive and complex problem of poverty." It is looking for "tangible results" and its "programs are geared to the real wants of the people." FUSE "aids the people in crystallizing their wants in specific areas of action" and then it "works *with* the people at all times." Id. at 103.

197 On the Rose Hill campus, the likelihood that this will happen is directly related to the number of non-Catholics who may become students. In some other branches of the University, which already enroll a substantial number of Jews and some Protestants, only the desire to create religious organizations is now absent.

198 See Gannon, note 114 above, at 286; Fordham University School of Education Catalog, 1967-1968, at 19.

diocesan instrumentality should be carefully avoided in the future. It would imply a judgment by the ecclesiastical authorities that the institution is in some significant respects distinctively Catholic—a judgment that others might well accept without further deliberation.

Another problem presented by the School of Education concerns the Graduate Division of Religious Education. Since the questions raised are similar to those with regard to the Ph.D. program in theology, this Division is discussed below.

The special case of the Graduate School of Arts and Sciences. Like the other branches of Fordham previously discussed, the student body of the Graduate School of Arts and Sciences is preponderantly Catholic. Of the 1570 men and women enrolled as full-time or part-time graduate students in 1967-1968, four out of five were believed to be Catholic. Most of these candidates for a master's or doctor's degree were graduates of avowedly Catholic colleges.[199]

Thus far the picture is essentially the same as elsewhere in the University. An unusual feature is added, however, by the fact that nearly a fourth of all degree candidates in the Graduate School are priests, nuns, and other religious—370, or 23 per cent of all enrolled in the School.[200]

So large a concentration of the religious naturally generates the question whether Fordham has become, to a significant degree, a training center for clerical educators, instead of remaining a center for advanced studies by all who are qualified to pursue them. Noting the question, we provide as an answer our own opinion that the Graduate School does not shape itself to suit special needs of the religious graduate scholars (if, indeed, special needs exist). Nor does it appraise the religious differently from laymen either in accepting them as candidates or in evaluating the quality of their work while at Fordham. If, contrary to what we have thus far been able to discover, any department within the Graduate School does in fact differentiate in any way between one category of degree candidates and the other, the differentiation should of course be ended at once. So long as parity is practiced in deed as well as in word, we perceive no reason why Fordham should discourage attendance in its Graduate

---

199 In 1962-63, 1307 graduate students were registered, of whom 6.8 per cent were non-Catholic and 82.0 per cent had graduated from Catholic colleges. The Self-Study of Fordham University 1963, at 178.

200 The percentage in 1962-1963 had been 35.9. Ibid.

School by religious personnel. No principle of civil law or educational wisdom requires or would justify Fordham's regarding an applicant as unsuitable solely because of his religious commitments. Fordham will not lose its repute as an institution of higher learning so long as it treats each candidate as a graduate student only—that is, as an academic person, not as a religious person with a status setting him or her apart from other graduate students.

8. THE TEACHING OF THEOLOGY AND PHILOSOPHY

Suspicion about the academic credentials and purposes of Philosophy and Theology departments in Catholic institutions is understandable. For many generations courses in these areas were taught —and in some institutions they apparently still are taught—for the purpose of sealing minds, not stretching them. Scornful of philosophy as presented in inferior institutions like Harvard, a Jesuit scholar of another day exclaimed proudly: "Only the Catholic colleges, if my observation is correct, have a vast, compact, thoroughly reasoned and tested body of philosophic truth, extending over the whole field, consistent in all parts, taught and drilled into every graduate by lecture, repetition, disputation and essay, until it becomes a part of his very mind and mode of thought."[201] In 1924 the then Prefect General of Studies of the Society of Jesus could declare (though not without the quickly expressed disagreement of a few other Jesuits) that the "main purpose in teaching philosophy to our students is to defend the faith. However much we may think of its disciplinary effectiveness; however strongly we may insist on its cultural value, down in our hearts we know very well that our controlling motive is to implant these principles which we have received from a higher source than mere reason—to render our students immune from those infections of scepticism and materialism that are in the air we breathe. The teaching of philosophy is propaganda in the justifiable sense of the word."[202] The student, thus immunized against doubt, became a well trained "swordsman in defense of a system."

Some Catholic colleges may continue to believe that this is the end to be sought by philosophy or theology teachers. Philosophy,

---

[201] Quoted in Gannon, note 114 above, at 107.
[202] Id. at 174.

they seem to feel, should be the handmaiden of Theology, and Theology should deny even the speculative worth of conceptions other than those already authoritatively approved.[203] Perhaps as a consequence of this rigidity present-day Catholic college students, according to a recent critique, have often received instruction in these fields "with a mixture of bored indifference and hostile resentment;" their instructors, some students believe, "still act as if they were dealing with students who wanted a pat catechism to memorize, regurgitate, and forget."[204]

Fordham has sought to move in a different direction. It is indubitably seeking to free itself from whatever may have been a past heritage of dogmatism, indoctrination, and intellectual delimitation. The Fordham Theology and Philosophy Departments are not closed to non-Catholic teachers, nor do they require instructors to promise they will never stray from defined paths. A recent University pronouncement asserts that theology, though "taken seriously," is "approached competitively as is any other respected, legitimate academic discipline. It is assumed that the student of theology wants to learn his subject without the prior judgment that all forms of theology are in error except one."[205] The Department of Theology declares its purposes in terms that might readily be adopted by any of the scientific or humanistic departments of the University. Its course offerings are not limited to microscopic analysis of the underpinnings of the Catholic faith, but include surveys of twentieth-century Protestant thought, Zen Buddhism, and Judaism past and present. The Department of Philosophy offers undergraduate courses that explore the ideas of Hegel, Kant, Marx, and the Existentialists as well as those of Aquinas and Catholic moralists. The two departments perceive themselves not simply as conservators of the old, but as developers of the new, with interests that bring them into intellectual association

---

203 See, e.g., J. Foster, "Some Effects of Jesuit Education," and J. E. Kearns, "Social Consciousness and Academic Freedom in Catholic Higher Education," in R. Hassenger ed., The Shape of Catholic Higher Education at 165, 247 (U. of Chicago, 1967).

204 Jencks and Riesman, note 125 above, at 369. And see also Greeley, note 126 above, at 172. "Are the theology courses lively, distinctive presentations of the best of contemporary theologizing? On the contrary, in most instances they present dull, lifeless, and pre-Vatican theology which young people are compelled to take and would escape from cheerfully if they could do so."

205 This is Fordham Today 10 (1968). A similar theme was developed by Christopher Mooney, Chairman of the Theology Department, in his remarks at the Spring Conference of the Fordham University Council, April 20, 1968.

with other academics.[206] Changes in tone have perhaps been unblatant, but still they have been sufficiently unsubtle to have aroused concern among Fordham graduates, some of whom have outspokenly wondered whether the University has not forsaken its loyalties and whether it may not be stimulating students to forsake theirs.

The nature of the offerings in Theology and Philosophy takes on particular importance in New York in light of the prohibition of aid to institutions "in which any denominational tenet or doctrine is taught." As has been suggested earlier, this limitation certainly does not foreclose academic treatment of religious subjects, else it would render ineligible a large number of universities and colleges in the state. Studies of religion and religious thinking are accepted elements of American higher education in institutions whose freedom from ecclesiastical control is unquestionable. What the Constitution does do is apparently to preclude public subsidization of institutions that indoctrinate. In judging theology and philosophy courses, a court might consider what subjects are taught, how they are taught, who teaches them, and whether they are required. At present, the range of subject matter in Fordham's offerings is undoubtedly broad enough to preclude a hasty judgment that their purpose is indoctrination. Neither judges nor officials, we predict, would feel well qualified to analyze the materials and the teaching methods in such courses as, say, "Johannine Theology" or "The Church in Theological Perspective" to determine whether coursework is academically noncommital or is, instead, religiously dogmatic. Inquiry into the specifics of the program would be distasteful because any outsider's and especially a public official's questioning about what professors do in their classrooms may seem a threat to academic freedom. Unless precisely such an inquiry were to be made, Fordham's extensive course offerings in the field of religion would not be a source of difficulty. Fordham has done enough—and will no doubt

---

[206] Compare "The Idea of the Catholic University," a statement prepared by R. J. Henle, S.J., based on discussions in 1967 among prominent educators under the auspices of the North American region of the International Federation of Catholic Universities, at p. 2: "In a Catholic university all recognized university areas of study are frankly and fully accepted and their internal autonomy affirmed and guaranteed. There must be no theological or philosophical imperialism; all scientific and disciplinary methods, and methodologies, must be given due honor and respect. However, there will necessarily result from the interdisciplinary discussions an awareness that there is a philosophical and theological dimension to most intellectual subjects when they are pursued far enough. Hence, in a Catholic university there will be a special interest in interdisciplinary problems and relationships."

in time do even more—to show persuasively that neither faculty members who are theologians and philosophers nor students who take their courses are doctrinally shackled.

If, however, Fordham is to gain full acceptance within the non-Catholic academic community from which it hopes to attract future teachers and also within the non-Catholic secondary schools from which it hopes to draw a desirably diversified student body,[207] Theology and Philosophy may need further analysis (or continued implementation of directions already decided upon) by Fordham itself. The present situation leaves open some questions that may create a "credibility gap" in the educational world. In terms of Fordham's long-range development, this may be even more important than officials' opinions concerning what Fordham does.

The purpose of the basic courses. Considerable evidence exists that the basic offering in Theology and Philosophy, especially the former, has until now had somewhat more to do with the student's faith than with his liberal education. Of course the two are not mutually exclusive.[208] Still, one could sense in the Fordham curriculum a continuing resolve to use academic discipline as a means of forcing engagement in denominational study, a policy unlikely to be applauded in academic circles.

Throughout the University's undergraduate branches—in Pharmacy and Business Administration and Education as well as in the liberal arts colleges of Thomas More and Fordham—all Catholic students, but not others, were until 1967-1968 required to complete a year-long introductory course in theology, defined as follows:

> Nature of religious experience; its relevance in changing periods of thought and culture; the Judeo-Christian experience in the context of modern biblical exegesis; development of the Christian doctrinal tradition culminating in Vatican II; status and future of current theological discussion.

To insist that all students, whatever be their special interests, should at some point open their minds to the complexities of religious philosophy or religious history or religious literature might be a sustainable judgment concerning educational values. To insist that

---

[207] See pp. 87-88, above.

[208] Compare This Is Fordham Today 10 (1968); ". . . . Fordham believes that to be liberally educated a man must understand and appreciate his own religious heritage and tradition. This understanding failing, the connection between a liberal education and a man's life and conduct is appreciably weakened."

Catholic students receive instruction from which others are excused suggests an effort to propagate a sectarian viewpoint. This is a religious, not an educational purpose, and would be difficult to square with the state constitution's limitation on teaching doctrine.

In Fordham and Thomas More Colleges, which at present enroll virtually no students who declare themselves to be non-Catholics, the required study of Theology has become all-embracive.[209] Elsewhere in the University, non-Catholic students can apparently be trained to become creditable school teachers or business executives or druggists without having mastered "Theology 11-12"—or, for that matter, any species of theology whatsoever if they prefer to enroll instead in other types of non-vocational courses.[210]

This kind of differentiation among students is inescapably a serious academic embarrassment. It runs counter to the main currents that now course through the University. Two recent developments suggest that the embarrassment can be eliminated or at least lessened gracefully.

First, at the new liberal arts college in Lincoln Center a freshly designed introductory course will be required of all entering students, without reference to their religious preferences. It will survey the literary and historical forces that have aggregately shaped the "Judeo-Christian tradition." Conducted by four instructors drawn from different religious backgrounds and possessing varied intellectual resources, the course will presumably shed light not only on Catholic doctrinal positions, but on other views concerning matters as to which Catholics and non-Catholics have disagreed or have arrived at similar conclusions by different routes. The success of the new survey course may not be assured. It ambitiously hopes to cover in a scholarly way,

---

[209] Compare Report of the President, Fordham University, 1965-1967, at 8: ". . . Fordham sees it has a responsibility to provide courses in Theology for all students, regardless of their religious heritage. The fact is now realized that the religious heritage of all our students is a part of their cultural backgrounds. A university which fails to reveal that part of a man's heritage is failing in its duty."

[210] See School of Education Catalog 1967-1968, at 21, 74 (Catholic undergraduate students must "take Theology 11-12" and two other Theology courses; those "not of the Catholic faith may, but are not required to, take the courses in theology. If they prefer not to take these courses, they must select in their place a set of courses with credit equivalency") ; School of Business Administration Catalog 1967-1968, at 23, 40 (to the same effect, with the added notation that "Theology introduces the student into a study of revelation's fact and meaning, the historical person of Christ and His work and teaching") ; College of Pharmacy Catalog 1967-1968, at 17, 26 (to the same effect; non-Catholics "may substitute approved electives") .

within the dimensions of a single year, the Old Testament, the New Testament, pre-Reformation history, and modern theological history. Whether or not all of this be accomplished, the course is planned as an unequivocal element of general education in a manner that a course "For Catholics Only" can only debatably be.

Second, the liberal arts colleges on the Rose Hill campus have recently generalized and, in so doing, liberalized their requirements. In past years each student was compelled to enroll for a specified number of course credits in various subject matters, including a generally required introductory course in Theology. At Fordham College in September 1967 and at Thomas More College in September 1968 the specifics were softened without, however, losing sight of the desirability of broadening and diversifying the student's intellectual experiences. Before he or she graduates, each student will have completed a total of thirty-two courses. Regardless of his chosen area of specialization, the student will sample the curriculum generously, for he must distribute sixteen of his courses among the following four general areas:

Philosophy and Theology	5 courses
Literature and Fine Arts	5 courses
History and Social Sciences	3 courses
Mathematics and the Natural Sciences	3 courses

Within these four divisions the student may choose widely. If, as we understand to be the case, Catholic students will not be channeled into particular courses and if the available offerings continue to include courses that are plainly not doctrinaire, a distribution requirement like this one can readily be sustained on educational grounds. Educators may debate whether other groupings might be preferable—for example, Humanities, Social Science, and Natural Science—but we believe that Fordham's present choice is readily sustainable as curricular planning without covert religious purposes.

The composition of the teaching staff. A further question about the detachment of Fordham's theologians and philosophers arises from their emphatically Catholic background.

The Philosophy Department in Fordham College in 1967-1968 had twenty-four members in professorial ranks. Seventeen were Jesuits, four were graduates of Catholic colleges (three of whom had also earned their doctorates in Catholic institutions), and only three were men whose education had been mainly outside Catholic influence. Of the ten persons holding the rank of instructor, two were Jesuits, another was a member of a different religious order, and the remaining seven were Catholic college products.

The Theology Department, in its professorial ranks, listed twenty-three Jesuits, four other Catholic religious, four laymen trained in Catholic institutions, and one non-Catholic layman. In the sub-professorial ranks were a Jewish visiting lecturer, a Catholic adjunct instructor, and a Catholic instructor.

We do not for a moment contend that the heavy preponderance of Catholics—and, specifically, of Jesuit priests—in these two departments connotes unprofessionalism or covert proselytizing. To some extent it undoubtedly reflects a process of self-selection, since the combination of religious and intellectual enthusiasms that led some of these able men to become Jesuits led them also to their choice of a professional specialty. Moreover, the subject matters with which some of these scholars deal are not in themselves crowded with opportunities for indoctrination of religious propositions— Hebrew, for example, or linguistic and philosophical analysis of papyri, or Aramaic or Syriac, or the documents of Qumran (all of which, we may note, are taught by Jesuits). We have been impressed, too, by what we have learned concerning the present professional tone of the two departments in question. Nevertheless we rather doubt that the academic world at large will cease thinking of Fordham as a special Catholic enclave unless these especially sensitive departments can gain a diversified membership. We also believe that public officials and courts would be impressed by a more diversified faculty in these departments, though they might well decide that the present distribution is consistent with an absence of indoctrination and denominational control.

We recognize that Fordham faces difficulty here. It cannot effectively compete for non-Catholic scholars of philosophy and subjects related to theology so long as non-Catholics suppose that Fordham is inhospitable. That supposition will probably continue so long as non-Catholics are rarities in these departments. Drawing in a few more non-Catholics—or, at the least, Catholics who have had a nonsectarian educational experience—will require intensive effort. But unless that effort is made, many people may continue to suspect that Fordham intends to remain aggressively denominational at heart, whatever may be the surface indications to the contrary.

Unfair this may be. Without having made a survey, we hazard the guess that the religion departments in some institutions which remain untroubled by academic or governmental doubts about their detachment are no more diverse than Fordham's. Does something like a double standard of morality require, then, that Catholic colleges be more ecumenical than others in this respect?

The answer to that question, we believe, is plain. The problem lies not in double standards but, rather, in the recency of change in Catholic institutions and in their emphasis on Theology and Philosophy as the integrating subjects for the curriculum. Having long regarded these as fortifications of the faith more than as academic subjects, some Catholic colleges—Fordham among them—have now altered their viewpoint. Persuading others that the alteration has in fact occurred may require more powerful proofs than would be demanded if the institutional past were not casting a shadow upon the present.

Training of teachers of religion. A question of a markedly different nature may be raised about the graduate program in Theology, within the Graduate School of Arts and Sciences, and the Master's degree program in Religious Education, formally part of the School of Education.

The Theology Department, which accepts none who aspire only to the Master of Arts degree,[211] is said to attract a particularly well qualified Ph.D. group. In 1967-1968, 111 graduate students were registered for work in Theology. Among them were 53 laymen and laywomen and 68 priests, nuns, and other religious, including two Protestant clergy. Although the Fordham program has begun to attract non-Catholics, over 90 per cent of those now enrolled in it are Catholic. Virtually every candidate—Catholic and non-Catholic, lay and religious—has teaching as his personal goal.[212]

---

[211] The Department does grant a Master's degree as the terminal degree for the occasional student who, contrary to initial expectation, is found not to be of doctoral caliber.

[212] Compare J. M. Lee, "Education: The Winds of Change," 107 Ave Maria 6, 9 (April 13, 1968) : Teachers of religion "are flocking in almost unbelievably large numbers to universities to receive graduate training in the many new catechetical programs which have sprung up there. At bottom, there are two distinct types of university-based training programs. The first, historically and numerically, is the type of training program which treats catechetics as fundamentally a mode of applied theology. The Catholic University of America pattern has become the exemplar for this type of program, which includes Fordham University, Manhattan College, The Loyola Pastoral Institute, Webster College and many others. The second type of program treats catechetics as primarily a mode of the teaching-learning process; i.e., the facilitation of the actual learning of religion in educational and familial settings. The University of Notre Dame program, in which the students major in eudcation and minor in theology, is the archetype of this pattern."

The Theology Department's graduate offering is plainly educational in the most professional sense, but its presence in the Graduate School may complicate Fordham's eligibility for federal grants under existing law. The Department of Health, Education, and Welfare is forbidden by law to help a university finance its expenditures for staff, research or building constructoin connected with the training of teachers of religion. From this follows the conclusion that future applications to the federal government for general assistance in support of Fordham's graduate enterprises must (in our best judgment) cautiously separate the Theology Department from the rest of the Graduate School.[213]

Graduate Division for Religious Education. Although officially an element of the School of Education, the Graduate Division for Religious Education is essentially an independent enterprise, located at Rose Hill rather than downtown, with its own faculty, and supervised only in the most nominal way by the Dean.* In 1967-68, this division enrolled 70 students (12 laymen and laywomen, 26 male religious, and 32 nuns). The faculty was composed of seven Jesuits and three lay persons. All teachers and all students were Catholic. The purpose of the division, which grants the Master's degree in religious education, is to train graduate students to teach the Catholic religion in parochial or other religious schools, and to prepare them to supervise other teachers of Catholicism. In recent years the emphasis has shifted from a fairly constant dose of Theology to include methodological aspects of teaching religion. Efforts have been made to strengthen connections with non-Catholic institutions, such as Union Theological Seminary. Nonetheless, despite such courses

---

[213] How this may be done we must leave for later analysis, which can best be undertaken in the light of discussions with Health, Education, and Welfare officials concerning a specific proposal. We note in passing that other activities in the Graduate School are unlikely to be regarded as training for a "religious vocation." A Washington official with whom we discussed present policies summarized his opinion as follows: "If a program prepares members of a religious order to perform secular tasks (such as treating lepers) in conjunction with the work of the order, this is training for a religious vocation." Notwithstanding that opinion, we believe that the nature of a program must be determined by its main purpose and not by the adventitious circumstance that a priest or nun might be able to utilize the program in furtherance of a religious vocation. In this view a medical school would not become a program to train persons for a religious vocation simply because some of its students were religiously motivated in seeking medical training. The determining factor would be the institution's purpose, not the students'.

* The Board of Trustees has eliminated this department from the School of Education and has created a Graduate Institute of Religious Education, without significantly altering the function of this element of the University.

as "The Psychology of Religion in the Adolescent," the curriculum is still heavy with more traditional offerings like "An Introduction to Salvation History." These courses are not taught critically, but are meant to convey the content which a teacher of religion should, in turn, convey to his pupils.

Quite clearly, a program of this type could not be supported by federal and state funds. "Denominational tenets and doctrines" are frankly taught in the Theology courses, which are purposefully designed to give instruction in Catholic dogmas. That suffices to create ineligibility to receive public grants in aid of this particular program. We doubt that the aggressive sectarianism of this one unit would determine the characterization of the entire Fordham enterprise, although in an otherwise close case it might be a factor of considerable weight. The real issue to be examined by Fordham is whether a university that aspires to independent status can justify continuing in its School of Education a program designed solely to train persons to teach a single religious faith. Fordham should perhaps consider whether its religious education division, which is seemingly remote from the rest of university life, might advantageously be shifted to a theological seminary or to some other ecclesiastical sponsor.

9. RELIGION ON THE CAMPUS

A Roman Catholic chaplain and three assistant chaplains are responsible for maintaining religious activity on the Fordham campus. In addition to the University Church, a number of small chapels facilitate attendance at Masses, of which fifteen are offered daily. Opportunities for making confessions are also scheduled daily. Attendance at religious services is voluntary throughout. It is encouraged by posted notices and, to some extent, by personal reminders, but the requirements that formerly led to outward displays of piety regardless of inner feelings have been altogether abandoned.[214]

---

[214] See Fordham University General Bulletin of the Undergraduate Colleges, Series 3, No. 11, at 10 (1967): "As a Roman Catholic University, Fordham is vitally interested in the religious and moral dimensions of its student body. . . . All students, including those not of the Catholic faith, are invited to share in the rich religious spirit that has always characterized Fordham University. No student, of course, is required to attend any religious services." To the same effect, see An Introduction to the Undergraduate Colleges of Fordham University 10 (1967). Two especially ceremonious occasions—an "annual Mass of the Holy Spirit to dedicate to God the work of the scholastic year" and a Baccalaureate Mass—are noted in the above-cited publications, but attendance is clearly voluntary.

Must the present Catholic religious activity and the organization that supports it under University auspices be altered if Fordham is to be regarded as free from religious domination?

First, we note again—with emphasis—that Fordham no longer prescribes, as once it did, its students' religious behavior. We have been assured, moreover, that Fordham would today (differently from the past) facilitate non-Catholic religious activity by students and faculty, were interest to be manifested. Here we imply no belief that a university must appoint and support religious counsellors for every significantly large religious grouping within its student body, or that it must provide on-campus facilities for counsellors paid for by others. We are aware of strong moves within nondenominational institutions to terminate altogether their provision of religious personnel and facilities (including employment of a college chaplain). Belief has grown not only in academic circles but also in ecclesiastical bodies that concern with students' religious activity should be transferred wholly from the universities to the churches. If Fordham wished to adopt a policy in accord with that view, it could do so safely. What it cannot do safely is to strain itself to be attentive to Catholic students while coldly ignoring the non-Catholics.

As matters now stand, Fordham's situation presents no problem of monopoly or exclusivity other than flows naturally from the numerical dominance of Catholics in the student body.

College chaplains. Certainly the presence of chaplains on campus does not in itself create a difficulty. To hold otherwise would be to call into question the status of a vast number of American colleges, in which clergymen and religious counsellors of various kinds have been appointed to advise and possibly to inspire students. The fact that Fordham's chaplains are Catholic has no more significance, for purposes of the present discussion, than does the Protestantism of the chaplains, at, say, Columbia and Wesleyan.[215]

---

[215] Compare The Faculty Handbook of Columbia University 1968, at 145: "The chapel program is under the direction of the chaplain of the University, who is an Episcopalian, in accordance with a tradition dating back to the origins of King's College;" Wesleyan University Catalog 1967-1968, at 40: "There are weekly Sunday morning services held in the Memorial Chapel, conducted in a broadly Protestant tradition, under the direction of the Minister to the College Church." We take note of the fact that both Wesleyan and Columbia make provision for religious counsellors who are not of the same faith as the chaplain (or minister), in order to meet the needs of their diversified student bodies.

Like the generality of college chaplains, Fordham's are chosen and appointed by the University, through its president. One may perhaps assume, however, that assignments to these posts would not be made in the face of opposition by the Society of Jesus or the Archbishop of New York. At least theoretically, nevertheless, the staff engaged in this branch of University activity is directly subject to the University and is not externally controlled by a religious organization. Whether Fordham could itself appoint and remove Roman Catholic chaplains if it were no longer to be regarded as a Jesuit institution, is another matter. The present power to choose religious counsellors, is in a sense, a reflection of Fordham's having been accepted as committedly Catholic. Were it not so accepted, possibly it would no longer be in a position to select, without ecclesiastical participation, the holders of priestly offices on its campus. As to this, contrary opinions have been expressed by persons presumably well versed in the law and practice of the Church.

The college church. The Fordham church both resembles and differs from the churches and chapels that are commonplace in independent colleges and universities. The main place of worship at Fordham is the Church of Our Lady, Mediatrix of All Graces, constructed in 1845. Until December 4, 1893, it functioned as parish church for the neighborhood. On that date its status changed and it became exclusively a devotional center for use by Fordham students and faculty, with no ties to the surrounding community.[216] In this respect it is like most other college churches, whatever be their religious coloration.

The University Church of Our Lady differs from most other campus churches, however, in that the University cannot confer upon its pastor a full measure of liberty to determine the religious expression that occurs within it, since the priests within the church are subject to ecclesiastical control over the content and form of worship. Nor may the University freely determine what use may be made of the church by others. Although legal title to the building and the land on which it stands is vested in the University's trustees, the church may not be devoted to non-Catholic religious services so long as the Archbishop withholds consent.[217]

---

[216] See Gannon, note 114 above, at 113.

[217] As to a collateral use of the church, see Fordham University Student Handbook 1967-1968, at 42: "Recently, the Archdiocese has granted permission for weddings in the University Church for members of the 'Fordham Family.' Each applicant must be approved by the bride's pastor and the Archdiocese."

Furthermore the ecumenical spirit has not yet led widely to multidenominational use of Catholic church premises, so that Fordham does not at present share other universities' freedom to allow use of the campus church by various religious and community groups.[218]

The campus church, viewed realistically, has in fact been a distinctively Jesuit, and not a distinctively Fordham, responsibility. Thought might well now be given to regularizing the legal position and, simultaneously, to eliminating any question about external control over activities on the University's property and ostensibly under its direction. This could be done by selling the church to the New York Province of the Society of Jesus or, if it be created as has been suggested, to the Fordham Jesuit Community Corporation.[219]

We are apprised that canon law imposes no obstacles other than the necessity of various notifications and formal approvals. The transfer of title could be accompanied by covenants and the granting of necessary easements—covenants to assure continued maintenance of the church for use by the "Fordham Family" and easements to assure continued access to the church across the surrounding University campus.

If this were done, the Fordham Chaplain would become, simply, the pastor of the Church of Our Lady, Mediatrix of All Graces, designated as such by appropriate ecclesiastical action without the University's participation. The assistant chaplains would become, simply, the pastor's assistants. Their changed designation would not lessen their availability. It would not alter the character of the

----

218 Compare Wesleyan University Catalog 1967-1968, at 40: Memorial Chapel, which is under the direction of a Protestant, is the scene of Sunday church services; it is also the scene of Sunday morning Mass. And see Columbia University, News and Comments from the Office of the Chaplain, Spring Term 1968, at 1, 2: "Having received assurance that St. Paul's is not an 'Episcopal Church,' the Archdiocese of New York (Roman Catholic) agreed two years ago to permit Catholic worship in the chapel;" the regular Sunday schedule includes Holy Communion (Lutheran) at 9:30, Holy Communion with Sermon (Book of Common Prayer) at 11:00, and Mass (Roman Catholic) at 5:00. Mass is celebrated in the chapel daily except Saturday. See also Columbia University Faculty Handbook 1968, at 145: "The University provides, through the office of the Chaplain, the fullest opportunity to students, staff, and faculty members for the conduct of the religious life and the pursuit of religious knowledge. St. Paul's Chapel is a University building open to the use of any religious group seeking to serve the University community."

219 For the relevant discussion of the possible incorporation of the Community, see pp. 83-86, above.

services rendered by them to the Fordham academic community.[220] It would not diminish the frequency or the richness of liturgical moments at Fordham.[221] It would simply make plain that the church is close to, but is nevertheless organically distinct from the academic corporation.

Were this step to be taken, Fordham would not be treading an unblazed trail. As long ago as 1757 the college church at Yale became "The Church of Christ in Yale University," a formally constituted ecclesiastical entity.[222] In 1916 what had been the college church of Wesleyan University was separately organized under the name "The Church of Christ in Wesleyan University," open to membership by Wesleyan students or staff who accept its purpose, which is defined as a "fellowship of students and members of the faculty for the purpose of common worship and mutual encouragement in seeking to discover and follow the Christian way of life."[223] And at St. Louis University, which is determinedly Jesuit, the church popularly identified as "the St. Louis University church" is in fact and in law the St. Francis Xavier Catholic Church, connected with the University by a walkway and by long usage, but not otherwise.

[220] Fordham University Student Handbook 1967-1968, at 42: "The University Chaplain is the 'quasi-pastor' for the University community. As such, he organizes all major religious functions of the community. . . . It is his responsibility, too, whenever the University is in operation, to provide the ordinary religious service such as Masses and confession periods, as well as to assist any individual or groups who wish special religious services. His office is always available for those who desire counseling or consultation."

[221] Compare J. W. Donohue, Jesuit Education 175-176 (Fordham, 1963), commenting on the significance of the liturgy in the educational setting: "A religious sense of the presence of God is directly and powerfully awakened by participation in the liturgical life of worship within the Church. From a brief communal prayer to the most splendid celebration of Solemn Mass, the liturgical moment always constitutes an actually holy situation highly effective for deepening faith in the Divine reality and an effective response to it. Moreover, the Mass also evokes and enlarges the Christians' sense of their oneness with each other in the Lord. Even at the level of sociological observation, it can be seen that a sharing in religious ritual unifies the members of a group. They not only act together but their fraternal feeling is strengthened by a spiritual transformation when it is brought into the very sanctuary. This vivid awareness of the Holy God and of the sacred character of the community when once it has been related to Him, contributes profoundly to growth in personal goodness. Consequently, cultivation of the liturgical life is a central element in the plan of Jesuit education for development of moral stature. This does not mean, of course, that the liturgy is thought of chiefly as a means for fostering individual devotion and social unity. Its primary function remains the worship of God and the offering of that homage to which both the person and the community are obliged. The Catholic educator, however, knows that the liturgical action also has these rich moral values and he hopes to cultivate them reverently. . . ."

[222] See Yale University Bulletin, series 63, no. 22, at 119 (1967).

[223] Wesleyan University Bulletin 1960-1961, at 85.

Chapels on campus. In addition to the Church of Our Lady, three chapels are maintained on the Rose Hill campus and one at the Intown Center. These mini-churches, as someone has called them, are at all times available for private prayer. In two of the chapels the Mass Schedule laid down by the Chaplain provides the liturgy at convenient hours on all class days.

We have gained the impression that non-Catholic use of some or all of the chapels, for meditation or for worship, might be arranged without great difficulty. On at least two occasions, when Fordham's campus has been the scene of conferences among clergymen of diverse faiths, a chapel has been utilized for Protestant religious services. Upon the assumption that slight physical changes may add to the chapels' flexibility, and upon the further assumption that ecclesiastical opposition would not block Fordham's permitting non-Catholics in addition to Catholics to use the University's facilities, we believe that preserving these religious adjuncts of the educational structure will generate no difficulties. Unless and until Fordham's student body and faculty membership change drastically, the chapels are not likely to be in heavy demand by others than Catholics. The University need not, in our view, seek to arouse the demand, but should be able to respond if it does become manifest. Possibly Fordham could respond simply by providing separate religious facilities for non-Catholics. This seems a needlessly expensive step, however, if the present chapels' use can instead be broadened in accord with the ecumenical spirit.

Prayer in the classroom. Until recent times Fordham classes were required to be opened by a prayer in unison. Today the University, officially, neither encourages nor discourages the practice, though some deans have called attention to "the tradition" at faculty conferences when a new academic year commences. It continues at the choice of individual professors. Some Jesuit professors both commence and end each class with an Our Father or a Hail Mary, but other Jesuits engage in no religious manifestation at all. Some of the older lay professors launch their classes with a prayer, and some Protestant and Jewish professors regularly ask that an opening prayer be led by a student.

Prayer in Fordham classrooms at the instructors' option does not raise the same issue as does a command that prayers be offered in public school classrooms. As to the latter, the courts have held that when governmental authorities introduce prayer into the classroom, they take a forbidden step toward the establishment of a state religion.[224] When, however, a non-governmental institution of higher learning allows but does not compel the murmuring of a prayer, no constitutional issue appears. And so long as prayer has been neither required nor strongly urged by a religious organ extrinsic to the institution, one cannot logically conclude that praying evidences the educational establishment's subservience to religious authority.

Our conclusion is, therefore, that incidental prayers, which are now said only upon individual instructors' initiative, need not be flatly forbidden in order to establish Fordham's independence or non-denominationalism.[225]

We nevertheless suggest that the opening of classes by prayers acceptable to Catholics will become far less feasible if and when Fordham gains a student body and faculty more religiously diverse than now. One comfortable consequence of Fordham's present homogeneity is, of course, the absence of sensitivities caused by differences in faith or practice. If, however, Fordham realizes its ambition of becoming a great metropolitan center of learning, its instructors will no longer be able to assume that none of their students will be upset by prayers whose wording Catholics take for granted.

We can only speculate as to whether attendance at Fordham by Protestant and Jewish and Muslim and agnostic students is not even now being discouraged by awareness that religiosity intrudes into Fordham's lecture halls. How much is gained by routinely mumbling prayers when young men and women have assembled for academic exercise rather than for religious expression, is a matter we are not competent to judge. We are dubious, however, that classroom prayers significantly advance either an academic or a religious purpose, and we fear they may diminish Fordham's ability to attract students who

---

[224] See Engel v. Vitale, 370 U.S. 421 (1962); and compare Stein v. Oshinsky, 348 F. 2d 999 (2d Cir.), cert. den., 382 U.S. 957 (1965).

[225] This conclusion is in general harmony with the pragmatic judicial attitude that has refused to find significance in conventional invocations of the deity, even in public matters. See, e.g., Lincoln v. Page, 241 A. 2d 799, 800-01 (N.H., 1968), holding that opening a town meeting with an invocation delivered by a clergyman invited by town officials does not violate the Establishment Clause of the First Amendment. The invocation was not required by law. "One voter . . . may regard an invocation as purely ceremonial, another as an historical throwback to another day and another as a religious practice which should be forbidden. But however any individual voter may describe the practice, it is not . . . an establishment of religion . . . in any pragmatic, meaningful and realistic sense. . . ."

are impatient with the formalities (as distinct from the content) of Catholicism.

We make no recommendation other than that deans and other senior administrators take pains not actively to encourage classroom praying by newly recruited teachers. They should instead clearly indicate that the University has no affirmative desires or expectations in this respect. The matter is probably not in itself grave enough to justify a prohibitory rule that would cause some of the older professors to be resentful. We do urge, however, that no effort be made to keep the old tradition alive by artificial respiration. Considerations of taste, related to the diversified academic community Fordham hopes to become, will, we think, lead faculty members to a new tradition if they feel free to choose.

Physical symbols of religion. At one time in its not very distant past, the Fordham campus was heavily dotted with conventional religious statuary. A prominent Jesuit, not himself associated with Fordham, recently remarked: "When I visited Fordham a few years ago, I felt a little bit like a stroller through the grounds of a convent. I didn't mind the number of the statues so much as their appallingly low aesthetic quality." Were he to visit Fordham today, he would have to hunt far to find the statuary that had offended him. Almost all of the University's outdoor representational art has been collected—perhaps one should say segregated—in an inconspicuous location. A few nostalgic faculty members have regretted the atmospheric change, but, for the most part, the disappearance of material reminders of saintliness has seemingly not been greatly noticed.

The crucifix remains prominently present in many classrooms and in other structures. It is of course a religious symbol intended to move those who perceive it. It is an object of veneration, not an interior decoration. Its display raises the question of whether Fordham forces on all its students a sectarian religious influence regardless of their wishes.

Minds react differently to symbolism. Some will undoubtedly believe that the presence of the classroom crucifix intimates an infusion of religion into the educational process. Others will probably regard it as simply a reminder of Fordham's genesis. In this day and age courts or governmental agencies are unlikely to hold flatly that Fordham must remove every crucifix or other token of religious belief as a precondition of being deemed an independent, non-denominational university. In the sixteenth century the smashing of idols in Cholula's four hundred massive temples evidenced the changing of religious commitment. We doubt that a similar smashing of crucifixes must occur in the twentieth century in order to strengthen Fordham's claim to educational status.

Even so, the University's retaining a powerfully moving religious symbol in each of its classrooms may have an unacknowledged effect upon others' appraisal of Fordham. Probably none will denounce Fordham simply because crucifixes are displayed; but the display might contribute as one relevant factor to a composite judgment that Fordham is religiously committed. Even more likely, it might subtly and perhaps even unconsciously intensify denunciation on some other ground.

Moreover, highly respected educators have insisted to us that among their own students who are not Catholics, and especially among those who are not Christians, some have been disquieted when working in a symbolically charged atmosphere. We know of no empirical data in support of this opinion, but we fully credit the sincerity of those who hold it. In a sense the significance non-Catholics may attach to the classroom crucifix is no more than a counterpart of the significance it avowedly has in Catholic eyes.

Having especially in mind Fordham's desire to nurture a pluralistic academic community, we incline toward the conclusion that institutional stress on a single religion's symbols should be ended.

Religious garb. Most of the clergymen who teach at Fordham wear religious garb in the classroom and during other academic engagements. This is not required by the Society of Jesus. The Archbishop of New York regulates the clothing style of priests as they pass to and fro within the archdiocese, but he does not formally have authority to impose his preferences on the campus itself. During the past several years half a dozen Fordham Jesuits have chosen not to wear cassocks or Roman collars when engaged in University work or when relaxing on campus. Their sartorial independence may possibly not have had the personal approval of colleagues eager to emphasize the "Jesuit presence," but it has violated no rule and is consistent with the belief some Jesuits entertain that students should address them as "Professor" and not as "Father."[226] Generally, how-

---

[226] We may note in passing that the course listings in the catalogs of the Rose Hill liberal arts colleges and Graduate School do identify the instructors in the various courses as Professor, without any added indication of religious status.

ever, priests and other religious at Fordham continue to be readily identifiable by their dress, and no mass movement toward laicized clothing seems imminent.

The wearing of religious garb has been regarded as weightily significant in schools attended by young children. A recent Catholic study of parochial education has characterized the "very presence of the religious" as "in itself a dominant, unforgettable symbol."[227] A Catholic law professor writes that this, conjoined with other holy symbols, may contribute toward creating a "pervasive atmosphere" which, among other things, "increases respect for the church as an institution to guide one's total life adjustment and undoubtedly helps stimulate interest in religious vocation."[228] No doubt some such belief underlies the litigation and the legislation that for more than seventy-five years have been generated when garb has appeared in public schools.[229]

The supposed impact of teachers' dress upon the minds of immature pupils does not, however, bear significantly on what should be done at Fordham. If a Fordham teacher is a member of a religious order (Jesuit or other) and chooses to dress in the approved style of that order instead of the approved style of the currently popular campus clothier, he should be wholly free, we think, to indulge his preference. Fordham students are not immature, impressionable school children; they are not continually under the dominance of a single teacher or a small number of teachers; at the most only a minor percentage of their teachers are religious personnel, distinctively garbed. In brief, we regard the effects of the religious dress that does appear on the Fordham campus to be too speculative and too minor to justify institutional concern. The matter should remain

---

227 R. Neuwien ed., Catholic Schools in Action 17 (Notre Dame, 1966).

228 D. A. Giannella. "Religious Liberty, Nonestablishment, and Doctrinal Development," Part II, 81 Harvard Law Rev. 513, 574 (1968).

229 See, e.g., O'Connor v. Hendrick, 184 New York 421, 77 N.E. 612 (1906) (". . . the effect of the costume worn by these Sisters of St. Joseph at all times in the presence of their pupils would be to inspire respect, if not sympathy, for the religious denomination to which they so manifestly belong"); Commonwealth v. Herr, 229 Pa. 132, 78 Atl. 68 (1910) (upholding statute that forbade public school teacher's wearing while on school duty "any dress, mark, emblem or insignia indicating the fact that such teacher is a member or adherent of any religious order, sect or denomination"); Zellers v. Huff, 55 N. Mex. 501, 236 P. 2d 949 (1951) ("Not only does the wearing of religious garb and insignia have a propagandizing effect for the church, but by its very nature it introduced sectarian religion into the school"). See, generally, D. E. Boles, The Two Swords 224-252 (Iowa State Univ., 1967).

—as it has in recent years become—one to be decided by the individual professor, who can choose which aspect of his personality to emphasize in his raiment. The choice he may make is unlikely to have significant consequences for Fordham.

10. PROFESSIONAL ASSOCIATIONS

Fordham University holds membership in the American Council on Education, the Association of American Colleges, the Association of Urban Universities, the Council of Higher Educational Institutions in New York City, and the Association of Universities and Colleges of the State of New York. It is an accredited member of the Middle States Association of Colleges and Secondary Schools. It is registered by the Board of Regents of the State of New York. Its various departments and schools are members of major professional bodies in their respective fields, such as the American Association of Colleges of Pharmacy, the Association of American Law Schools, and the American Association of Collegiate Schools of Business.

None of these academic identifications suggests that Fordham may fit into a special educational category. But Fordham is also a member of the National Catholic Educational Asociation, the Jesuit Educational Association, and the International Federation of Catholic Universities. The significance, if any, of these additional memberships in religiously restricted associations must be examined.

No one of these distinctively Catholic groups has legislative power or otherwise exercises control over Fordham's policies or acts.

The National Catholic Educational Association concerns itself with every level of education, from kindergarten through graduate school. One of its departments deals particularly with colleges and universities, but only as a stimulator of discussion, transmitter of ideas and experiences, and organizer of special studies.[230] Its stated objectives are to promote the welfare of Catholic education, in part by providing regional and national spokesmen; to foster cooperation and professional growth; and to "enable Catholic education to interpret itself to the public."

[230] Compare Greeley, note 126 above, at 166. "Are there national agencies through which the Catholic institutions can operate? The unfortunate answer is that for all practical purposes there are not. There is a college division of the National Catholic Educational Association with a small and competent staff in Washington that tries manfully to keep the channels of communication open and to bring the educators together for discussion at an annual meeting."

The Jesuit Educational Association includes all twenty-eight colleges and universities under American Jesuit auspices, and also the more than one hundred other Jesuit educational institutions. Its constitution clearly defines it as an advisory agency, designed to serve its members and not in any degree to govern them. It has departments of higher and secondary education, as well as permanent "commissions" that focus more particularly on liberal arts colleges, graduate schools, and professional schools (among others).[231]

The International Federation of Catholic Universities maintains a secretariat in Paris. It is essentially a discussion body, aimed at the mutual stimulation of its member universities. For purposes of interchange the Federation is subdivided into regional groups (including one for North America), which prepare background papers and carry on conversations concerning major topics that will then be considered at an international meeting of the Federation. During 1967 the discussions related to the broad question: "What is the nature and role of the contemporary Catholic university?"

Clearly, organizations like those just sketched raise no spectre of external domination or control. Even the Jesuit Educational Association, which might be thought to be a forceful body, has no actual authority and, seemingly, no great influence.[232] In these circumstances, continued membership does not instantly create grave legal problems.

Doubt may arise, however, concerning the propriety of Fordham's remaining within the Jesuit Educational Association if, by altering

231 The 1948 constitution of the Jesuit Educational Association is substantially quoted in M. M. Pattillo, Jr. and D. M. MacKenzie, Church Sponsored Higher Education in the United States 263-269 (Am. Council of Educ., 1966).

232 Compare Greeley, note 126 above, at 166: "Most surprisingly, there is very little cooperation across provincial lines even within the Jesuit order, so that the university in any one of the eleven provinces of the Society of Jesus in the United States might well cooperate with another Jesuit university in a different province, but such cooperation would be quite accidental. We found not only considerable differences in the quality and goals of the various Jesuit provinces, but also considerable rivalry among the provinces and a strong disinclination on the part of educators in one province to make any sort of sacrifice that could conceivably give another province an advantage over their own. So great were the differences among Jesuit provinces that it almost seemed we were speaking to members of different religious orders and that within the Jesuit community there was at least as much pluralism as in the whole of Catholic higher education." Cf. Jencks and Riesman, note 125 above, at 390, stating the authors' belief that the Jesuit Educational Association and the Conference of Presidents of Jesuit Colleges and Universities "have no real authority," but do tend to "make Jesuits more self-conscious about the fact that none of their institutions ranks academically with leading secular institutions."

its governing body, the University chooses not to be identified as an institution under the exclusive auspices of the Society of Jesus.

Moreover, wholly without reference to analytical niceties, Fordham may advantageously consider new academic linkages that will fully accord with the realities of its present-day development and its probable future.

Finally, we note as we did in an earlier branch of the discussion that self-characterization provides an especially important indicator of institutional personality. So long as Fordham declares itself eligible to belong to organizations whose members must be distinctly Catholic, questions will probably continue to be raised concerning the University's freedom from religious constrictions. The University's severing some of its present inter-institutional ties would still leave its individual faculty members entirely free to maintain professional associations linked with religion, if they so desired.

11. PUBLICATIONS

Fordham has become a major publisher of scholarly works and journals. Serials published under its imprint are the following:

TRADITIO: Studies in Medieval History, Thought and Religion.

INTERNATIONAL PHILOSOPHICAL QUARTERLY, edited jointly by Fordham's Philosophy Department and a Jesuit philosophy faculty in Belgium, "to promote mutual understanding and fruitful dialogue between the Orient and the West."

THOUGHT: A Review of Culture and Idea, a quarterly magazine which "aims to survey all fields of contemporary learning and affairs from the point of view of an American, Catholic and Jesuit university."

MONUMENTA IURIS CANONICI, produced under the auspices of the Institute of Medieval Canon Law.

The Fordham University Press, as of the spring of 1968, had published 103 books still in print. They dealt with many subject matters and had been written by authors of varied background. Included in the list are thoroughly secular titles.[233] The humanities have their innings, too.[234] Political and social affairs receive attention.[235] Among the authors are distinguished non-Catholics, including professors at Chicago, Columbia, Harvard, and Princeton.

Nonetheless, despite this diversity, nobody reading the Fordham list could doubt that it emphasizes Catholic topics and Catholic authors; indeed, almost half of the published books—48 out of 103—were written or edited by religious personnel. Biography tends to the religious—as, for example, "Eugene de Mazenod, Bishop of Marseilles," "Margaret Clitherow: Apostle and Martyr," and "The Life of Sir Thomas More." History tends to the religious—as, for example, "Byzantium and the Roman Primacy," "Cistercian Settlements in Wales and Monmouthshire, 1140-1540," "The English Church and the Papacy in the Middle Ages," "The Intellectual Conquest of Peru: The Jesuit College of San Pablo, 1568-1767," and "The Spanish Elizabethans: The English Exiles at the Court of Philip II." Philosophy tends to the religious—as, for example, "The Acton-Newman Relations: The Dilemma of Christian Liberalism," "The Philosophy of Gabriel Marcel," "The Presence and Absence of God," and "The Thomist Spectrum." Sociology and social affairs tend to the religious—as, for example, "Research in Religion and Health," "The Sociology of Religion," "Three Reforms of the Church," and "Anatomy of a Church: Greek Orthodoxy Today." Vocational discussion tends to the religious—as, for example, "Local Leadership in Mission Lands," "Religious-Apostolic Formation for Sisters," "The Role of Communication Arts in Mission Lands," "The Local Superior: Capstone of Formation," and "Personality and Sexual Problems in Pastoral Psychology."

These comments are meant to be descriptive, not critical. The present emphases of the Fordham University Press are not legally objectionable. We repeat our strong opinion that Fordham's achiev-

---

233 Among those noted in the current listing are "The Antitrust Structure of the European Common Market," "Economic System Analysis," "The Steel Import Problem," and "Mental Illness, Due Process and the Criminal Defendant."

234 Among recently published works are "The Errand of Form: An Assay of Jane Austen's Art," "Latin Manuscript Books Before 1600," "Henry James and the Dramatic Analogy," "Symbol and Myth in Ancient Poetry," "The Heritage Plaques of New York," and "Demosthenes, on the Crown."

235 Examples are "Why War Came in Korea," "Economic Planning in the Underdeveloped Areas," "From Failing Hands: The Story of Presidential Succession," "Problems in Addiction: Alcoholism and Narcortics," and "Race and Nationalism: The Struggle for Power in Rhodesia-Nyasaland."

ing ever wider professional and governmental recognition as an independent university does not hinge upon its disavowing interest in intellectual matters of possibly special moment to Catholics. The book titles used illustratively above suggest serious scholarly activity. So do the contents of Thought, which has a Catholic focus. The direction that activity has taken does not necessarily lead it away from academic detachment. One need not be Catholic to appreciate the importance of Catholic studies or to think that they belong in a university setting (as witness Yale University's creation of a special professorship of Roman Catholic Studies) or to believe that they have yet to receive as much general attention as they may perhaps merit.[236] Fordham's support of scholarly publications, through the medium of Fordham University Press, is not so narrowly focused as to cast doubt upon the breadth of the University's present academic accomplishments or its ambitions for the future. It need not erase past interests in order to embrace new ones.

---

[236] See. e.g., the Minutes of the Board of Directors, American Council of Learned Societies, May 18, 1968, at 7: "The Board had before it a request from Fordham University for a grant in support of a Symposium on The Jesuit Contribution to Art and Art History which the University's Department of Fine Arts hopes to hold, under the chairmanship of Professor Rudolf Wittkower, in the spring of 1969. Mr. Lee commented that this is a thoroughly good subject, which has not received adequate attention. Voted: To approve a grant . . . ."

Epilogue

A paleontologist charged with reconstructing the past by analyzing fossil fragments can focus on fixed material. Fossils do not change their shape while in the process of being described. The authors of this book have not dealt with similarly static data. Happily for its future, Fordham University is far from being a fossil. It is a living, constanly changing organism. During the short interval that elapsed between the completion of this study and the final preparation of a manuscript for the printer, many of the changes recommended in preceeding pages actually occurred. Description of Fordham's past is necessary to understand the recommendations that were given, and it is necessary also if the recommendations are to have meaning for other institutions that confront problems like those under discussion in this work. But the account cannot be closed without mention of some of the major developments that have changed and strengthened Fordham itself between June 1968, which was the originally intended termination date of this institutional exploration and the forepart of 1969, when the authors delivered their book to the publisher. Alterations in Fordham's tone and contours have been too significant to be ignored. They may well suggest steps that other institutions may wish to consider, and they may also have an impact upon future governmental decisions.

GOVERNING BODY AND ADMINISTRATION

On October 25, 1968, New York's Education Department approved an amendment to Fordham's charter that authorized enlarging the membership of the University's board of trustees from nine to not more than thirty-one. Subsequently new trustees were chosen, supplanting the all-Jesuit board previously in office. The present board consists of twenty-six members. Eleven of these are Jesuits. Not all of the fifteen laymen are Catholics. The only University official who serves as a board member is the President of the University. The chairman of the board is a layman. The Jesuits who were chosen as trustees were elected by the board itself, rather than selected by the Society of Jesus, which was not consulted in advance. They have no power that differentiates them from the other board members, all of whom share equally in policy-making decisions.

The trustees' by-laws explicitly declare that the trustees alone possess power to elect and to remove the President of the University. In December 1968 the then President, Rev. Leo McLaughlin, S.J., resigned. He was succeeded in office by another Jesuit, Rev. Michael P. Walsh, S.J., who had previously been a Fordham trustee and had only recently retired as President of Boston College. Father Walsh was elected by the board rather than designated for the post by ecclesiastical authorities, as had been the previous practice whenever a Fordham presidential change occurred. Nothing in the by-laws of the board of trustees nor any other express or implied mandate in any of the constituent documents of the University requires that the President (or, for that matter, any other officer or employee) be a Jesuit or a Roman Catholic.

THE JESUIT COMMUNITY

Jesuits as individuals remain prominent in Fordham's affairs. Eighty-six of the 463 members of the University's teaching staff are Jesuits. Among the ninety-one "line" administrators in ranks above that of Department Chairman, eighteen are Jesuits. The deans of five of the fourteen colleges, schools, and special sessions of the University are Jesuits. Only one Jesuit is among the twelve individuals who hold "staff" positions reporting to the "line" administrators.

The "contributed services" of these and other members of the Society of Jesus have been an important element of Fordham's past success as well as of its present well-being. But neither the Society of Jesus nor any other external body within the Church now provides financial assistance to the University. The individual Jesuits who are connected with Fordham have formed a separate corporation, The Jesuits of Fordham, Inc. The University has agreed that Jesuits employed by it are to receive precisely the same compensation as is paid for similar services rendered by other comparable personnel. Their own corporation maintains and supports the resident Jesuits, reimbursing the University for any special expenses incurred by the University for facilities not accorded to comparable University employees. The resident Jesuits have indicated that they intend to contribute to the University, or some similar organization, the difference between their collective earnings and their collective expenses. But The Jesuits of Fordham, Inc. has expressly reserved entire discretion as to whether, when, and in what amounts contributions are to be made. Were The Jesuits of Fordham, Inc. to decide voluntarily to donate the maximum amount of income received from the University, less expenses, for the fiscal year 1968-69, the amount would be approximately $400,000. This would represent 1.8 percent of the University's operating budget for the fiscal year, and appromately 5½ percent of the University's gift income.

Among other important changes in Fordham's Jesuit community has been separation of the rectorship of the community from the presidency of the University. Early in 1969 an associate professor of history became Rector of The Jesuits of Fordham, Inc., thus replacing Fordham's President as head of the religious community. The Rector has no power over University matters; the President has no power over religious personnel, other than that he may exercise as to all other Fordham personnel.

GROUP FACILITIES AND INSTITUTIONAL RELATIONSHIPS

During the autumn of 1968 the University's board of trustees adopted formal policies to govern the use of Fordham's facilities—its buildings, lands, and other property. Recognizing that these facilities are intended "primarily for academic use," the trustees nevertheless were cognizant that the University's premises might have "other appropriate uses at times and under circumstances which do not conflict with the needs or purposes of the University." These other "appropriate uses" have been spelled out in detail. One of them is "Meetings of recognized religious organizations," a phrasing undoubtedly sufficiently broad to counter any suggestion that Fordham's facilities have been reserved for denominationally identifiable bodies. The trustees have provided, moreover, that rental charges are to be made for use of the premises by bodies not immediately connected with the University itself.

At the same time, steps have been taken to disentangle Fordham and its properties from relationships that might have ambiguous connotations.

Thus, for example, Mitchell Farm, used principally as a summer resort for Jesuits, has been transferred outright to The Jesuits of Fordham, Inc.

Fordham Preparatory School, which has been an integral element of the University, is in the process of being separated from the parent institution. It will be incorporated as an autonomous educational enterprise, owning its own property and conducting its own affairs, perhaps close by Fordham in its physical location, but discernibly apart from it structurally and manegerially.

The University's relationships with the College of Philosophy and Letters, which had been located on a separate campus at Shrub Oak, New York, and which was maintained specifically for the training of Jesuit collegians, will terminate in June 1969. The Society of Jesus will then close the Shrub Oak facility and will assign its Jesuit faculty and student body elsewhere. The College of Philosophy and Letters will no longer be an extension of Fordham University.

— AND ON MORE GENERAL THEMES

Even since this manuscript was prepared, public aid to private education has undergone important developments.

New York has already begun to pay public moneys to support many private colleges and universities, under its so-called Bundy Law.[1] But as was foreseen state funds have thus far been denied to church-related institutions. The way in which the law has been administered may further encourage moves toward independence by schools which in times past had stressed the closeness of their religious ties. Partly, no doubt, because of the disparity in treatment between sectarian and nonsectarian institutions under the Bundy Law, and partly because parochial elementary and secondary schools have been under increasingly heavy financial pressure, Governor Nelson Rockefeller in early 1970 advocated repeal of New York's constitutional prohibition of public aid to sectarian educational institutions.[2] Both houses of the state legislature have since approved such a change. In the meantime, many other states have recently considered statutory

[1] See p. 37.
[2] For discussion of the New York State Constitutional provision and its interpretation, see Section III of Appendix A.

proposals to liberalize the use of tax moneys for the benefit of sectarian schools, with varying results. And fresh litigation has been commenced to challenge federal grants to sectarian colleges, despite the purported secular purposes of those grants.

The Administration of Section 6401 of the New York Education Law. As explained in earlier pages, New York's Legislature, guided by the report of the Select (Bundy) Committee on the Future of Private and Independent Higher Education in New York State, authorized annual subventions of private educational institutions, at the rate of $400 for each earned bachelor's or master's degree and $2400 for each earned doctorate.[3] No institution could receive funds. however, if it were ineligible under the state or federal constitution. Payments were to commence in July, 1969. In the summer of 1968, the Commissioner of Education wrote to each private college and university within the state, outlining the information needed by him to determine its eligibility for funds, as follows:

1. What are the stated purposes of the institution, as set forth in its charter or legislative authority (please quote verbatim), and in other relevant documents?

2. Is the institution wholly or in part under the control or direction of any religious denomination? If the answer is in the affirmative, indicate the nature and extent of such control or direction in all areas of the life of the institution.

3. Does the institution receive financial assistance from any religious body? If the answer is in the affirmative, please indicate fully the nature, extent and frequency of such assistance and indicate the proportional relationship which such assistance bears to other sources from which the institution derives funds.

4. Do the policies of the institution with respect to the selection of members of its governing board, its administrative officers or its faculty provide that the faith or creed of a candidate shall be relevant in any way to his selection? If the answer is in the affirmative, please set forth in full the text of any such policy which is in writing, and indicate

---

[3] Actual payments have been about 5% less these figures would indicate because of the state's own acute financial difficulties.

fully the nature and extent of any such policy which is not in writing.

5. Do the policies of the institution with respect to the admission of students provide that the faith or creed of an applicant shall be relevant in any way to his admissibility to the institution? If the answer is in the affirmative, please set forth in full the text of any such policy which is in writing, and indicate fully the nature and extent of any such policy which is not in writing.

6. Do the policies of the institution with respect to the awarding of scholarship, fellowship or other financial assistance to its students provide that the faith or creed of an applicant shall be relevant in any way to the awarding of such assistance? If the answer is in the affirmative, please set forth in full the text of any such policy which is in writing, and indicate fully the nature and extent of any such policy which is not in writing.

7. Is any denominational tenet or doctrine taught in the institution? If the answer is in the affirmative, please provide full information concerning the nature and extent of such instruction and indicate whether it is mandatory or optional. If mandatory for some students, but not for all, please indicate the circumstances under which it is mandatory.

8. Does the institution award any degree or degrees in the field or religion? If the answer is in the affirmative, please indicate the name of such degree or degrees and provide full information with respect to the requirements for the conferring of such degree or degrees.

9. Does the institution include within its structure, or is it affiliated with any seminary or schools of theology? If the answer is in the affirmative, please provide a full description of the seminary or school of theology, and indicate the nature and extent of the relationship or affiliation.

10. What is the place of religion in the programs of the institution? (Please indicate the character and extent of required religious observance, if any.)

11. Do the policies of the institution with respect to the use of any institutional facility or program by other than the staff, faculty and student body provide that the faith or creed of an individual applicant, or the denominational affiliation of an organizational applicant is relevant in any way to the granting of such use? If the answer is in the affirmative, please set forth in full the text of any such policy which is in writing, and indicate fully the nature and extent of any such policy which is not in writing.

12. Has the institution filed with the State Education Department a Certificate of Religious or Denominational Institution pursuant to Education Law section 313? If so, please indicate the date of filing, and indicate whether such certificate was subsequently withdrawn.

13. Is there any other information which the institution deems pertinent to a determination of its eligibility for state aid under the constitutional provisions referred to above?[4]

Responses were sought by November 1, 1968, but delays were dealt with liberally. From November 1968 to November 1969 the State Education Department received from the concerned institutions the materials they deemed relevant. After carefully analyzing each institution's characteristics, the Department announced in late July 1969 that fifty-two grants would be made for the 1969-70 academic year, aggregating $24,112,000.[5] New York University at $4,400,000 was the largest grantee; the College of Insurance at $16,000, the smallest.

At that time, the Commissioner wrote to the other institutions, all of which had some church affiliation, indicating that he had tentatively found them to be ineligible. But he added that each of those institutions could submit further documentation that would permit an up-to-date consideration of their status, and he suggested that a conference with the Department be arranged. The great majority of the affected institutions availed themselves of the opportunity to be further considered by the Department. They provided additional documents, including new catalogues and by-laws, and

---

[4] Memorandum on Constitutional Eligibility of Certain Non-Public Institutions of Higher Education for State Aid Pursuant to Chapter 677 of the Laws of 1968, August 5, 1968, circulated to Chief Executive Officers attached to a memorandum of August 12, 1968, from Commissioner of Education James E. Allen.

[5] N.Y. Times, July 26, 1969, p. 1, col. 5.

state education officials consulted extensively with representatives of these colleges and universities. The initial decision had been made provisionally because the Department was aware that church-related institutions were in a period of rapid change; even so, officials were surprised by the number of changes revealed in the analysis and discussions that followed in late 1969.[6] Some were perhaps only superficial, consisting of little more than renaming the Department of Theology the Department of Religious Studies. Others, however, such as changes in the composition of the governing board, were indeed substantial. On January 5, 1970, Commissioner Ewald B. Nyquist announced that twenty-one institutions had been adjudged by him to be ineligible, and that one, Keuka College founded by the Baptists, had been found to be eligible.[7] Of the twenty-one deemed barred from receiving state aid, nineteen have Roman Catholic ties, one has Lutheran connections[8] and one is nondenominational fundamentalist.[9] Seven other institutions had withdrawn their applications in the expectancy of being denied aid.

On February 19, the Commissioner announced that Fordham, Manhattanville College, and St. John Fisher College were eligible for aid, with Fordham to receive over $1,000,000 for this fiscal year.[10] After careful examination of relevant documents and the report of an outside theologian who studied the university's offerings in Theology and Philosophy, the Department had concluded that Fordham was no longer a sectarian institution.[11]

When asked what factors determined eligibility, the Department's Legal Counsel responded that "no single factor can be identified as controlling; a judgment must be made on everything that is known about the institution.[12] Plainly, the Department has adhered to the "mosaic" approach intimated in its original letter to the college presidents, applied in the Horace Mann case[13] and in the present study. Equally plainly, the Department accepts the view, propounded throughout this volume, that institutions do change and that a

---

[6] Interview with Robert D. Stone, Legal Counsel and Deputy Commissioner for Legal Affairs, Jan. 16, 1970.

[7] N.Y. Times, January 6, 1970, p. 29, col. 1.

[8] Wagner College.

[9] The King's College. See Catalogue 1968-1970. The Statement of Doctrine for the College, p. 9, includes a belief in the inerrancy of the Bible.

[10] See News Release of New York State Education Department, February 19, 1970.

[11] The Ram, vol. 52, No. 8 ,Feb. 20, 1970, p. 1, col. 1.

[12] Interview with Robert D. Stone, see note 6 above.

[13] See pp. 35-36.

sectarian institution can evolve into one eligible for public aid under New York's constitution as it is now written.

Whether church-related colleges and universities should undergo change—or, rather, should accelerate the pace of change—in order to be able to dip into the public purse is, of course, an entirely different matter. This questions, which is properly the subject of debate by those who are devoted to the particular institutions involved, is not one that the authors of this book have sought to answer. The concern of this monograph has been with changes that might be needed to establish eligibility for state subvention; but whether the benefits to be gained were outweighed by the costs has been for others to consider.[14]

Possible Amendment of Article XI, Section 3. The controversy over whether Catholic institutions of higher learning should stress their Catholicism or their learning will in all probability intensify in the years to come. At the same time, so long as sectarian schools and colleges do exist, those who are devoted to them will generate strong pressure to eliminate the prohibitions against their receiving public money. At present, Article XI, Section 3 of the New York Constitu-

---

[14] Compare C. M. Whelan, S.J., "Catholic Universities and the Gellhorn Report," *America*, Nov. 16, 1969, 474, 479. Father Whelan, a member of the Fordham Law School faculty, commented on an earlier draft of this book (which had been submitted to Fordham officials for their information) in the following terms: "Fordham, of course, is only one of many Catholic universities manifesting the symptoms of an identity crisis. Every American Catholic university has serious financial and academic problems. The most important question, therefore, is whether the Gellhorn Report offers an acceptable solution.

"In my judgment, it emphatically does not. I do not see how any university that honestly executed the Gellhorn recommendations could seriously call itself Catholic. Gellhorn and Greenawalt, understandably misled by the questions they were asked to answer, lost sight of the real problem at Fordham: not how to change it into another Columbia, but how to develop it into a first-rate Catholic university. . . .

"It seems obvious to me, without extended financial or legal analysis, that it is altogether fanciful to think that the other public and private universities in New York would stand by and let the State Legislature propel Fordham, secularized or not, into the forefront of American Education. . . .

"Is Fordham, then, condemned to be second-best? The answer depends on the standard of excellence you choose. If Harvard, Yale and Columbia are the models, then I have no doubt that, in certain areas, Fordham for the present and the foreseeable future is and will be second-best. If, on the other hand, the standard of excellence is that found in the best traditions of Catholic universities throughout the world, I think that Fordham has an enormous opportunity, in many areas, to achieve and maintain the summit.

"If only the goal be kept clear, the means can be found. Patience, sacrifice and perseverance will be necessary, as they are necessary to any great enterprise. Let the goal, however, become confused, and no amount of money or talent will make any Catholic university what it ought to be: an intellectual community centered on the Truth that is Christ."

tion, inexactly described as the "Blaine Amendment," is a seemingly impenetrable bar to aid.[15] During 1969 Governor Rockefeller had believed himself compelled by the constitution to veto a bill providing aid to church-related colleges. In 1970, however, perhaps in response to well publicized suggestions that Catholic parochial schools might not survive without state assistance,[16] the Governor urged the New York Legislature to eliminate the constitutional restriction. In his address that opened the Legislative Session, he spoke of creating a special Commission to inquire into "the fiscal problems of the private schools, with the objective of developing appropriate ways in which the state can help further to insure the quality of education for children attending private schools." To assure a positive response to the recommendations he foresaw, Governor Rockefeller recommended that, "at this session, there be a first passage of a Constitutional amendment to repeal the Blaine Amendment to the State Constitution and to substitute the less restrictive language of the Federal Constitution on separation of church and state."[17]

The Governor's proposal immediately stirred the opposition of the New York State Teachers Association, the American Jewish Congress, and the New York Times among others.[18] Nevertheless, since the Governor's address, both the Senate and Assembly have passed measures as a first step toward repeal.[19] Since opposition to repeal was widely assumed to have been instrumental in defeating the proposed 1967 constitution (which had embodied the result now desired by the Governor), softening of New York's constitutional language will plainly not be achieved without bitter public debate. whose outcome cannot confidently be foretold.

Some Developments in Other States. The ferment over aid to religious education has by no means been confined to New York. In many states, proposals to provide financial assistance to sectarian

---

[15] See Section III of Appendix A. Even were that bar eliminated, general aid like that of the Bundy Law would be highly dubious under the federal constitution. See discussion at end of Section I of Appendix A.

[16] See, e.g., N.Y. Times, June 22, 1969, Sect. E, p. 9, col. 1; Manhattan Tribune, Jan. 17, 1970, p. 15, col. 1. See also the report of the strike-averting settlement with lay teachers in parochial schools. N.Y. Times, Jan. 19, 1970, p. 29, col. 1. Compare Manhattan Tribune, Jan. 31, 1970, p. 11, col. 1.

[17] N.Y. Times, Jan. 8, 1970, p. 30, cols. 1, 2.

[18] See id., at p. 31, col. 1; p. 40, col. 1.

[19] N.Y. Times, Feb. 17, 1970, p. 1, col. 2. As noted in the text, amendment of the state constitution requires passage by two successive legislatures and adoption at a general election.

schools were extensively considered in 1969.[20] Few of these proposals
were in fact adopted, but the Connecticut and Rhode Island legislatures authorized payment of a portion of the salaries of the teachers
of secular subjects in parochial schools, and Ohio passed a somewhat
similar law. Iowa, Oregon, and Washington provided grants for students in private colleges and universities, and Michigan and Wisconsin
aided medical branches of two church-related universities.

During 1969, also, the New Hampshire Supreme Court was called
upon to advise the Senate of that state concerning the constitutionality
of a number of bills, including one that would provide for the free
loan of textbooks to private school pupils.[21] The Justices concluded
that the bill was constitutional. Although the state constitution
states that "no money raised by taxation shall ever be granted or applied for the use of the schools or institutions of any religious sect
or denomination,"[22] the Justices indicated that support by tax money
is permissible "if sufficient safeguards are provided to prevent more
than incidental and indirect benefit to a religious sect or denomination."[23]

A federal three-judge district court in Pennsylvania upheld as
consistent with the federal constitution a plan that goes well beyond
"fringe" benefits.[24] It authorizes the state to contract with parochial
as well as other schools to educate students in mathematics, physical
sciences, modern foreign languages, and physical education. With
one judge dissenting, the court sustained this plan on the ground
that the services were connected with the secular functions of the
schools.[25] The Supreme Court of Maine reached an exactly opposite
conclusion in response to a broader legislative proposal. Asked to
advise on a bill to provide more general funds to private schools for

---

20 See Commission on Law and Social Action of the American Jewish Congress,
Public Aid to Religiously-Affiliated Schools—Developments in the 1969 State
Legislatures, Aug. 13, 1969, and Supplemental Report, Dec. 22, 1969.

21 Opinion of the Justices, Oct. 31 (1969), in response to Request of the
Senate, No. 5969.

22 New Hampshire Constitution, Part 2, Art. 83.

23 Opinion of the Justices, note 18 above.

24 Lemon v. Kurtzman, Nov. 28, 1969, Civil Action, No. 69-1206 (E.D. Pa.). The
case had been appealed to the Supreme Court of the United States when this
book went to press.

25 Compare Board of Education v. Allen, 392 U.S. 236 (1968), discussed in
Section I of Appendix A, involving the provision of textbooks for use by
parochial school pupils.

"secular educational service," four of six participating judges expressed the view that it was unconstitutional under the federal standard.[26]

  While pressures increase for more extended aid to sectarian
institutions, a major test case has been brought in the federal court
in Connecticut challenging the use of federal funds to help sectarian
colleges and universities construct additional facilities.[27] The plaintiffs
contend that funds under Title I of the Higher Educational Facilities
Act of 1963[28] cannot constitutionally be expended to provide buildings at church-related institutions of higher education. The issues
presented are precisely those decided by the Maryland Court of Appeals in Horace Mann League v. Board of Public Works in 1966[29]:
can sectarian colleges receive public funds for nonreligious purposes?
If not, are the institutional defendants to be deemed sectarian? The
plaintiffs clearly hope that this case will lead the Supreme Court to
endorse the principles of the Horace Mann decision. Should their
hope be realized, the immediate consequence would be a sharp cut-
ting back of federal aid now available for sectarian colleges, and the
longer-term prospect would be for the invalidation of many forms
of assistance now proposed in various states. Although the result is
far from certain, we doubt that the Supreme Court will accept the
Horace Mann rule for funds which, like those now in controversy,
have been given for a specific secular purpose.[30]

  A Final Word About the Law. If the Supreme Court does
eventually decide the merits of the case already appealed from the
district court in Pennsylvania and the pending challenge in the district
court in Connecticut, it will greatly clarify the federal limits on assistance to sectarian educational institutions and their pupils.[31] Even
were that to occur, continuing conflicts of legal interpretation and
policy can be expected in the various states for years to come. A

---

[26] Opinion of the Justices, January 15, 1970.

[27] Tilton v. Finch, Civil Action No. 12767 (D. Conn.).

[28] 20 U.S.C. §§ 701-721, 751-758. See Section II of Appendix A.

[29] 242 Md. 645, 220 A.2d 51, appeal dismissed and cert. denied, 385 U.S. 97
(1966). See Section I of Appendix A.

[30] See Section I of Appendix A. We believe the Court would more probably
be in accord with the approach of the State Supreme Court in Vermont Educational
Buildings Financing Agency v. Mann, 127 Vt. 262, 247 A.2d 68 (1968), appeal
dismissed, 396 U.S. 801 (1969).

[31] The Supreme Court heard argument late in 1969 on the contention that
tax exemptions may not validly be granted to religious bodies, an important
related problem. Walz v. Tax Comm'n, 24 N.Y. 2d 30, 298 N.Y.S. 2d 711, 246
N.E. 2d 517, prob. juris. noted, 395 U.S. 957 (1969).

church-related college, if it is pushed toward independence by economic factors, must consider not only present patterns of aid and existing legal barriers, but the likely developments in subsequent years. As these pages have suggested, this task is by no means easy. Most important of all, of course, those responsible must consider the kind of institution they want, for public aid is not worth having if it can be gained only by ignoring the goals a college or university is striving to attain.

Appendix A

THE SECTARIAN UNIVERSITY UNDER THE FEDERAL AND NEW YORK CONSTITUTIONS AND LAWS

I. THE FEDERAL CONSTITUTION

All federal and state grants and loans must comply with the First Amendment of the Constitution of the United States.[237] It thus sets the outer limits of permissible aid at both levels of government.[238] The amendment, like most parts of the Constitution, is cryptic: "Congress shall make no law respecting an establishment of religion, or prohibiting the free exercise thereof. . . ." Obviously this language gives no plain directive about the permissibility of aid to sectarian colleges and universities. Nor does the history of the amendment's adoption shed clear light on the matter, though opinions have some-

---

[237] As originally written, the amendment limited only the federal government. See Barron v. Baltimore, 32 U.S. (7 Pet.) 243 (1833). The Supreme Court has held that it was made applicable against the states by the Fourteenth Amendment, which forbids state deprivations of "life, liberty, or property, without due process of law." See Cantwell v. Connecticut, 310 U.S. 296 (1940); Everson v. Board of Education, 330 U.S. 1 (1947). Although the extension of the Establishment Clause to the states occurred only two decades ago and has been challenged by some critics, see E. S. Corwin, Constitution of Powers in a Secular State 109-18 (Michie, 1951); W. Parsons, The First Freedom 69-73 (McMullen, 1948), these critics have yet to win over a single Justice and the applicability to the states of both the Establishment and Free Exercise clauses is firmly established. See Abington School Dist. v. Schempp, 374 U.S. 203, 215-17 (majority opinion), 230, 253-58 (concurring opinion of Brennan, J.), 308, 310 (dissenting opinion of Stewart, J.) (1963); L. Pfeffer, Church, State and Freedom 139-49 (Beacon, rev. ed. 1967).

[238] Until 1968, the enforcibility of the theoretical limits on federal expenditures was uncertain. The problem was finding someone with standing to bring a suit against dubious grants. In Frothingham v. Mellon, 262 U.S. 447 (1923), the Supreme Court had held that a federal taxpayer did not have a sufficiently direct or immediate interest to justify his challenging the legality of the ways in which Congress has chosen to use his taxes. Under this doctrine, Congress might spend money in violation of the Constitution without the possibility of judicial scrutiny. See H. W. Jones, "Church-State Relations: Our Constitutional Heritage," in H. M. Stahmer ed., Religion and Contemporary Society 156, 197 (Macmillan, 1963). See generally K. C. Davis, Administrative Law Treatise §§22.09, 22.10 (West, 1958); L. L. Jaffe, Judicial Control of Administrative Action 459-500 (Little, Brown, 1965); Comment, "Taxpayers' Suits: A Survey and Summary," 69 Yale Law Jour. 895 (1960). But in 1968 the Court sharply restricted the principle of the Frothingham case, when a taxpayer challenged expenditures for

131

times been written as though the intent of the Framers was unmistakable.[239] The religion clauses of the First Amendment were cast in such general terms that, inevitably, their content has been marked out for the most part in the decisions of courts, and particularly the Supreme Court. The courts' efforts to elucidate the First Amendment have themselves lacked lucidity or, even, continuity of attitude. As one commentator has said: "Legal doctrine on church-state relations is unclear. This topic has remained more confused than any other major aspect of American public law, not excluding commerce, desegregation, reapportionment, civil liberties, or even due process. In the handful of leading cases which have arisen from strikingly different visions of the role of religion in American society the Court has failed to demonstrate a consistent line of development."[240]

The Supreme Court has fully considered the validity of aid to parochial education under the First Amendment in only two cases, Everson v. Board of Education and Board of Education v. Allen.[241]

---

parochial school students under the Elementary and Secondary Education Act of 1965, 20 U.S.C. §§241a et seq., 821 et seq. (Supp. 1967). Flast v. Cohen, 392 U.S. 83 (1968), decided that a federal taxpayer may attack what is essentially a spending program if he claims that the program violates a specific constitutional limit upon spending, such as the Establishment Clause of the First Amendment, rather than merely the distribution of powers between state and federal authorities, the issue in *Frothingham*. Taxpayers' suits had long provided a convenient vehicle for Establishment Clause claims against spending in many states. See, e.g., Everson v. Board of Education, 330 U.S. 1 (1947); Horace Mann League v. Board of Public Works, 242 Md. 645, 220 A. 2d 51, appeal dismissed and cert. denied, 385 U.S. 97 (1966). Flast v. Cohen indicates that they will now be equally effective at the federal level. For the possible effect of *Flast* on New York's restrictive rule on taxpayers' suits, see footnote 387, below.

[239] See Everson v. Board of Education, 330 U.S. 1, 8-15 (majority opinion), and 33-34 (dissenting opinion of Rutledge, J.) (1947). Compare M. de W. Howe. The Garden and the Wilderness 1-31 (U. of Chicago, 1956); C. J. Antieau, A. T. Downey & E. C. Roberts, Freedom from Federal Establishment (Nat. Cath. Welf. Conf., 1964).

[240] R. G. Dixon, Jr. "Religion, Schools, and the Open Society: A Socio-Constitutional Issue," 13 Journal of Pub. Law 267, 288 (1964).

[241] Everson v. Board of Education, 330 U.S. 1 (1947); Board of Education v. Allen, 392 U.S. 236 (1968). The Court has on occasion dismissed appeals from decisions of state courts, e.g., Snyder v. Town of Newtown, 365 U.S. 299 (1961). Technically dismissals for "want of a substantial federal question," unlike discretionary denials of certiorari, are decisions on the merits; but the Court has on occasion dismissed cases it does not wish to hear as well as those it believes were correctly decided below. Philip Kurland has called a ruling that an issue is not a substantial federal question "technical language for saying 'don't bother us.'" "Politics and the Constitution: Federal Aid to Parochial Schools," 1 Land and Water Law Rev. 475, 476 (1966). See A. M. Bickel, The Least Dangerous Branch 126-127 (Bobbs-Merrill, 1962); G. Gunther, "The Subtle Vices of the 'Passive Virtues'—A Comment on Principle and Expediency in Judicial Review," 64 Columbia Law Rev. 1, 10-13 (1964).

Neither case involved an institution of higher learning; the Court was divided in both; and in both the majority opinions are subject to varying intepretations. Thus they provide no sure guide to the future. In this area more than most, the complexity of the issues and the multiplicity of possible directions in which the law may develop make prediction hazardous. Because judicial attitudes are still not fully formed, the extensive commentaries of scholars merit analysis along with the few decided cases themselves.

We start our analysis with a description of four cases—the Everson and Allen cases mentioned above; Abington School District v. Schempp,[242] the so-called school prayer case, which apparently represents an important shift in the Court's doctrinal treatment of the Establishment Clause; and Horace Mann League v. Board of Public Works,[243] a Maryland case in which aid to sectarian colleges was challenged. We then consider the spectrum of possible interpretations of the Establishment Clause and conclude with our own suggestions about the likely future development of the law.

A. THE CASES.

1. *Everson v. Board of Education.*[244] In 1947 the Supreme Court first tested a state program against the Establishment Clause. Under New Jersey law the board of education in each school district could decide to pay for the transportation of children to nonprofit private as well as to public schools. In the district in which plaintiff was a taxpayer, the Board authorized payment for transportation to Catholic Schools. Since the record contained no evidence that other children attended non-Catholic private schools and did not receive transportation, the majority of the Court treated the case as if transportation were offered to all school children. By a 5-4 vote the Court sustained the board's action. After an analysis of the intent of the Framers of the Establishment Clause, Justice Black, in one of the most famous passages in church-state literature, wrote for the majority:

> The establishment of religion clause of the First Amendment means at least this: Neither a state nor the Federal Government

---

[242] 374 U.S. 203 (1963).

[243] 242 Md. 645, 220 A.2d 51, appeal dismissed and cert. denied, 385 U.S. 97 (1966).

[244] 330 U.S. 1 (1947).

can set up a church. Neither can pass laws which aid one religion, aid all religions, or prefer one religion over another. Neither can force nor influence a person to go to or to remain away from church against his will or force him to profess a belief or disbelief in any religion. No person can be punished for entertaining or professing religious beliefs or disbeliefs, for church attendance or non-attendance. *No tax in any amount, large or small, can be levied to support any religious activities or institutions, whatever they may be called, or whatever form they may adopt to teach or practice religion.* Neither a state nor the Federal Government can, openly or secretly, participate in the affairs of any religious organizations or groups and *vice versa.* In the words of Jefferson, the clause against establishment of religion by law was intended to erect "a wall of separation between church and State."[245]

Nonetheless, the Court did not bar the provision of bus transportation. "[W]e must not strike that state statute down if it is within the state's constitutional power even though it approaches the verge of that power." Although the state can not support religion, neither can it inhibit the free exercise of religion.

> Consequently, it cannot exclude individual Catholics, Lutherans, Mohammedans, Baptists, Jews, Methodists, Nonbelievers, Presbyterians, or the members of any other faith, *because of their faith, or lack of it,* from receiving the benefits of public welfare legislation. While we do not mean to intimate that a state could not provide transportation only to children attending public schools, we must be careful, in protecting the citizens of New Jersey against state-established churches, to be sure we do not inadvertently prohibit New Jersey from extending its general state law benefits to all its citizens without regard to their religious belief.[246]

In the majority's view the provision of bus fares, though it helped children attend religious schools, was analogous to general governmental services, like police and fire protection and collections for sewage disposal, which are obviously not forbidden to parochial schools and school children by the First Amendment.

---

[245] Id., at 15-16. [Italics added.]
[246] Id., at 16. [Italics in the original.]

That amendment requires the state to be a neutral in its relations with groups of religious believers and non-believers; it does not require the state to be their adversary. . . .

The State contributes no money to the schools. It does not support them. Its legislation, as applied, does no more than provide a general program to help parents get their children, regardless of their religion, safely and expeditiously to and from accredited schools.[247]

Justice Jackson, in his dissenting opinion,[248] emphasized the importance for the Catholic Church of parochial education and its religious purpose. He considered the bus subsidy a form of aid, and found inapposite Justice Black's allusion to general governmental services. In a lengthy dissent, Justice Rutledge, joined by three other Justices, including Justice Jackson, wrote:

The prohibition broadly forbids state support, financial or other, of religion in any guise, form or degree. It outlaws all use of public funds for religious purposes.

* * *

Payment of transportation is no more, nor is it any the less essential to education, whether religious or secular, than payment for tuitions, for teachers' salaries, for buildings, equipment and necessary materials. Nor is it any the less directly related, in a school giving religious instruction, to the primary religious objective all those essential items of cost are intended to achieve. No rational line can be drawn between payment for such larger, but no more necessary, items and payment for transportation."[249]

Until 1968, *Everson* was the only Supreme Court case dealing with aid to sectarian education under the First Amendment, and discussions of relevant issues have frequently taken the form of argument over what *Everson* "really" stands for. Though the holding of the case is permissive of aid, the language of all three opinions is restrictive. So much of this has been quoted because there is such divergence over its significance.

---

[247] Id., at 18.
[248] Id., at 18.
[249] Id., at 28, 33, 48.

2. *Abington School Dist. v. Schempp.*[250] In 1963, the Supreme Court held Bible reading in the public schools unconstitutional. The result was hardly startling, since the Court had previously struck down recitation of a state-authorized nondenominational prayer in *Engel v. Vitale.*[251] The interest of the case lies in the Court's effort to rectify the limited amount of theoretical analysis in the *Engel* opinion.[252] What emerges from the 116 pages of opinions is a strong emphasis on the concept of "neutrality" and a test of constitutionality under the First Amendment apparently more hospitable toward aid of sectarian schools than the *Everson* dicta, though *Everson* itself is cited as authority for the test.

Discussing the interrelationship and overlap between the Free Exercise and Establishment Clauses, the majority opinion (written by Justice Clark) emphasizes that the government's role under these clauses is to be "neutral" toward religion.

> The test may be stated as follows: what are the purpose and the primary effect of the enactment? If either is the advancement or inhibition of religion then the enactment exceeds the scope of legislative power as circumscribed by the Constitution. That is to say that to withstand the strictures of the Establishment Clause there must be a secular legislative purpose and a primary effect that neither advances nor inhibits religion.[253]

Since the primary purpose and effect of the challenged Bible reading was religious, the practice was impermissible. In an extensive concurrence in which he also stressed "neutrality" and the conjunction of the two religion clauses, Justice Brennan stated:

> What the Framers meant to foreclose, and what our decisions under the Establishment Clause have forbidden, are those involvements of religious with secular institutions which (a) serve

---

250 374 U.S. 203 (1963).

251 370 U.S. 421 (1962).

252 That decision enjoyed widespread unpopularity. One of the reasons was that the concurring opinion of Justice Douglas cast doubt on the validity of many practices not touched on by the majority, including the provision of chaplains for the armed forces, grants of money to religious hospitals, and tax exemptions for religious institutions. 370 U.S. 421, 437. Justice Douglas regretted his vote with the majority in *Everson* which "seems in retrospect to be out of line with the First Amendment. . . . Mr. Justice Rutledge stated in dissent what I think is durable First Amendment philosophy." Id. at 443.

253 374 U.S., at 222.

the essentially religious activities of religious institutions; (b) employ the organs of government for essentially religious purposes; or (c) use essentially religious means to serve governmental ends, where secular means would suffice.[254]

In discussing tax exemptions available to religious institutions, Justice Brennan commented, "If religious institutions benefit, it is in spite of rather than because of their religious character. For religious institutions simply share benefits which government makes generally available to educational, charitable, and eleemosynary groups."[257] In a brief concurring opinion joined by Justice Harlan, Justice Goldberg made this general observation:

> It is said, and I agree, that the attitude of government toward religion must be one of neutrality. But untutored devotion to the concept of neutrality can lead to invocation or approval of results which partake not simply of that noninterference and noninvolvement with the religious which the Constitution commands, but of a brooding and pervasive devotion to the secular and a passive, or even active, hostility to the religious. Such results are not only not compelled by the Constitution, but, it seems to me, are prohibited by it.[256]

The "purpose and primary effect" criterion of *Schempp* was not wholly novel. It had been utilized before in cases sustaining Sunday Closing Laws against claims under both the Establishment and Free Exercise Clauses.[257] Specifically in answer to the assertion that these laws infringed the religious liberty of Sabbatarians, Chief Justice Warren wrote, in a plurality opinion, that a general law might be valid despite an indirect burden on religious observance if its "purpose and effect" are to advance the State's secular goals.[258] The theoretical significance of *Schempp* is its implication that "purpose and primary effect" may be an all-encompassing test for Establishment Clause cases. Still, the case did concern Bible reading in public schools, an issue quite different from financial aid to parochial schools, and it is hazardous to apply language directed at one kind of problem to the

---

[254] 374 U.S. 203, 230, 294-95.

[255] Id., at 301.

[256] 374 U.S. 203, 306.

[257] McGowan v. Maryland 366 U.S. 420 (1961); Braunfeld v. Brown, 366 U.S. 599 (1961).

[258] Braunfeld v. Brown, 366 U.S. 599. 607.

solution of another. Moreover, the central terms of the standard contain considerable ambiguity.

3. *Board of Education v. Allen.*[259] In June of 1968 the Court confirmed the intimations of *Schempp* and exhibited an even more permissive attitude toward aid than it had in *Everson.* The case concerned a textbook law in New York,[260] under which local school boards are required to purchase textbooks for loan without charge to students in any public or private school that complies with the compulsory education law. The texbooks for use in private schools must be books that are required for courses in those schools and are either books designated for public school use or approved by the boards of education or other school authorities. By a 6-3 vote, the Court upheld the law. In his relatively brief opinion for the majority, Justice White invoked the *Schempp* rule. That is to say, he considered whether providing textbooks for parochial school children was in furtherance of a "secular legislative purpose" and has a primary effect that neither advances nor inhibits religion. The New York Legislature, he noted, had expressly said that it sought only to further the educational opportunities of children. Those who now attacked the law's validity, he added, "have shown us nothing about the necessary effects of the statute that is contrary to its stated purpose. The law merely makes available to all children the benefits of a general program to lend school books free of charge. Books are furnished at the request of the pupil and ownership remains, at least technically, in the State. Thus no funds or books are furnished to parochial schools, and the financial benefit is to parents and children, not to schools."[261]

Justice White conceded that providing textbooks free of charge might possibly encourage attendance at a sectarian school. But he regarded that as of little significance, remarking that "that was true of the state-paid bus fares in *Everson* and does not alone demonstrate an unconstitutional degree of support for a religious institution."

As for the books that were to be bought with public funds, the opinion noted that they must be approved by the public school authorities and that "only secular books may receive approval."

---

[259] 392 U.S. 236 (1968). For background history bearing on the case, see R. E. Morgan, The Politics of Religious Conflict 98-102 (Pegasus, 1968).

[260] Education Law §701.

[261] 392 U.S. 236, 243-244.

Books—unlike the bus transportation involved in the earlier Supreme
Court case—are concededly "critical to the teaching process;" but
sectarian schools are not engaged solely in teaching religion, for, as
"this Court has long recognized," they "pursue two goals, religious
instruction and secular education."[262]

Justice White's opinion continued with the following comments
concerning the educational contributions made by institutions outside
the public school system:

Underlying [earlier] cases, and underlying also the legislative
judgments that have preceded the court decisions, has been a
recognition that private education has played and is playing a
significant and valuable role in raising national levels of knowledge, competence and experience. Americans care about the
quality of the secular education available to their children. . . .
Considering this attitude, the continued willingness to rely on
private school systems, including parochial systems, strongly suggests that a wide segment of informed opinion, legislative and
otherwise, has found that those schools do an acceptable job of
providing secular education to their students. This judgment is
further evidence that parochial schools are performing, in addition to their sectarian function, the task of secular education.

Against this background of judgment and experience, unchal-
lenged in the meager record before us in this case, we cannot
agree with appellants either that all teaching in a sectarian school
is religious or that the processes of secular and religious training
are so intertwined that secular textbooks furnished to students
by the public are in fact instrumental in the teaching of religion.
This case comes to us after summary judgment entered on the
pleadings. Nothing in this record supports the proposition that
all textbooks, whether they deal with mathematics, physics,
foreign languages, history, or literature, are used by the parochial schools to teach religion.[263]

Concurring, Justice Harlan expressed his belief that the religious clauses of the First Amendment do not forbid governmental
activity aimed at achieving a permissible non-religious purpose, so
long as "the activity does not involve the State 'so significantly and

---

[262] Id., at 245.
[263] Id., at 247-248.

directly in the realm of the sectarian as to give rise to . . . divisive influences and inhibitions of freedom.' "[264]

Two of the three dissenting judges, Justices Black and Douglas, are the only members of the *Everson* court still on the bench. Justice Black, the author of the prevailing opinion in *Everson,* contended that neither that nor any other opinion of the Court supported the present holding. Upholding a state's power to pay for schoolchildren's transportation, he maintained, "cannot provide support for the validity of a state law using tax-raised funds to buy books for a religious school." In a sectarian school, he contended, even the books that relate to secular subjects "will in some way inevitably tend to propagate the religious views of the favored sect." Furthermore, since books are "the most essential tool of education" and are "the heart of any school," they are readily distinguishable from bus fares, which merely assure convenient transportation to the schoolhouse. State financial aid in supplying books, Justice Black asserted, "actively and directly assists the teaching and propagation of sectarian religious viewpoints in clear conflict with the First Amendment's establishment bar," in a way that does not occur when it finances "a general and nondiscriminatory transportation service in no way related to substantive religious views and beliefs." He concluded with a categorical statement of belief that "tax-raised funds can not constitutionally be used to support religious schools, buy their school books, erect their buildings, pay their teachers, or pay any other of their maintenance expenses, even to the extent of one penny."[265]

Justice Douglas, in a separate dissenting opinion, expressed belief that New York school authorities would inevitably find themselves under pressure to approve books with sectarian overtones. "Can there be the slightest doubt," he asked, "that the head of the parochial school would select the book or books that best promote its sectarian creed?"[266] Even when an author's treatment of particular topics is not "blatantly sectarian," he added, a school textbook "will necessarily have certain shadings that will lead a parochial school to prefer one text over another."[267] Neutral treatment of historical events like the Crusades and the Reformation, Justice Douglas observed, is virtually impossible. Like Justice Black, he thought that

---

[264] 392 U.S. 236, 248.
[265] 392 U.S. 236, 250, 252-54.
[266] 392 U.S. 236, 254, 256.
[267] Id., at 260.

a large gulf separated the bus transportation law upheld in *Everson* from the schoolbook law now under discussion. A school might well survive without a bus, but "the textbook goes to the very heart of education in a parochial school. It is the chief, although not solitary, instrumentality for propagating a particular religious creed or faith."[268]

In the view of the third dissenter, Justice Fortas, the central feature in the case was that the texts furnished were chosen by the sectarian school officials.[269] In *Everson* students in sectarian schools were merely extended the same service as those in public schools; here, however, a special and separate service was provided, and this, to Justice Fortas, constituted the use of public money to aid sectarian establishments.

Although the *Allen* case certainly does not settle all the complex issues involved in aid to sectarian education, this recital of the views that prevailed and of the views that were so forthrightly expressed in dissent shows that the Court's judgment was not casually rendered. The decision indicates a willingness to give the *Everson* opinion considerably greater significance than its author, Justice Black, is now willing to attach to it. The Court's most recent expression seems, in summary, to affirm the possibility of compartmentalizing the secular and the religious elements of education in a denominational school.

4. *Horace Mann League v. Board of Public Works.*[270] When the State of Maryland decided to give financial help to four colleges so that they could construct two science buildings, a science wing and dining hall, and a dormitory and classroom building, suits were promptly brought to block the gifts. Ultimately a 4-3 majority of Maryland's highest court decided that the First Amendment is a bar to giving state aid to sectarian institutions, even for such mainly secular purposes as eating and sleeping accommodations. The decision was rendered in 1966, two years bofore the *Allen* case discussed in preceding paragraphs. Whether the result would have been different had the *Allen* decision then been available, is of course only a matter of speculation. In any event, the *Horace Mann* case deserves close attention because it embodies a sustained judicial discussion of grants to higher educational institutions.

---

[268] Id., at 257.

[269] 392 U.S. 236, 264, 269-270.

[270] 242 Md. 645, 220 A. 2d 51, appeal dismissed and cert. denied, 385 U.S. 97 (1966).

The Maryland court guided itself by what it thought to be the spirit of the *Schempp* case—the case that forbade Bible reading in public schools because public authorities must remain neutral toward religion and religious organizations. To support a religious institution by outright financial assistance, the majority concluded, was to abandon the required posture of neutrality. Maryland, the judges said, planned to go far beyond the kind of general welfare legislation permitted by *Everson*. The state proposed to make its gifts to specific institutions of higher learning. For the Court, therefore, the central issue was whether, purely as a matter of fact, the benefiting institutions were or were not sectarian. For those found to be dominantly religious (as were three of the four colleges involved in the litigation), the constitutionally requisite "neutrality" precluded public generosity.

We believe the case to be of very limited authority as a source of constitutional insight, even though the Supreme Court of the United States declined to review it.[271] The pertinent language in the Maryland case is somewhat at odds with the Supreme Court's subsequent decision in *Allen*. Moreover, the majority opinion is not noteworthy for clarity in tone and reasoning.[272] And yet, when the *Horace Mann* case has been discounted as an analysis of the First Amendment, it still has significant utility as a guide to measuring the character of an educational institution. In some situations and for some purposes a categorization of institutions is a necessity. The Maryland court, seeking to decide whether one college was denominational and another not, formulated criteria which have a commonsensical appeal and they may retain validity even if subsequent

---

[271] In regard to the three grants declared invalid, the Supreme Court denied certiorari, a discretionary determination. 385 U.S. 97 (1966). In regard to the sustained grant, it did dismiss an appeal. 385 U.S. 97. Although technically this may have been a decision on the merits, see discussion note 241 above, it is much more likely that the Court wished to avoid consideration of the three denied grants and did not choose to take only one part of what had been an integrated case.

[272] For critical commentary, see generally R. F. Drinan, "Does State Aid to Church Related Colleges Constitute an Establishment of Religion?,—Reflections on the Maryland College Cases." 1967 Utah Law Rev. 491 (1967); P. G. Kauper, "Religion, Higher Education and the Constitution," 19 Alabama Law Rev. 275 (1967) See also Vermont Educational Buildings Financing Agency v. Mann, 127 Vt. 262, 247 A.2d 68 (1968), appeal dismissed, 396 U.S. 801 (1969), upholding construction assistance for a classroom and science building to a church-related college by a corporate instrumentality of the state. Relying on *Schempp* and *Allen*, the court sustained the aid, because "There is no suggestion that the cause of religion will be served or obstructed by the facilities to be constructed . . . ." Id., at 74.

decisions do not hold that sectarian institution are barred from receiving the kinds of funds involved in *Horace Mann*.

B. POSSIBLE PRINCIPLES OF INTERPRETATION

The few cases just summarized leave many unanswered questions concerning the scope of the Establishment Clause and the limits it sets on financial assistance. State cases other than *Horace Mann* have been relatively numerous, but on the whole not very revealing.[273] Stable legal doctrines have not as yet emerged—nor, for that matter, have religious attitudes toward Church-State relations been altogether stable, especially during recent years which have been marked by mutual forbearance and ecumenicity.[274] Although what is proper constitutionally remains a matter of debate, the logic of events pushes both the federal and state governments to come to at least tentative conclusions before the debate ends. They are being pressed to take an increasingly central role in financing private higher education, and they seem likely to do so. In this area constitutional law remains malleable. It is likely to be influenced at least in part by the writings of speculative scholars—perhaps, indeed, more than by the writings of the Framers of the Constitution. As the following pages show, however, no single theoretical approach commands united support.

1. *No Aid—Absolute Separation*

The "no aid" theory is that all goverment financial aid to religious institutions, direct or indirect, is forbidden by the First Amendment. According to this position, the Establishment Clause erected, in the language of Jefferson and *Everson*,[275] a " 'wall of separation between church and state,' " which is breached if any expenditures are made on behalf of religion. Both opinions in *Everson* give very strong support to this position, though some language in the majority opinion has provided ammunition for proponents of other views.

---

[273] Of the many state cases concerned with these problems, most turn on language in state constitutions. But see the recent case in Vermont, cited in the preceding footnote. The comments of state courts and lower federal courts on the federal Establishment Clause are not a very reliable indicator of what the Supreme Court is likely to decide.

[274] See M. R. Konvitz, Religious Liberty and Conscience 3-26 (Viking, 1968); Morgan, note 259 above, at 133-139; Cf. R. C. Casad, "The Establishment Clause and the Ecumenical Movement," 62 Michigan Law Rev. 419 (1964) (describing some of the legal issues raised by church mergers).

[275] 330 U.S. 1, 16.

With minor qualifications, the Department of Health, Education, and Welfare under President Kennedy accepted the principle of "no aid" to primary and secondary sectarian education.[276]

The supporters of the "no aid" position believe it is justified by the historical meaning of the First Amendment and the *Everson* case, as well as by independently sound policy reasons.[277] Aid to religious institutions, they believe, is an unfair use of the funds of those who are nonreligious. And since any plan of aid will confer a larger benefit on some religions than others, aid is also unfair to the members of the religions that benefit less. Parochial schools provide an excellent example; since the vast majority are Roman Catholic,[278] aid to them plainly helps Catholicism more than other denominations. Moreover, if aid to religious institutions is allowed, the result will be a bitter and divisive political struggle over shares of the pie. A further consequence, opponents claim, will be to undercut the cultural unity promoted by the public schools: "[T]he public school, as the ally of social tolerance, class fluidity, and the open mind, is so valuable that alternatives to it should not be encouraged and certainly should not receive public support."[279]

Another argument is that substantial aid would create serious dangers of secular interference with religious enterprises, as well as religious interference in state matters. Advocates of strict separation also believe that no constitutional line can be drawn to limit aid except no aid, that to permit a little aid is to permit unlimited aid. As Justice Rutledge put it: "Payment of transportation is no more, nor is it any less essential to education, whether religious or secular, than payment for tuitions, for teachers' salaries, for buildings, equipment and necessary materials."[280]

As simple as the "no aid" theory appears on its face, it presents certain difficulties. As Justices Douglas's concurring opinion

---

[276] See "Constitutionality of Federal Aid to Education in Its Various Aspects," Sen. Doc. No. 29, 87th Con., 1st Sess., (1961) reprinted in 50 Georgetown Law Jour. 349 (1961).

[277] See generally L. Pfeffer, Church, State and Freedom 524-526 (Beacon, Rev. ed. 1967).

[278] Over 90 per cent of all children who attend non-public schools are in Catholic schools. R. F. Drinan, "State and Federal Aid to Parochial Schools," 7 Jour. of Church and State 67, 71 (1965).

[279] Center for the Study of Democratic Institutions, Religion and American Society 49 (1961). See also A. M. Bickel, Politics and the Warren Court 201-204 (Harper & Row, 1965).

[280] Everson v. Board of Education, 330 U.S. 1, 48 (1947).

in the school prayer case pointed out,[281] American society is honey-combed with direct and indirect aids to religion, among them grants to religious hospitals and tax exemptions for churches. A thorough-going proponent of absolute separation would be compelled to argue that these practices are unconstitutional, a position not likely to be endorsed by the courts.[282] One may, of course, distinguish these practices on various grounds. Not taking money may be different from giving it. The secular benefits conferred by hospitals may be relatively unrelated to the religion of their operators, while parochial education, according to those opposed to aid to schools, is "per-meated" with religion, making any aid to education aid to the re-ligious purposes of the church itself.

Since no one would care to deny parochial schools and school children the benefits of community existence, such as police protec-tion, a second difficulty for the no aid position is drawing the line between prohibited aid to the school and incidental benefits extended to all buildings or persons. Most adherents of strict separation be-lieve that the Supreme Court erred when, in *Everson,* it regarded bus transportation for parochial schoolchildren to be simply the ex-tension of a public service rather than an aid to private school systems.[283] As the 5-4 split in that very case shows, separating the allowed from the forbidden is not easy even when agreement on general principles has been reached.

Critics of the "no aid" position press these difficulties as evidence of the theory's inherent weakness. They argue that some of the policy contentions supporting the theory are misconceived. They maintain, for example, that since Catholics will be embittered if aid be denied, "no aid" is as likely to be socially divisive as some aid.[284] And even if the underlying policy judgment, such as the cul-tural assimilation promoted by public schools, do have merit, the critics think they are not of constitutional dimension.[285]

---

[281] Engel v. Vitale, 370 U.S. 421, 437 (1962).

[282] See, e.g., Murray v. Comptroller 241 Md. 383, 216 A. 2d 897, cert. denied 385 U.S. 816 (1966); Truitt v. Board of Public Works, 243 Md. 375, 221 A. 2d 370 (1966). The Hill-Burton Act, 42 U.S.C. §291 (1964) authorizes grants and loans for the construction of hospitals, including those that are church-affiliated, and no one has suggested that a challenge to them would be likely to be suc-cessful. Cf. R. F. Drinan, Religion, The Courts and Public Policy 33-34 (McGraw-Hill, 1963).

[283] See Pfeffer, note 277, at 566-71.

[284] See, e.g., A. Schwarz, "No Imposition of Religion: The Establishment Clause Value," 77 Yale Law Jour. 692, 710-711 (1968).

[285] Id., at 715-718.

Despite its problems, some version of the "no aid" principle, but by no means its most absolute one, appeared to be in the Supreme Court's mind when it decided *Everson*.[286] The majority admitted that bus transportation approached the "verge" of what the Constitution permitted, and the four dissenters thought the verge had been passed.

Equally clearly, however, the language of the *Allen* case rejects the "no aid" theory. This was perceived by the two Justices who had participated in the *Everson* decision as members of the majority. In *Allen*, they strongly dissented precisely because the Court had cast off the limitations suggested by the earlier case. The rationale in *Allen* is not that textbooks are a "welfare benefit," like school lunches and medical treatment, but rather that education in secular subjects meets a secular need that is properly the concern of the state.

One aspect of the no aid theory remains well established. That is that the state can not itself engage in or finance religious education. The *Engel* and *Schempp* cases forbid religious exercises in the public school.[287] In an earlier case, *McCollum v. Board of Education*,[288] the Court had struck down a "released time" system, under which children received religious instruction from teachers of their own faith for one hour a week in the public school. It said, "This is beyond all question a utilization of the tax-established and tax-supported public school system to aid religious groups to spread their faith."[289] Although some of the breadth of *McCollum* was undercut by *Zorach v. Clauson*,[290] which upheld a released time system with classes outside the school, the principle that public money can not

---

286 See Jones, note 238, at 196-97.

287 These decisions do not preclude teaching about religion as a relevant part of the experience of man. Abington School Dist. v. Schempp, 374 U.S. 203, 225 (1963). Whether religion can ever be taught "objectively," particularly at the lower levels, is a troubling question and one with whose implications the Court has yet to deal. See, e.g., D. A. Giannella, "Religious Liberty, Nonestablishment, and Doctrinal Development," Part II, 81 Harvard Law Rev. 513, 568-71 (1968); R. Ulich, "The Educational Issue," in P. A. Freund & R. Ulich, Religion and the Public Schools 42-45 (Harvard, 1965); P. Phenix, "Religion in American Public Schools," 1965 Religion and Public Order 82, 84; P. G. Kauper, Religion and the Constitution 96 (Louisiana State, 1964); W. G. Katz, Religion and American Constitutions 50-56 (Northwestern, 1964); H. Stahmer, "Religion and Moral Values in the Public Schools," Religious Education, Jan.-Feb. 1966, p. 20.

288 333 U.S. 203 (1948).

289 Id., at 210.

290 343 U.S. 306 (1952).

finance religious instruction seems firmly embedded, and is reflected in the federal and state legislative plans to provide aid to education.[291]

2. Aid Permitted For Secular Purposes

Proponents of aid repeatedly argue that parochial schools serve a secular purpose, by providing education that equips students for life in American society.[292] Since education is a public function, they argue, government may help finance it wherever the function may happen to be performed.

Bradfield v. Roberts, decided in 1899,[293] upheld an agreement of the District of Columbia to construct a building for a hospital to be administered by a religious order. Relying on the absence of any reference to religion in the certificate of incorporation of the hospital, the Court declared it immaterial under the First Amendment that in fact the Roman Catholic Church "exercises great and perhaps controlling influence over the management of the hospital." In any event, the Court said, the hospital must be managed wholly in accord with the defined purposes and powers of the "non-sectarian and secular corporation" that legally owned it. The influence of the Church upon the corporation did not convert it into a religious body or alter its legal character, which was fixed beyond change by the act of incorporation.[294]

The language of *Bradfield* seems broad enough to include any educational institution whose religious ties are not spelled out in the charter. Its applicability to education obtained oblique support in *Quick Bear v. Leupp,*[295] in which the Court considered a government contract to pay the Bureau of Catholic Indian Missions for

---

291 A possible exception was the original G. I. Bill of Rights, Servicemen's Readjustment Act of 1944, 58 Stat. 287, under which military veterans were given financial aid to permit them to study as and where they wished, including religious seminaries. See HEW memorandum, note 276 above, at 19, 50 Georgetown Law Jour. at 370-71; R. M. Sullivan, "Religious Education in the Schools," 14 Law and Contemporary Problems 92, 109-110 (1949); J. H. Choper, "The Establishment Clause and Aid to Parochial Schools," 56 California Law Rev. 260, 317 (1968).

292 See, e.g., Legal Department of National Catholic Welfare Conference, "The Constitutionality of the Inclusion of Church-Related Schools in Federal Aid to Education," 50 Georgetown Law Jour. 397, 401 et seq. (1961); R. F. Drinan, Religion, The Courts, and Public Policy 116-135 (McGraw-Hill, 1963).

293 173 U.S. 291.

294 Id., at 298.

295 210 U.S. 50 (1908). The central issue was whether Congressional legislation forbidding the use of public money to educate Indians in sectarian schools extended to the "Treaty Fund" involved in the case.

educating Indians. The government urged that *Bradfield* established the constitutional validity of spending public money for education under sectarian auspices, comparing the instruction in morality and religion which accompanied education in secular subjects to the religious ministrations in a sectarian hospital. The Court apparently accepted this view: "It is not contended that [the contract] is unconstitutional, and it could not be. . . . Bradfield v. Roberts . . . ."[296]

A case upholding the right of parents to send their children to parochial schools, *Pierce v. Society of Sisters*,[297] lends some indirect support to the secular benefit argument. The Court struck down an Oregon statute requiring all children to go to public school because it "unreasonably interferes with the liberty of parents and guardians to direct the upbringing and education of children under their control."[298] Since a state has a sufficient secular interest to compel children to go to school regardless of their parents' wishes, and since the state cannot constitutionally decide that parochial schools are in general inadequate to provide schooling, proponents of aid contend that the state must recognize the secular benefit provided by the schools, and can (or must), therefore, finance them. Robert Drinan has said, "Public money... cannot logically be withheld from the private school if it is publicly accredited as an institution where children may fulfill their legal duty to attend school."[299]

---

[296] Id., at 81. In Everson v. Board of Education, 330 U.S. 1 (1947), and subsequent cases, the Court has not, of course, followed the broader implications of *Bradfield* and *Quick Bear*. And see Justice Rutledge's dissenting opinion in *Everson*, 330 U.S. 28, 44, n. 35.

[297] 268 U.S. 510 (1925).

[298] Id., at 534-535. See also Meyer v. Nebraska, 262 U.S. 390 (1923) (invalidating statute forbidding teaching a foreign language); Farrington v. Tokushige, 273 U.S. 284 (1927) (invalidating excessively detailed control of private schools by government). At the time of *Pierce* the Court gave the Fourteenth Amendment an expansive reading to strike down laws it deemed unreasonable. Since the principle of "substantive" due process has since been very narrowly circumscribed, see R. G. McCloskey, "Economic Due Process and the Supreme Court: An Exhumation and Reburial," 1962 Supreme Court Review 34 (U. of Chicago, 1962), most decisions based on it have been overruled or are of doubtful authority. Not so with *Pierce*. The Court has recently cited it with approval, Griswold v. Connecticut, 381 U.S. 479, 481-483 (1965), and few doubt it would be decided the same way today, though the opinion would read differently.

[299] R. F. Drinan, "The Constitutionality of Public Aid to Parochial Schools," in D. H. Oaks ed., The Wall Between Church and State 60 (U. of Chicago, 1963). See the same author's discussion in Religion, The Courts and Public Policy, 123-127 (McGraw-Hill, 1963). Another author has called this "the strongest argument to sustain . . . aid to parochial schools . . . ." P. B. Kurland, "Politics and the Constitution: Federal Aid to Parochial Schools," 1 Land and Water Law Rev. 475, 491 (1966).

A later decision cited in support of the secular function argument is *Cochran v. Louisiana State Board of Education.*[300] The Court sustained the use of state funds to supply textbooks to children in parochial and other private schools, holding that the expenditure was for a public—and, one may presume, secular—purpose.[301]

Of course the proposition that sectarian schools serve some secular purpose is one with which few would quarrel. The central question is whether the government can aid worthwhile secular endeavors when they are undertaken by religious institutions, particularly when the religious and secular purposes are as intermingled as they are in the parochial educational process.[302] The flatly negative answer *Everson* seemed to provide has been revoked by *Allen.* If the government's purpose is to aid secular education and the primary effect is to promote secular education, then, under *Allen,* aid may be permissible. But even *Allen* does not clearly establish that financial aid can go directly to a sectarian school, for expenditure by it. The benefit that was involved in the *Allen* litigation was, at least in outward form, conferred upon the child (to whom textbooks were loaned) rather than upon the schools; accordingly, the decision could be read as limited to "child benefits," discussed below.

If a broader reading of *Allen* is correct and sectarian schools can receive public largess beyond the fringe welfare benefits apparently contemplated by *Everson,* what are the constitutional limits to aid? Many possibilities have been advanced. One is that implied by *Bradfield.* If the school is incorporated for a public purpose and aid is given in support of that purpose, the state has no need to inquire

---

300 281 U.S. 370 (1930).

301 The case was decided, we must note, before the First Amendment had been held to be a limitation upon what states as well as the federal government could permissibly do in the way of giving aid to religion. For Leonard Manning, given the prior extension of the free speech guarantee to the states, "it is hard . . . to conceive how those Justices would lightly turn aside, indeed ignore, the first amendment." L. F. Manning, "Aid to Education—Federal Fashion," 29 Fordham Law Rev. 495, 515 (1961).

302 That parochial education is permeated with religion is something that Catholic educators themselves have often claimed. According to one Jesuit: "It is a commonplace observation that in the parochial school religion permeates the whole curriculum, and is not confined to a single half-hour period of the day. Even arithmetic can be used as an instrument of pious thoughts, as in the case of the teacher who gave this problem to her class: 'If it takes forty thousand priests and a hundred forty thousand sisters to care for forty million Catholics in the United States, how many more priests and sisters will be needed to convert and care for the hundred million non-Catholics in the United States?'" J. H. Fichter, Parochial School: A Sociological Study 86 (Notre Dame, 1958).

how the school is operated so long as the public function is realized.[303] This theory would permit total subsidization of sectarian schools, including their explicitly religious endeavors.

A similar consequence might be arrived at under the "neutrality" theory of the Establishment Clause developed by Philip Kurland.[304] In his view that clause coalesces with the Free Exercise Clause to require the government to be neutral, neither to aid nor to inhibit religion. "[T]he proper construction of the religion clauses of the First Amendment is that the freedom and separation clauses should be read as a single precept that government cannot utilize religion as a standard for action or inaction because these clauses prohibit classification in terms of religion either to confer a benefit or to impose a burden."[305] If the government decides to aid all schools or all non-public schools in a certain way, religious schools can participate with the others, not because they are religious, but because the state must be blind to whether they are religious or not.[306] Some secular purpose would, of course, have to underlie the general granting of aid, but a religious institution's using all or part of its aid for religious purposes would not be prohibited. Thus, a tax exemption extended to all charitable enterprises would be proper even though freedom from taxation would assuredly though indirectly further a church's capacity to carry on the religious activities that justify its being.

Initially advanced by the National Catholic Welfare Conference, a somewhat different rationale for sustaining general aid has recently been supported by Professor Jesse Choper, who contends that parochial schools may be directly or indirectly financed by governmental resources "so long as such aid does not exceed the value of the secular

---

303 In fact in *Bradfield* the city's money was spent to acquire a direct reciprocal benefit. In return for having a building or ward constructed by the city, the hospital promised to treat poor patients sent to it by the city. The opinion, however, did not rely on this *quid pro quo*.

Another point noted in *Bradfield* is that the hospital apparently did not confine itself to Catholic patients. An institution so limited might have been treated differently.

304 See P. B. Kurland, Religion and the Law (Aldine, 1962).

305 Id., at 18. The language in *Everson* against discrimination in the distribution of public welfare benefits, 330 U.S. at 16, gives qualified support to this view.

306 As Professor Kurland has himself noted, this theory, strictly applied, leads to invalidation of plans, such as shared time, whose purpose is the accommodation of parochial school needs. See Kurland, note 299 above, at 494.

educational service rendered by the school."[307] The basic argument is that the government can properly pay for secular benefits, though the Establishment Clause forbids its financing religious purposes. As Professor Choper himself recognizes, his proposed approach would enable publicly-assisted sectarian schools to divert to directly religious purposes the resources they would otherwise have had to spend on secular subjects; but this, he believes, is not unconstitutional as long as the state actually receives the secular benefits for which it has paid.

Others, alarmed by the support that general grants may give to a school's religious purposes, have advocated more limiting criteria for aid. The most obvious of these and the one reflected in many of the present federal statutes authorizing aid to higher education, discussed in the next section, is that public funds must be earmarked for specific secular purposes. Thus, the government might be constitutionally able to pay for the construction of a science building, but it could not help meet a sectarian institution's general budgetary needs. Of course funds that have been provided to an institution for one of its secular purposes will enable the institution to devote correspondingly more of its own funds to religious purposes; for this reason, the distinction between limited and general aid has been attacked as fallacious.[308] Possibly this objection would lose its force if a grant were made solely to provide a facility or to finance an activity the recipient would not otherwise have been able to afford.[309] Unfortunately, ascertaining precisely how money might be spent in the future would be extremely difficult, particularly if an institution were to become aware that by proclaiming its own inability to meet a need, it might legalize the state's meeting the need in its behalf.

---

[307] J. H. Choper, "The Establishment Clause and Aid to Parochial Schools," 56 California Law Rev. 260, 266 (1968) ; see National Catholic Welfare Conference, Legal Department, "The Constitutionality of the Inclusion of Church-Related Schools in Federal Aid to Education," 50 Georgetown Law Jour. 397, 411, 434-437 (1961) ; cf. Schade v. Allegheny County Inst. Dist., 386 Pa. 507, 126 A. 2d 911 (1956). It is conceivable, though no court has yet held this, that an institution very heavily financed by government funds would be considered an agency of the state, limited in regard to its religious activities as would be the government. Cf. Simkins v. Moses H. Cone Memorial Hosp., 323 F. 2d 959 (4th Cir., 1963), cert. denied, 376 U.S. 938 (1964), (forbidding racial discrimination in hospital aided by government).

[308] "Statutory Note on Higher Education Facilities Act," 77 Harvard Law Rev. 1353, 1354 (1964).

[309] See HEW Memorandum note 276 above, at 18, 50 Georgetown Law Jour. at 370; 20 U.S.C. §823 (a) (5) (Supp., IV 1969) (forbidding grants for materials if institutional funds would ordinarily be used for them).

Another suggested distinction is between grants and loans. Money that has been loaned must be repaid, and is therefore less likely than an outright gift to free other funds that may further some religious undertaking.[310] If, however, the loan is a "soft" loan—that is, one that is made on terms more favorable than would normally govern a financial transaction—it is the equivalent of a "hard" loan plus a small subsidy, so the danger of released funds is not eliminated. Perhaps the kind of "aid" that is easiest to detach from religious purposes is the contract for a specific piece of research or other work not likely to be undertaken as an ordinary function of a school or university.[311]

Yet another possible criterion for judging the constitutional propriety of aid turns not on the nature of the aid itself, but on the alternative possibilities open to the government. In his separate opinion in the Sunday Closing Law cases, Justice Frankfurter wrote, "[I]f a statute furthers both secular and religious ends by means unnecessary to the effectuation of the secular ends alone—where the same secular ends could be equally attained by means which do not have consequences for promotion of religion—the statute cannot stand."[312] Applying this criterion to parochial education presents real difficulties. The test requires weighing alternative means to a given end but much depends on how a permissible secular end is defined. If the end is the general raising of educational standards, it makes sense to speak of aid to public education and aid to all education as alternatives. If the end is defined, however, as improving the education of all students, then assistance to sectarian schools may be the only means of aiding students in those schools.[313] Even if improvement of general educational quality is viewed as the end, once a legislature has determined that educational institutions of diverse types (including the sectarian) must be aided, a court might be embarrassed to substitute its own contrary belief that the objectives could be achieved equally well by excluding sectarian schools.

---

310 See HEW Memorandum, note 276 above, at 18, 50 Georgetown Law Jour. at 369-370.

311 Id., at 18-19, 50 Georgetown Law Jour. at 370.

312 McGowan v. Mayland, 366 U.S. 420, 466-67 (1961). Justice Brennan's concurring opinion in *Schempp*, 374 U.S. at 295, employs somewhat similar language; the government is forbidden to "use essentially religious means to serve governmental ends, where secular means would suffice." Since it is not clear whether he would regard parochial schools as "essentially religious means," it is hard to know whether he thinks this test relevant to the problem of aid to education.

313 See Choper, note 307 above, at 308-311.

Yet another possible means of limiting public expenditures for education outside the public schools would be a requirement that control over the expenditures must be maintained by the state. If a governmental authority must approve each outlay of funds, so the proponents of this suggestion have said, adequate protection will be provided against using the public's money for religious purposes.[314] The advocates of this device have failed, however, to spell out the precise nature of the fiscal control they have in mind, nor have they shown how it would preclude freeing equivalent funds for other institutional (including religious) purposes.[315]

Despite these various doubts and difficulties that inhere in the "secular purpose" theory no matter how it may be formulated, the theory has unquestionably been reinforced by the recent *Allen* decision, sustaining the public purchase of textbooks for parochial school children. The majority opinion in *Allen* does not deny the essentiality of textbooks in the educational process carried on by parochial schools. Rather, it stresses that those schools have dual purposes; it relates the state-provided textbooks to the purpose characterized as secular. Though the Court mentions that, technically, the books were simply loaned and were not given away permanently, it does not seem to regard that as significant. The Court does remark that the record had not established the religiosity of the secular courses, and it might have decided against the law or restricted its application to subjects taught in a secular way if all or some courses had been proved to have heavy religious overtones. Since the case involved only marginal expenditures, the Court might possibly have viewed more substantial aid differently.[316] Subject to these uncertainties, the decision strongly supports the secular function standard, at least when aid is strictly confined to specified secular purposes.

3. Aid Permitted As Benefit To The Child

The "child benefit" or "pupil benefit" theory falls somewhere betweeen the "no aid" and "secular function" approaches; indeed

---

[314] M. A. Gordon, "The Unconstitutionality of Public Aid to Parochial Schools," in D. H. Oaks ed., The Wall Between Church and State 73, 92 (U. of Chicago, 1963).

[315] See Choper, note 307 above, at 333-335.

[316] Justice Harlan in his concurrence indicated that government activity would be unconstitutional if it involved the state " 'so significantly and directly in the realm of the sectarian as to give rise to . . . divisive influences and inhibitions of freedom.' " 392 U.S. 236, 249 (1968). Conceivably much more substantial aid would fall over this line, though it is impossible to tell from the quoted standard exactly where the line would be drawn.

in some of its guises it is virtually indistinguishable from one or the other. Put most simply, the theory would allow aids to children and forbid aids to parochial schools. In *Cochran v. Louisiana,* in which the Supreme Court upheld supplying textbooks to private school children, it quoted with approval an exposition of the "child benefit" approach by the state court:

> One may scan the acts in vain to ascertain where any money is appropriated for the purchase of school books for the use of any church, private, sectarian or even public school. The appropriations were made for the specific purpose of purchasing school books for the use of the school children of the state, free of cost to them. It was for their benefit and the resulting benefit to the state that the appropriations were made. True, these children attend some school, public or private, the latter, sectarian or non-sectarian, and that the books are to be furnished them for their use, free of cost, whichever they attend. The schools, however, are not the beneficiaries of these appropriations. They obtain nothing from them, nor are they relieved of a single obligation, because of them. The school children and the state alone are the beneficiaries.[317]

Cochran, of course, involved a due process rather than Establish-ment Clause challenge, and the case cannot be taken as upholding the validity of "child benefits" under the First Amendment. *Everson,* however, in forbidding aid to schools and permitting the extension of welfare benefits to all citizens, gave impetus to the argument that aid to children was permissible under the Establishment Clause.

One of the problems with this approach is its almost infinite elasticity.[318] If it is taken to mean only that benefits marginally related to the educational process may be granted to school children, then it accords with the holding of *Everson.* If it is meant to allow tuition payments and textbook assistance, it represents a genuine mid-point between no aid and more general aid. It can, however, become simply a way of phrasing a principle of general aid. In 1955 an editorial in The Catholic World contended:

> The questions really resolve themselves in one main question: is the Federal Government planning to offer any help toward the building of non-public schools?. . . [I]n the matter

---

[317] 281 U.S. 370, 374-375 (1930).
[318] See, e.g., L. Pfeffer, Church, State and Freedom 568 (Beacon, rev. ed., 1967).

of erecting new school buildings, it's obvious that American children are entitled to the benefits of public welfare legislation regardless of race, creed, or color. That was the decision of the United States Supreme Court in February 1947, upholding a New Jersey state statute providing free bus transportation for children attending Catholic schools. American youth, whether Catholic, Protestant or Jewish, have a right to be educated in school buildings that have decent physical facilities.[319]

Not only is "child-benefit" a very flexible theory, it may, by focusing on the recipient of aid, be unresponsive in particular circumstances to the danger posed to Establishment Clause values.[320] The construction of a science laboratory may, in actuality, aid the religious purpose of a school far less than an across the board tuition grant (or tax exemption) given to parents.

Some commentators, though conscious of these problems, have nevertheless defended the child benefit approach. Harry Jones has written, "It is my own judgment, based on some experience with the practical legislative problem since the federal aid-to-education bill of 1949, that the 'pupil benefit' theory, reasonably applied, is a workable compromise interpretation of the First Amendment and no threat to the integrity of American constitutional church-state relationships."[321]

George LaNoue has suggested that implicit in *Everson* and *Cochran* are limits that preclude too expansive a version of the child benefit standard and that keep it responsive to the principle of nonestablishment. The grants whose validity was upheld in those cases, he has pointed out, had three common factors:

1. No religious institution acquired new property by reason of the challenged state action;

2. Complete fiscal control of the administration and spending of public funds remained in the hands of government; and

319 181 The Catholic World 1-2 (1955), quoted in G. R. La Noue, "The Child Benefit Theory Revisited: Textbooks Transportation and Medical Care," 13 Jour. of Public Law 76, 88 (1964).

320 See Choper, note 307 above, at 313-318. Like most of the other aid theories, it cannot prevent the freeing of funds that may then be devoted to religious uses.

321 See Jones, note 238 above, at 196. See also H. W. Jones, "The Constitutional Status of Public Funds for Church-Related Schools," 6 Jour. Church & State 61, 71-73 (1964); D. A. Giannella, "Religious Liberty, Nonestablishment, and Doctrinal Development," Part II, 81 Harvard Law Rev. 513, 576-581 (1968).

   3. The benefaction conferred by the state was not put to a religious use.[322]

He would allow bus transportation, shared time used of facilities operated by the state, and medical care; would forbid tuition grants (which could be used for religious purposes); and would permit textbook grants only, if at all, when their unadaptability for religious use was incontestable.[323]

The "child benefit" theory underlies much of the Elementary and Secondary Education Act of 1965, which, for example, requires approval by public authorities and public ownership of materials made available to parochial schools.[324] The theory is reflected in parts of the *Allen* opinion. The Court does say:

> The law merely makes available to all children the benefits of a general program to lend school books free of charge. Books are furnished at the request of the pupil and ownership remains, at least technically, in the State. Thus no funds or books are furnished to parochial schools, and the financial benefit is to parents and children, not the schools.[325]

Yet neither the "secular purpose and primary effect" test that the Court purports to apply nor the language of the rest of the opinion indicates that the decision would have been different if the textbooks had gone directly to the schools. Indeed what seems remarkable is how little emphasis was placed on "pupil benefit," especially in light of the stress on that theory in the New York Court of Appeals.[326] Yet the result is certainly consistent with a "child benefit" rationale, and a majority opinion rarely manages to embody the shades of emphases each of the Justices would have expressed had he written the opinion. In some future case "child benefit" may still emerge as the central analytical tool.

---

[322] La Noue, note 319 above, at 90-91.

[323] Id., at 91-94.

[324] 20 U.S.C. § 825 (Supp. IV, 1969). See D. M. Kelley & G. R. LaNoue, "The Church-State Settlement in the Federal Aid to Education Act," 1965 Religion and the Public Order 110; Giannella, note 321 above, at 578-579.

[325] 392 U.S. 236, 243-244 (1968).

[326] 20 N.Y. 2d 109, 228 N.E. 2d 791, 281 N.Y.S. 2d 799 (1967).

4. *Aid Permitted To Promote Free Exercise Of Religion And Prevent Establishment Of Secularism*

Two other, somewhat interrelated, arguments are advanced to support aid to parochial schools. One is that when parents choose to send their children to a parochial school, they are exercising their religious liberty, an exercise constitutionally protected by *Pierce*. Protecting the exercise of religion is perhaps the predominant and certainly one basic value in the religion clauses of the First Amendment. Whatever marginal danger public aid might create in the direction of establishing a state-supported religion must, it is argued, be weighed against the benefit to free exercise.[327] This view finds some, albeit not very direct, support from later cases that, unlike *Pierce*, were decided under the First Amendment.

In *Zorach v. Clauson*, in upholding New York's released time system, Justice Douglas wrote for the Court:

We are a religious people whose institutions presuppose a Supreme Being. We guarantee the freedom to worship as one chooses. We make room for as wide a variety of beliefs and creeds as the spiritual needs of man deem necessary. We sponsor an attitude on the part of government that shows no partiality to any one group and that lets each flourish according to the zeal of its adherents and the appeal of its dogma. When the state encourages religious instruction or cooperates with religious authorities by adjusting the schedule of public events to sectarian needs, it follows the best of our traditions. For it then respects the religious nature of our people and accommodates the public service to their spiritual needs. To hold that it may not would be to find in the Constitution a requirement that the government show a callous indifference to religious groups. That would be preferring those who believe in no religion over those who do believe.[328]

---

[327] See generally R. F. Drinan, "Does State Aid to to Church-Related Colleges Constitute an Establishment of Religion?—Reflections on the Maryland College Cases," 1967 Utah Law Rev. 491, 511-515 (1967); cf. P. G. Kauper, *Religion and the Constitution* 42-44 (Louisiana State, 1964).

[328] 343 U.S. 306, 313-314 (1952).

In *Sherbert v. Verner*,[329] the Court upheld the right of a Sabbatarian to receive unemployment compensation, despite a general state rule that only those available for work, including Saturday work, could receive the benefits. It would, the Court said, deny Mrs. Sherbert's free exercise of religion so to penalize her for her beliefs. Although excluding individuals otherwise eligible from a general welfare system is different from declining to finance education, the analogy is clear; parents who choose religious schools for their children are arguably in the same position as Mrs. Sherbert if aid is denied to them.

The related argument is that for the state to refuse to finance parochial schools is in effect an establishment of a religion of secularism.[330] Such cases as *McCollum, Engel,* and *Schempp,* it is argued, effectively exclude religion from the public school. *Torcaso v. Watkins*,[331] invalidating a religious test for state office, and *United States v. Seeger*,[332] broadening the religious criterion for conscientious objection, indicate that irreligion and secular humanism enjoy the protection of the First Amendment as do orthodox religions.[333] If this is so, then favoring them, the argument goes, is as much a constitutional violation as would be penalizing them, and it is precisely this that the public school does. Strict separationists give a short answer to the crude form of this argument. The public school, they say, inculcates neither religion nor irreligion; efforts to influence value development in that area are not among a schoolteacher's responsibilities.

But this short answer does not entirely satisfy proponents of religious schools. As Robert Drinan, a prominent Jesuit scholar, puts the matter:

---

[329] 374 U.S. 398 (1963). See also In re Jenison, 267 Minn. 136, 125 N.W. 2d 588, sustaining a religious claim to exemption from jury duty after the Supreme Court had remanded the case for reconsideration in light of Sherbert v. Verner, 375 U.S. 14 (1963); Arlan's Department Store v. Kentucky, 371 U.S. 218 (1962), dismissing an appeal from state decision upholding a legislative exemption for Sabbatarians from Sunday Closing Laws.

[330] See L. F. Manning, "Aid to Education—Federal Fashion," 29 Fordham Law Rev. 495, 522-524 (1961).

[331] 367 U.S. 488 (1961).

[332] 380 U.S. 163 (1965). Technically a reading of congressional intent, the decision has strong constitutional overtones.

[333] See W. B. Ball, "Religion in Education: A Basis for Consensus," 108 America 528 (1963).

[T]he public school's curriculum is 'permeated' by a secular or nonsectarian atmosphere and is therefore also 'religious' or 'non-religious.' No education can exist without a 'permeation' of some outlook on life and human existence. An education without an ideological orientation is an impossibility.[334]

This comment may overstate the point since the average public school does not purport to provide an all encompassing system of values in the same way as a Catholic school, but the difficulty remains. In the words of Alan Schwarz:

[S]ecular treatment unavoidably tends to belittle both Protestant and Catholic dogma and hence may perhaps be characterized as indoctrinating anti-religionism or secular religionism. Similarly, a civics class in racial discrimination would invoke the equality value but would ignore its religious source, associating the value with Americanism or some other secular ethic. Ignoring the theological source of the imperative—and, worse, supplying an alternative secular source—tends to belittle, perhaps even negate, the theological. Religion is most necessary, and hence most believable, when it provides the sole explanation for all phenomena. A system which provides answers without reference to religion or which teaches that there are no answers makes religion less necessary and hence less believable.[335]

Both the "free exercise" and "nonestablishment of secularism" arguments have interesting consequences if pushed to their logical extremes. In the first place they could provide a basis for general and complete aid, since, given the very nature of the arguments, aid to the religious purposes of the parochial school would not necessarily be foreclosed. The second consequence, perhaps more significant for this study, is that they might not only permit but require aid. If it is actually a denial of free exercise or an establishment of religion to withhold aid, then the government has no choice in the matter. Such a conclusion would mean striking down some

---

[334] See Drinan, note 292 above, at 157.

[335] A. Schwarz, "No Imposition of Religion: The Establishment Clause Value," 77 Yale Law Jour. 692, 700-701 (1968). This point may be weakened in so far as aspects of religion can be conveyed in the public school. See materials cited in note 287 above, and P. A. Freund, "The Legal Issue," in P.A. Freund and R. Ulich, Religion and the Public Schools 17-24 (Harvard, 1965).

state constitutional provisions that forbid aid to religious educational
institutions.

The *Everson* opinion provides some scanty support for this
position; it says that the state cannot exclude persons from welfare
benefits "because of their faith, or lack of it;" but it immediately
denies any intent "to intimate that a state could not provide transportation only to children attending public schools."[336] Even if the
state can permissibly differentiate public and private schools, it might
possibly be barred from treating private religious schools differently
from private nonreligious schools.[337] This, of course, is the result
that would be reached under a strict application of Philip Kurland's
"neutrality" standard, since only a forbidden religious criterion would
separate the two classes of schools.

If the "free exercise" and "nonestablishment of secularism" contentions do not require aid, they may still be sufficient to make aid
permissible that would otherwise be proscribed. For many scholars,
they are important factors to be balanced against conflicting values.
Wilber Katz, who favors a "neutrality" that is less formal than
Professor Kurland's, has written:

> [I]n many fields where laws affect religion incidentally, the
> promotion of neutrality requires affirmative provision for re-
> ligion. Here legislatures have been left with discretion; in this
> area provisions affirmatively fostering religious freedom are not
> invalid as 'establishing' religion, but their omission does not
> make the legislation invalid as a restraint on 'free exercise'. . . .[338]

Paul Kauper, for whom "religious liberty is the central concern
of the constitutional order as it relates to the subject of religion,"[339]
advocates a degree of accommodation or cooperation between government and religion; like Professor Katz, he would approve inclusion
of parochial schools in a program that included aid to all children
or all schools. Alan Schwarz reaches a similar conclusion because he
believes that the fundamental objective of the Establishment Clause

---

[336] 330 U.S. at 16.

[337] Cf. L. F. Manning, "Aid to Education—State Style," 29 Fordham Law Rev.
525, 546-548 (1961), arguing that such a classification is inherently unreasonable
at the college level and is a violation of the equal protection clause of the
Fourteenth Amendment.

[338] W. G. Katz, Religion and American Constitutions 91 (Northwestern, 1964).

[339] P. G. Kauper, Religion and the Constitution 13 (Louisiana State, 1964).

value is protection against *imposition* of religion.[340] Assistance that maximizes opportunities for proselytizing is, in his view, the most pernicious. The danger of aid to parochial schools, however, he regards, as relatively speculative and as offset by "the obvious state interest in quality education for all children and the parochial child's equality, free exercise and establishment claims."[341]

Donald Giannella argues that the underlying value for the religion clauses is voluntarism:

Religious voluntarism . . . conforms to that abiding part of the American credo which assumes that both religion and society will be strengthened if spiritual and ideological claims seek recognition on the basis of their intrinsic merit. Institutional independence of churches is thought to guarantee the purity and vigor of their role in society, and the free competition of faiths and ideas is expected to guarantee their excellence and vitality to the benefit of the entire society.[342]

In interpreting the Establishment Clause, he believes that a principle of "political neutrality" will best promote that value.[343] This is not Professor Kurland's rigid no-classification standard, for, like Professor Katz's neutrality, it will at times require government to accord a special place to religious activities.[344] Professor Giannella considers aid to parochial schools a difficult problem to which to apply his test, since no aid will put the schools in a worse position than "voluntarism" would justify, and too much aid would put them in a better position. He concludes that the "child benefit" standard is an appropriate compromise.[345]

The "religious liberty" and "nonestablishment of secularism" arguments were apparently regarded as having no relevance in *Allen,* if one judges from the opinion. But with the possible exception of *Sherbert v. Verner,* the Court has not favored explicit use of a balanc-

---

[340] A. Schwarz, "No Imposition of Religion: The Establishment Clause Value," 77 Yale Law Jour. 692 (1968).

[341] Id., at 737.

[342] D. A. Giannella, "Religious Liberty, Nonestablishment, and Doctrinal Development," Part II, 81 Harvard Law Rev. 513, 517 (1968).

[343] For an energetic criticism of this view, see A. Schwarz, "The Nonestablishment Principle: A Reply to Professor Giannella," 81 Harvard Law Rev. 1465 (1968).

[344] See Giannella, note 342 above, at 527.

[345] Id., at 572-581.

ing approach to Establishment Clause cases, and these contentions may conceivably have influenced some of the Justices to some degree in a way not expressed.

5. *Aid Permitted To Colleges Even If Not To Schools*

Thus far, we have assumed that the relevant principles for aid to parochial elementary and secondary schools are equally applicable to sectarian colleges and universities. Since the Supreme Court has never dealt with aid to higher education, its opinions provide no basis for knowing whether it would treat colleges differently from schools, but others have contended that it should do so when the occasion presents itself. With one possible exception, no differences between the two levels of education have been advanced that would suggest more restrictive criteria for aid to colleges, but a number might lead to a more permissive standard.

At the same time that the Department of Health, Education and Welfare defended a fairly strict separationist position in regard to school aid, it took a very different view of public assistance to higher education. Responding to a Senatorial request for a position statement, the Department's general counsel remarked, first, that colleges, unlike the lower schools, were not available to all students. He continued:

> The process is more selective, the education more specialized, and the role of private institutions vastly more important. There are obvious limitations upon what the Government can hope to accomplish by way of expanding public or other secular educational facilities. If the public purpose is to be achieved at all, it can only be achieved by a general expansion of private as well as public colleges, of sectarian as well as secular ones. . . . [I]mportant are the distinctive factors present in American higher education: . . . the fact that free public education is not available to all qualified college students; the desirability of maintaining the widest possible choice of colleges in terms of the student's educational needs in a situation no longer limited by the necessity of attending schools located close to home; the extent to which particular skills can be imparted only by a relatively few institutions; the disastrous national consequences in terms of improving educational standards which could result

from exclusion of, or discrimination against, certain private institutions on grounds of religious connection; and the fact that, unlike schools, the collegiate enrollment does not have the power of State compulsion supporting it.[346]

This 1961 memorandum contains at least the seeds of most of the arguments for more favored treatment for colleges. The weakest point is the fact that school education is compulsory whereas college education is not. In both instances the student, or his parent, has voluntarily chosen a sectarian school and the argument for aid may debatably be even stronger if he can claim he was compelled to choose between sectarian and secular education.[347] Nor does the availability of free public education seem of more than historical relevance, since the possibility of free public higher education should not affect the issue of aid to sectarian education.

Certainly one of the fundamental points is that private higher education plays a much more important role than does private education at the school level. And few regard this as unhealthy.[348] If creative diversity rather than cultural homogeneity is desired at the college level and if, as now is the case, injections of public funds are needed to keep many private institutions above water and many more at an acceptable level of academic excellence, some form of assistance is required. Exclusion of sectarian institutions from this assistance would raise serious problems. The argument that the student who chooses a sectarian institution is discriminated against is much stronger if the comparison is with students at other private institutions rather than at public schools.[349]

The "discrimination" may extend in some form to faculty members as well. Religiously concerned scholars are said to feel less inhibited to pursue their interests in an institution with religious direction.[350] Permitting secular institutions to receive public funds

---

346 HEW Memorandum, note 276 above, at 26; 50 Georgetown Law Jour. at 379-380.

347 P. G. Kauper, "Religion, Higher Education and the Constitution," 19 Alabama Law Rev. 275, 295 (1967).

348 Compare Giannella, note 342, at 584: ". . . the staunchest advocates of a dominant public school system for the lower levels of education admit the value and necessity of the private college and university."

349 See, e.g., Kauper, note 347 above, at 291; L. F. Manning, "Aid to Education —State Style," 29 Fordham Law Rev. 525, 546-547 (1961).

350 M. M. Pattillo, Jr. and D. M. MacKenzie, Church-Sponsored Higher Education in the United States 167-170 (Am. Council on Educ., 1966).

while withholding them from church-related institutions, Professor Giannella has argued, would discriminate against teachers "who find a religiously oriented institutional commitment congenial" and would therefore (in his view) be basically inconsistent with full academic freedom.[351]

A difficulty of a different order is the sheer number of church-related colleges. Of 1,189 private colleges and universities in 1966, 817 were said to have significant church relationships.[352] Presumably not all of these would be found to be "sectarian" for purposes of legal classification, but enough would be to make the exclusion numerically large if all were to be deemed ineligible for public aid.[353] Further, the exceeding difficulty of winnowing the sectarian from the secular would in itself perhaps be a reason for not drawing a line that would require the task to be undertaken.

If reasons for aiding private higher education seem more clearly compelling than the reasons for aiding private lower schools, so too do the dangers to Establishment Clause values seem markedly less. Whatever is the case at parochial schools and despite some declarations about "permeation" by religious colleges themselves, most sectarian colleges apparently teach most secular subjects in an essentially non-religious style.[354] In any event, students of college age to whom religious themes are presented, whether in secular or avowedly religious courses, are better able than elementary and high schools pupils to evaluate what they are told and to avoid the passivity that makes indoctrination easy. Moreover, since courses in religion are offered in many private nonsectarian universities as well as in public universities, the difference between sectarian and other education, even though still significant, is not as striking as at the school level. Finally, since only 41 per cent of the church-related institutions are Catholic, aid to sectarian colleges is not, as is aid to sectarian schools, overwhelmingly aid to one faith.

---

[351] Giannella, note 342 above, at 586. Professor Giannella also asserts that "the development of a departmental or institutional point of view might prove academically desirable. In a sympathetic atmosphere a band of scholars dedicated to the same values and ideals can encourage and reinforce one another's efforts." Ibid.

[352] Pattillo and MacKenzie, note 350 above, at 19.

[353] See "Statutory Note on Higher Education Facilities Act," 77 Harvard Law Rev. 1353, 1358 (1964).

[354] Compare R. F. Drinan, 'Does State Aid to Church-Related Colleges Constitute an Establishment of Religion?—Reflections on the Maryland College Case," 1967 Utah Law Rev. 491, 503 (1967). And see discussion in Chapter III, above.

In terms of the test of secular purpose and primary secular effect employed in *Allen*, these differences might lead a court concerned solely with the implications of the federal Constitution to accept aid more easily when it goes to a sectarian college than when it goes to a parochial school. Colleges might also enjoy a favored position if an "alternative means" standard,[355] or the "principle of political neutrality,"[356] or some other balancing test were used.

C. CONCLUSION

Predicting the course of Supreme Court decisions is hazardous. Without intimating absolute confidence in our estimate of how judges will treat future cases, we regard a reversion from *Allen* to the restrictions of *Everson* as unlikely. Federal and state aid to private education seems virtually certain to increase rather than diminish in years to come. We strongly doubt that the Court will insist that none of the aid be allowed to flow to sectarian institutions. Conceivably the Court will rest its permissive decisions on a moderate "child benefit" rationale, but we suspect that it will find nothing constitutionally objectionable in aid that goes directly to schools for earmarked secular functions. On the other hand, we think that general aid to parochial schools will not be judicially sustained, if legislatively attempted, for some time to come.

Aid to higher education, as distinct from aid to the lower levels, seems to us to be likely to gain ready judicial acceptance whether given in the form of "pupil benefits" or directly in support of identifiably secular functions. This judgment, we recognize, implies belief that issues like those in the *Horace Mann* case, in which the Maryland Court of Appeals invalidated grants, would be differently decided if they were now to come before the Supreme Court.

The Court's readiness to allow general aid to sectarian colleges is far more doubtful. We think the greatest chance for approval would occur in connection with a program of across-the-board grants to private colleges based on some principle that excludes those students not pursuing a primarily secular course, but even a program limited in that manner might well be held invalid.

To some extent, these estimates are based on the present and probable future patterns of aid, discussed in the following sections,

---

[355] See Kauper, note 347 above, at 289-290.
[356] See Giannella, note 342 above, at 583-590.

since the Court gives at least some deference to the judgments of legislatures, particularly those of Congress. We deem it unlikely that in the near future the Court will strike down state constitutional provisions which forbid aid to sectarian colleges while allowing it to other private colleges. In this field, we believe, the states will be given a very large range of choice.

A single prediction can be made with near certainty: This will be a heavily litigated area.

II. FEDERAL LEGISLATION

Legislative provisions permitting the flow of federal funds to institutions of higher education fill hundreds of pages in the United States Code. Many of them are parts of a few major acts designed to assist colleges and universities, but many more are items in programs undertaken essentially for other purposes. For example, the Atomic Energy Act of 1946, as amended, authorizes the Atomic Energy Commission to make grants to institutions of higher education for such things as nuclear laboratory equipment and research reactors.[357]

Before engaging in a relatively brief description of the major educational programs, we can state three simple but significant conclusions. Every existing federal program is for a secular purpose, usually stated with clarity. In no program are sectarian institutions treated differently from other private colleges and universities, though only public institutions are eligible for some forms of aid. Many of the programs, but not all, specifically declare the ineligibility of divinity schools and institutions or departments preparing students for a religious vocation or for teaching careers in religion.

Extensive federal aid to higher education, or, indeed, any education outside federal territories, is a relatively recent phenomenon. In the first half of the nineteenth century the federal government did make some monetary grants to states for general educational purposes, and in the latter half of the nineteenth century aids for certain specialized purposes were developed. Perhaps the most notable of these was the establishment under the Morrill Act of 1862 of land grant colleges. Although proposals for general federal assistance to

---

[357] 42 U.S.C. §2051 (1964) ; See HEW Memorandum, "Federal Programs Under Which Institutions With Religious Affiliation Receive Federal Funds Through Grants or Loans," Sen. Doc. 29, p. 37, 87th Cong., 1st Sess. (1961) ; A. E. Sutherland, "Establishment of Religion—1968," 19 Case Western Reserve Law Rev. 469, 479-82 (1968).

education were often discussed in Congress, they were not enacted. Increasingly in this century such proposals foundered on the issue of aid to parochial schools. Catholics opposed aid limited to public education and many others thought that financing parochial education would be unconstitutional or unwise. Not until 1965 was this logjam broken by the compromise Elementary and Secondary Education Act of 1965. Meanwhile, however, important legislation relating to higher education had been adopted without the rancor that marked discussion of aid to schools.[358]

In 1944, the G.I. Bill of Rights provided tuition for veterans who wished to attend colleges and universities, including theological seminaries.[359] As originally approved the payments were made directly to the institution attended, but the law was changed to provide payments to the veterans themselves. Subsequent programs with similar benefits have also involved payments to the veterans. As in the original act, no distinction has been drawn between study at secular and sectarian institutions, and the funds may be used at each recipient's option for theological, as well as other professional education.[360]

In 1958 the National Defense Education Act provided fresh aids for higher education, some in the form of funds for students and some in the form of funds for institutions. Title II authorizes the allotment of funds to public and nonprofit private institutions of higher education, without limitation as to their nature, so that they can make low-interest loans to students.[361] Title IV establishes National Defense Fellowships,[362] primarily designed for graduate students interested in teaching at colleges and universities, with stipends going to both the students and the institutions they attend. Sectarian institutions are not excluded but in 1964 the following restriction on eligibility was passed:

No fellowship shall be awarded under this subchapter for study at a school or department of divinity. For the purposes of this

---

[358] For a historical summary of federal aid to education, see L. Pfeffer, Church, State and Freedom 579-604 (Beacon rev. ed. 1967); W. A. Mitchell, "Religion and Federal Aid to Education," 14 Law and Contemporary Problems 113 (1949).

[359] Servicemen's Readjustment Act of 1944, 58 Stat. 287.

[360] See HEW Memorandum, note 357, at 44; 38 U.S.C. §§1651-1687 (Supp. IV, 1969).

[361] 20 U.S.C. §§421-26, as amended (Supp. IV 1969).

[362] 20 U.S.C. §§461-65, as amended, §§462-64 (Supp. IV 1969).

subsection, the term 'school or department of divinity' means an institution, or department or branch of an institution, whose program is specifically for the education of students to prepare them to become ministers of religion or to enter upon some other religious vocation or to prepare them to teach theological subjects.[363]

Two other programs in the act—grants to improve the training of guidance counselors[364] and grants, authorized in 1964, to set up institutes of advanced study[365]—are available to sectarian universities without limitation.

The Higher Education Facilities Act of 1963[366] represented a considerable breakthrough in aid to higher education. It authorizes direct grants to institutions of higher education to construct both undergraduate and graduate "academic facilities." Church-related colleges and universities are eligible, but

The term 'academic facilities' shall not include . . . (C) any facility used or to be used for sectarian instruction or as a place for religious worship, or (D) any facility wich (although not a facility described in the preceding clause) is used or to be used primarily in connection with any part of the program of a school or department of divinity. . . . [T]he term 'school or department of divinity' means an institution, or a department or branch of an institution whose program is specifically for the education of students to prepare them to become ministers of religion or to enter upon some other religious vocation or to prepare them to teach theological subjects.[367]

As the Senate debates on the bill make plain, this formulation was designed to avoid constitutional doubts.[368] Senator Ervin proposed an additional amendment that would have had the effect of barring any assistance at all to church-related colleges, contending that their receiving federal grants was unconstitutional. Many senators opposed

---

[363] 20 U.S.C. §463 (d) (1964).

[364] 20 U.S.C. §491, as amended (Supp. IV 1969).

[365] 20 U.S.C. §591, as amended (Supp. IV 1969).

[366] 20 U.S.C. §§ 701-758, as amended (Supp. IV 1969).

[367] Id., §751 (2).

[368] See 109 Cong. Rec. 19467-96, 88th Cong., 1st Sess. (1963).

the amendment on the purely pragmatic ground that eliminating church-related colleges might arouse political opposition that would spell the end of the whole bill; but Senator Ribicoff, among others, responded to the constitutional point. He argued that the bill conformed with the secular purpose and primary secular effect test of *Schempp,* and added:

Aid for the religious aspects of church related colleges has been specifically excluded. There will be no assistance for sectarian instruction, for places of worship or for schools of divinity. We are concerned with providing these young men and women with the best in educational opportunities. . . .

That is our purpose, and that will be our effect. The constitutional issue has been met and answered by the terms of the bill itself.[369]

Two years later yet additional funds for various purposes were authorized by the Higher Education Act of 1965.[370] Title I provides grants that flow through the states to institutions of higher education for community service and continuing education programs.[371] No grant can be made for programs, activities or services related to sectarian instruction or religious worship, or provided by a school or department of divinity (defined as in the other statutes).[372] Title II-A,[373] which authorizes grants for the acquisition of library materials, contains a similar limitation. Title III[374] authorizes funds for cooperative arrangements that would allow "developing institutions" to draw on the talent and resources of the country's finest universities; developing institutions are defined to exclude institutions and branches of institutions that prepare students for the ministry, some other religious vocation, or to teach religion.[375] The provisions of Title

---

369 Id., at 19494-95.
370 20 U.S.C. §§1001-1144 (Supp. IV 1969).
371 Id., §§1001-1011. Arguably, a state with a strict prohibition on giving money to sectarian institutions could not even expend the time and manpower necessary to plan the use of federal funds and to serve as their conduit. Were this argument to succeed in any number of state courts, Congress would probably alter the legislation to avoid the difficulty by designing some other mechanism for disbursing its grants.
372 Id., §1011.
373 Id., §§1021-1028.
374 Id., §§1051-1055.
375 Id., §1052 (h).

IV-A and -B,[376] which authorize grants to high school graduates of exceptional need and which strengthen programs of low interest insured loans, contain no such restrictions. The only relevant limit in the work study grants of Title IV-C[377] is that students may not help construct, operate, or maintain facilities used for sectarian instruction or religious worship. Title V-C[378] allots fellowships to teachers, but not to those at schools or departments of divinity.

The Higher Education Amendments of 1968[379] extend and expand some of these programs, but without fundamentally altering their content or their treatment of sectarian institutions.

Whatever may utimately be the constitutional law on this subject, the provisions described here, as well as others in these and different acts, demonstrate that Congress has been much more willing to channel funds to church-related colleges and universities than to parochial schools.[380] We have no reason to doubt that the pattern in the near future will continue to be grants, loans, and contracts, earmarked for specific secular purposes, with all private nonprofit colleges and universities (other than "divinity" schools and branches as broadly defined) having equal access to benefits.

If the Supreme Court were to follow the same course as the *Horace Mann* case which disallowed Maryland's grants to sectarian colleges, institutions of higher learning having close church ties would, obviously, be deprived of considerable federal help that has only recently been tendered. As indicated earlier, we believe this will not occur. Federal programs of the same general type as those just described are, in our opinion, likely to be sustained.

If, as we now deem to be probable, the basic pattern of federal laws does not change in any very dramatic way, and if, as we have forecast, church-related colleges will not be judicially blocked from sharing in the benefits Congress has provided or is likely soon to

---

[376] Id., §§1061-1086.

[377] 42 U.S.C. §§2751-2757 (Supp. IV 1969).

[378] 20 U.S.C. §§1111-1118 (Supp. IV 1969).

[379] Public Law 90-575, 82 Stat. 1014; see S. Rep. No. 1387, H. Rep. No. 1649, Conf. Rep. No. 1919, 90th Cong., 2d Sess., 1968.

[380] Compare the provisions of the Elementary and Secondary Education Act of 1965, 79 Stat. 27, as amended (codified in different sections of U.S.C.). See also G. R. La Noue, "Church-State Problems in New Jersey: The Implementation of Title I (ESEA) in Sixty Cities," 22 Rutgers Law Rev. 219 (1968). His careful study of the operation of this title indicates a number of abuses of the guarantees intended to avoid unconstitutional applications of the act.

provide, one must conclude that a church-related college would gain little, if any, additional *federal* money by severing its present religious links. "Independence" would make for economic advantage only if Congress were to become markedly more openhanded or the Supreme Court were to become markedly more restrictive than we have predicted.

But these comments, we emphasize once more, relate to eligibility for *federal* funds. Independence may have substantially greater significance in respect of benefits conferred by the *state*.

III. THE NEW YORK STATE CONSTITUTION

Whatever be its status under federal law, a sectarian college or university is seriously disadvantaged under the constitution and statutes of New York.[381] These have counterparts in many other states. Although our discussion here will be confined to New York law, much of the commentary that follows may bear significantly on the legal position of church-related institutions in other states.

In the second half of the nineteenth century numerous states, New York among them, debated whether parochial schools should or could receive public funds.[382] Since this was long before the First Amendment's applicability to the states had been established, political leaders—sometimes moved by a genuine concern for Church-State separation and sometimes moved simply by hostility to Catholicism—attempted to establish in federal and state constitutions prohibitions against state involvement with religion. The high water mark of the federal effort was the amendment proposed by James G. Blaine in 1875, which stated:

> No state shall make any law respecting an establishment of religion or prohibiting the free exercise thereof; and no money raised by taxation in any State for the support of public schools or derived from any public funds therefor, nor any public lands devoted thereto, shall ever be under the control of any religious sect or denomination; nor shall any money so raised or lands so devoted be divided between religious sects or denominations.[383]

---

[381] We assume for the rest of this chapter that the relevant portions of New York's constitution do not themselves conflict with the federal constitution, a question discussed in Section I of this Appendix.

[382] See L. Pfeffer, Church, State and Freedom 530-34 (Beacon, rev. ed. 1967).

[383] 4 Cong. Rec. 5580, 44th Cong., 1st Sess. (1876).

The amendment failed of adoption in Congress, but Blaine-like provisions sprang up in the constitutions of most states. New York was no exception, though its restrictions differ from most in being limited to education. What is popularly though inexactly called the Blaine Amendment in New York's fundamental law was adopted by the Constitutional Convention of 1894, virtually two decades after Blaine's unsuccessful efforts at the federal level. Located in the Education article rather than in the Bill of Rights, it provided:

> Neither the state nor any subdivision thereof shall use its property or credit or any public money, or authorize or permit either to be used, directly or indirectly, in aid or maintenance, other than for examination or inspection, of any school or institution of learning wholly or in part under the control or direction of any religious denomination, or in which any denominational tenet or doctrine is taught.[384]

This language, plainly much more specific than the First Amendment, provides answers on the state level to many of the questions left open in federal constitutional law. That direct monetary assistance to private sectarian schools has been foreclosed seems clear.[385] Nor are sectarian institutions of higher learning in any better position.[386]

Though most of the litigation arising under the provision has concerned the meaning of "aid," two cases, at least, have arisen because direct grants had been made to institutions. One of these was dismissed on the ground that the plaintiff (suing simply as a taxpayer who objected to the manner in which his tax payments were being spent) lacked standing to challenge a grant from the Emergency Housing Board to build a dormitory at Canisius College,

---

[384] Now, as amended, in Article XI, §3. For background shedding light on the purpose of the provision, see Morgan, note 261 above, at 109-111.

[385] But cf. Schade v. Allegheny County Institution Dist., 386 Pa. 507, 126 A. 2d 911 (1956).

[386] Leonard Manning has advanced an intricate argument that the section might be deemed inapplicable to higher education. See "Aid to Education—State Style," 29 Fordham Law Rev. 525, 544-546 (1961). Both the legislative and the executive branches apparently now assume that the section does apply to higher education and we doubt that a court would reach a contrary interpretation in the face of its broad language. But cf. Sargent v. Board of Education, 177 N.Y. 317 (1904).

a Jesuit institution.[387] In the other case, New York's highest court sustained payments to a Catholic orphan asylum and to its teachers.[388] Another constitutional provision particularly dealt with orphanages; New York had had a long history of aid to them; and discussions at the Constitutional Convention had focused on schools rather than on homes for waifs. All these considerations led easily to the conclusion that orphan asylums were not "institutions" of the kind to which no public help could be extended.

Most of the cases in which the courts have tried to define "aid" have turned on the viability of the "child benefit" theory under the state constitution. One exception was *64th. St. Residences, Inc. v. City of New York*.[389] In that case the city had condemned property in the Lincoln Center area and set aside part of it for educational purposes. Fordham University submitted a bid, as did other educational institutions. The property was ultimately sold to it at a price below its fair value on the open market. The Court of Appeals, in a unanimous decision, held that the sale involved no forbidden grant or subsidy; the court even intimated that an unconstitutional discrimination would have occurred if Fordham had been excluded from the bidding.[390]

In the first of the "child benefit" cases, the state's intermediate court, the Appellate Division, held in 1922 that textbooks could not legally be furnished to parochial school pupils by a governmental body.[391] Even though the books were given to the schoolchildren and not to the schools, the court deemed the legislative generosity to be clearly prohibited by the New York Constitution. The gift, the judges

---

387 Bull v. Stichman, 273 App. Div. 311, 78 N.Y.S. 2d 279, aff'd, 298 N.Y. 516, 80 N.E. 2d 661 (1948). The present status of the rule of this case is somewhat unclear. Traditionally, New York has not permitted mere taxpayers to challenge state expenditures, although the status of a taxpayer has been sufficient to attack municipal outlays. See Schieffelin v. Komfort, 212 N.Y. 520, 106 N.E. 675 (1914). The United States Supreme Court in 1968, however, did allow federal taxpayers standing to challenge federal grants claimed to violate the Establishment Clause, Flast v. Cohen, 392 U.S. 83 (1968) (discussed in footnote 238 of this Appendix), and the effect of that decision on state law is uncertain. It is also conceivable that some plaintiff other than a taxpayer would be found for a suit against a grant to a sectarian institution. Cf. Board of Education v. Allen, 20 N.Y. 2d 109, 228 N.E. 2d 791, 281 N.Y.S. 2d 799 (1967), aff'd, 392 U.S. 236 (1968).

388 Sargent v. Board of Education, 177 N.Y. 317 (1904).

389 4 N.Y. 2d 268, 150 N.E. 2d 396, 174 N.Y.S. 2d 1, cert. denied, 357 U.S. 907 (1958).

390 Id., at 276; 150 N.E. 2d at 399; 174 N.Y.S. 2d at 5.

391 Smith v. Donhue, 202 App. Div. 656, 195 N.Y. Supp. 715 (3rd Dept. 1922).

said, was certainly an indirect aid to the parochial schools. The pupils, the court pointed out, "do not use textbooks and ordinary school supplies apart from their studies in the school. They want them for the sole purpose of their work there. There is no question but that the textbooks and ordinary supplies are furnished direct to the public schools; there is no thought that they are furnished to the scholars as distinct from the schools; neither can there be such a thought in the case of the parochial schools.[392]

Sixteen years later, in *Judd v. Board of Education*,[393] the Court of Appeals, 4-3, struck down a law authorizing the use of public funds to pay for bus transportation for parochial school pupils. It strongly rejected a child benefit contention:

> The argument is advanced that furnishing transportation to the pupils of private or parochial schools is not in aid or support of the schools within the spirit or meaning of our organic law but, rather, is in aid of their pupils. That argument is utterly without substance. It not only ignores the spirit, purpose and intent of the constitutional provisions but, as well, their wording. The object of construction as applied to a written constitution is to give effect to the intent of the people in adopting it, and this intent is to be found in the instrument itself unless the words or expressions are ambiguous. . . . There is nothing ambiguous here. The wording of the mandate is broad. Aid or support to the school 'directly or indirectly' is proscribed. The two words must have been used with some definite intent and purpose; otherwise why were they used at all? Aid furnished 'directly' would be that furnished in a direct line, both literally and figuratively, to the school itself, unmistakably earmarked, and without circumlocution or ambiguity. Aid furnished 'indirectly' clearly embraced any contribution, to whomsoever made, circuitously, collaterally, disguised, or otherwise not in a straight, open and direct course for the open and avowed aid to the school, that may be to the benefit of the institution or promotional of its interests and purposes.[394]

The dissenters contended that payments for transportation did not aid or maintain the institutions themselves and were not proscribed

---

[392] Id., at 661, 195 N.Y. Supp. at 719.
[393] 278 N.Y. 200, 15 N.E. 2d 576 (1938).
[394] Id., at 211-12, 15 N.E. 2d at 582.

by the Constitution.[395] The Constitutional Convention of that year sided with the dissenters, at least on the issue of bus transportation, adding what is now the last clause of the section "but the legislature may provide for the transportation of children to and from any school or institution of learning."

The most recent case dealing with Section 3 is *Board of Education v. Allen*,[396] discussed in Section I. The textbook law under attack was challenged in the state courts primarily on the basis of the state constitution. The Court of Appeals sustained the loan of textbooks by a bare majority, explicitly rejecting the reasoning of *Judd*:

> The architecture reflected in Judd would impede every form of legislation, the benefits of which, in some remote way, might inure to parochial schools. It is our view that the words 'direct' and 'indirect' relate solely to the means of attaining the prohibited end of aiding religion as such.

> The purpose underlying section 701, found in the legislature's own words . . . belies any interpretation other than that the statute is meant to bestow a public benefit upon all school children. . . .

> Since there is no intention to assist parochial schools as such, any benefit accruing to those schools is a collateral effect of the statute, and therefore, cannot be properly classified as the giving of aid directly or indirectly.[397]

The three judges in dissent would have adhered to *Judd* as consistent with the meaning of Section 3 and reflective of wise policy.[398]

The main thrust of the majority opinion is to justify only assistance that can be rationalized as child benefit. As to what may be regarded as, factually, a benefit to the child and not to his school, the opinion intimates a rather broad readiness to accept measures that might have been looked at askance in earlier years. Depriving parochial school children of many of the benefits now enjoyed by other school children under state and federal programs

---

[395] Id., at 218, 15 N.E. 2d at 585.

[396] 20 N.Y. 2d 109, 228 N.E. 2d 791, 281 N.Y.S. 2d 799 (1967), aff'd, 392 U.S. 236 (1968).

[397] Id., at 116, 228 N.E. 2d at 794, 281 N.Y.S. 2d at 805.

[398] Id., at 118, 228 N.E. 2d at 795, 281 N.Y.S. 2d at 805.

was simply regarded as an unfairness. One may anticipate that the majority would be likely to resolve other borderline cases (such as scholarship or, perhaps, tax exemptions for parents) in favor of aid rather than in favor of strict construction. Although some isolated language in the opinion could conceivably be stretched to suggest acceptance of aid to church-related educational institutions for secular purposes, as a whole it does not indicate that grants or any other public assistance going directly into the school's hands would receive judicial approval. And of course one cannot wholly ignore the danger that the precarious majority will shift back to the *Judd* approach, in which event aid to students, let alone aid to schools, would again be in jeopardy.

The New York courts have as yet given no indication of readiness to approve the constitutionality of indirect financial assistance like that embodied in a recent Massachusetts plan. The Massachusetts Constitution, in language similar to that of New York, provides:

> . . . no grant, appropriation or use of public money or property or loan of public credit shall be made or authorized by the commonwealth or any political division thereof for the purpose of founding, maintaining or aiding any school or institution of learning . . . wherein any denominational doctrine is inculcated, or any other school, or any college . . . which is not publicly owned . . .[399]

Massachusetts law permits the judges of the Supreme Judicial Court to give the legislature advisory opinions concerning the constitutional propriety of pending bills. In 1968 the judges were asked to evaluate a proposal to create a state authority which would raise money selling bonds and then lend sums to colleges and universities, sectarian and nonsectarian alike, for new construction projects. Repayment of the loans was expected to be made out of the revenue derived from the projects (such as dormitories and dining facilities), and the state authority was in turn to pay off its indebtedness as its loans were repaid. Since the authority's revenues from the sale of its bonds were not to be public moneys, and since the bonds were not to be backed by public credit, the Massachusetts judges concluded that the state constitution would not prevent effectuation of this plan.[400] The decision is noteworthy because the state-created authority

---

[399] Mass. Constitution, Article 46, Sec. 2 of the Amendments.
[400] Opinion of the Justices, 236 N.E. 2d 523 (Mass., 1968).

was clearly expected to provide participating institutions with less expensive financing than they could otherwise obtain. The case suggests that even fairly absolute prohibitions of financial assistance may possibly be circumvented by ingenuity and a sympathetic state court. Nonetheless, such efforts, even if successful, are unlikely to provide the massive financial support that colleges and universities may need to survive.

IV. NEW YORK STATE LEGISLATION

Until 1968, the primary vehicles for assistance to private higher education in New York have been scholarships and loans to students. This is not a coincidence; the aim has been to find mechanisms through which sectarian institutions may benefit on a parity with independent colleges and universities.

Each year New York provides about 20,000 scholarships, with an annual stipend of up to $1,000, to support four years of study in colleges within the state.[401] In addition to these so-called Regents scholarships, virtually every New York resident studying in an undergraduate or graduate school within the state has been eligible since 1961 for a scholar incentive award of $100 per semester.[402] According to the Select Committee on the Future of Private and Independent Higher Education, the $144 million disbursed by the state during the first six years of the Scholar Incentive Program "accounted for about two and one-half times more state scholarship money than was provided by all the other states combined . . . ."[403] The recipient of one of these awards, as well as the Regents scholarship winner, may choose whichever college and whichever program of study he prefers, with but one exception: "no such scholarship or assistance shall be provided to a student for professional instruction in theology or for a specific program for religious aspirants or leading to a divinity or religious education degree . . . ."[404]

In addition to these basic programs, various scholarships and fellowships have been authorized for specific purposes.[405] College and

---

[401] Education Law §601.

[402] Education Law §601 (a). See Morgan, note 261 above, at 99.

[403] Report of the Select Commitee on the Future of Private and Independent Higher Education in New York State/1968, "New York State and Private Higher Education" 26 (1968).

[404] Education Law §607.

[405] Education Law §§608-632.

vocational students have also been made eligible to receive loans of state funds.[406] None of the pertinent statutes have sought to confine their benefits to students enrolled in nonsectarian institutions.

Certain kinds of New York aid can go directly to institutions of higher education to help meet the needs of "medical schools, research centers and similar institutions or facilities operating specified training or research programs or projects pursuants to contracts with the state university."[407]

If grants of this kind have been made, their validity has apparently not yet been challenged. Conceivably a state contribution toward the costs of a medical school or research center operated by a sectarian university might be deemed unconstitutional. On the other hand, state aid might, in this setting, be regarded simply as the purchase price of a benefit sought by the state, and therefore not really "state aid" of the prohibited variety.[408]

This rationale was not serviceable, however, in regard to the Albert Schweitzer chairs in the humanities. In 1964 the legislature set up these distinguished professorships, along with Albert Einstein chairs in science, to attract renowned scholars to the state's universities. The Regents are authorized "to contract with outstanding scholars" to fill the chairs and

> to contract with any college in this state . . . in relation to the provision of proper facilities, equipment, supplies, professional assistants, clerical and other personnel and such other services as may be . . . appropriate to enable the holder . . . to carry out his work. . . . Every college in this state is hereby authorized to enter into such a contract with the regents.[409]

The Board of Regents awarded a Schweitzer Chair for 1967 to Fordham, to be filled by H. Marshall McLuhan. The Attorney General decided that the proposed contract with Fordham, involving payments up to $70,000, constituted "direct aid to a sectarian institution" in violation of Article XI, § 3.[410] "Although the grant of an Albert Schweitzer Chair to Fordham does not involve a financial

---

[406] Education Law §§650-658.
[407] Education Law §358.
[408] Cf. Bradfield v. Roberts, 175 U.S. 291 (1899).
[409] Education Law §239.
[410] Letter from Louis J. Lefkowitz, Attorney General, to Honorable James E. Allen, Jr., Commissioner of Education, September 13, 1967, p. 3.

gain to the strictly religious posture of that institution," the Attorney General wrote, "the award of such chair to the University enhances the general reputation of the school and in turn benefits the 'whole living organism.' "[411] The proposed contract with Professor McLuhan was also declared invalid, because interlinked with the Fordham contract. Fordham, rather than contesting the decision of the state's executive branch, undertook to compensate Professor McLuhan and to provide the proper accoutrements out of its own funds.

Far more disadvantageous than the occasional loss of compensation for a Schweitzer or Einstein Chair is the position of sectarian universities under the legislation approved in June of 1968 upon the recommendation of the Select Committee, popular called the Bundy Committee.[412] The committee, with an imposing membership appointed by the Governor and the Regents, unequivocally found a pressing need for public financing of higher education. The state's scholarship program, the committee said, had usefully benefited students, but had not produced fresh income for the educational institutions as a whole, partly because their tuition charges had not risen to absorb the amount of the grants.[413] Direct assistance to higher educational institutions was urgently needed, the committee concluded. Candidly facing the impediment of Article XI (3), it recommended unanimously that the section be repealed as it applies to higher education, so that grants could be made to all private colleges and universities, whether or not of a denominational character, so long as they were essentially devoted to education and not to religion. In words that echo some of the policy arguments outlined in earlier pages of this Appendix, the Bundy Committee stated:

> The democratic argument for a single comprehensive public school system in each community does not apply, in our view, at the level of the four-year college and the university. The clear-cut tradition of this country is that there should be a wide variety of colleges and universities, supported in a wide variety of ways. Moreover, there has been a general recognition for many generations that privately controlled colleges and universities—if they are good—serve the public interest in a wider and deeper way than most private elementary and secondary

---

[411] Id., at p. 2.
[412] See Report of Select Committee, note 165 above.
[413] Id., at 26.

schools. We intend no criticism of private schools; we are simply making the point that there is a pronounced and recognized difference between the public contribution of Columbia or Cornell and the public contribution of even the most distinguished of private elementary and secondary schools. The service of the schools is almost entirely a service through the students to whom they may offer unusual educational advantages. The service of the colleges and universities is wider—including as it does the learning of the faculties, the public value of their libraries, the professional service of the lawyers, doctors and engineers they train, and their general civic meaning as major institutions serving the community as a whole.

We are far from concluding all religious institutions should have state assistance. On the contrary, we would oppose any assistance to institutions whose central purpose is the teaching of religious belief. We suggest that each institution applying for state funds be examined as a whole to determine if it is primarily a religious institution or primarily an institution of higher education. Clearly no seminary should have state help, in our view. We do not favor aid to those which are mainly concerned with the indoctrination of their own faithful. Nor should there be state assistance to any institution which discriminates in its admissions on religious grounds, any more than there should be aid to any which discriminates on grounds of race or color.

But we firmly reject the wider argument that all institutions of higher education having any religious connection should be ineligible. We think this kind of rigidity flies in the face of both logic and experience. History demonstrate that there is no automatic connection between the presence or absence of religious affiliation and the presence or absence of those qualities which make a college or university a major instrument of public service. There are secular institutions which are narrow and restrictive in their conception of their task; there are religious institutions which stretch outward to all men and to all human concerns.[414]

Though the proposal to amend the New York constitution was laid aside without action, the state legislature did enact the basic

---

[414] Id., at 49.

authorizations proposed by the Committee.[415] After July 1, 1969, private institutions of higher education will receive an annual apportionment of $400 for each earned bachelor's or master's degree and $2,400 for each earned doctorate; but to qualify, "The institution must be eligible for state aid under the provisions of the constitution of the United States and the constitution of the state of New York."[416]

Under the new law, a church-related college or university that is precluded from participation by Article XI will suffer badly in comparison (and in competition) with independent educational institutions. Part or all of Section 3 of Article XI may of course be eliminated in the fullness of time, but repeal is by no means certain.[417] And repeal would not, in any event, guarantee the consistency of this aid with the Federal Constitution, under which it might also be held invalid. Meanwhile, state funds will be poured into the general treasuries of the eligibly independent, to be expended for whatever may be their needs as they themselves perceive them—while the institutions that preserve their religious identity will have to make do with their own resources. In absolute terms, their position will be no worse than at present, because it will be no different. In comparative terms, however, they may find that the independent institutions, taking advantage of their state subsidies, may move faster and farther on the road to academic excellence—or possibly even on the road to academic survival.

---

[415] Chapter 677, Laws of New York 1968, approved June 16, 1968, Education Law §6401.

[416] Id., Subsection 2 (d).

[417] Persons sensitive to New York political currents have stressed to us that the proposed revision of New York's constitution in 1967 was defeated in large measure because it would have eliminated that section's restriction on aid. See also Morgan, note 261 above, at 109-127.

Appendix B

STATE CONSTITUTIONAL PROVISIONS
CONCERNING SUPPORT OF SECTARIAN EDUCATION

INTRODUCTORY NOTE.

State constitutional provisions bearing upon use of public funds in aid of sectarian education are extraordinarily diverse. Whatever may be the boundaries they may set, and whatever may be the degree of their specificity or vagueness, they are in any event to be read with the federal Establishment Clause in mind. The provisions of the United States Constitution are the bedrock. The States may go beyond the Federal Constitution in restricting the use of public funds, but may not allowably be more lenient in this respect.

This Appendix includes the state constitutional provisions most likely to be relevant if state aid were extended to sectarian higher education and were then subjected to attack by a taxpayer's suit or in some other manner. Tangentially related general provisions—such as broad protections of religious liberty and the common provision that "no preference shall be given by law to any religious sect"—have been omitted. Many constitutions protect citizens against compelled payments for the support of any religion; these have been included when no other provisions would clearly be of more direct relevance, but they have been omitted when some other section would plainly govern. Limitations on aid to sectarian education have been included even when they appear to apply only to lower schools; but limitations referring explicitly to the use of public school funds without making reference to sectarian schools have not been set out. Moreover, provisions that generally restrict the state's making gifts of public money or using its credit in aid of private individuals and associations have been excluded from this compilation, because they are not directed specifically at educational or sectarian institutions. Conceivably, however, provisions of that type might be interpreted

183

to block all or some forms of assistance.[418] Inclusion of a provision does not necessarily connote a conclusion that it would be interpreted to be more severely restrictive than the general Establishment Clause of the Federal Constitution. For example. may states protect citizens against paying taxes to support places of religious worship and ministers. If a state constitution contained no provision other than that, most state courts would probably hold that the state restrictions on educational aid were no more severe than those created by the United States Constitution alone.

Important differentiations among the various constitutions are discernible. Some bar public aid not only to sectarian institutions, but also to private institutions generically; hence, attaining independence would not improve the position of a sectarian institution under state law. Some of the constitutional prohibitions are explicitly directed at sectarian colleges and universities as well as at lower schools; some appear to cover only primary and secondary schools; others leave unclear the precise extent of their scope. Some generally worded limitations on aid to religious sects are at least arguably inapplicable to sectarian schools that provide satisfactory secular education. Whether the relevant prohibitions apply only to specific funds or to all state money is a variable, also.[419]

References have been made to decisions of the highest courts of the respective states and to opinions of their attorneys general, when these bear directly on questions of aid. Excluded from this compilation are determinations concerning tax exemptions (almost invariably sustained), prayer and Bible reading in the public schools, Sunday closing laws, released time, chaplains and chapels connected with public institutions, and leasing and purchasing arrangements between the state and sectarian institutions. Needless to say, a careful lawyer would study such cases closely to determine their possible application to the question of aid. Even the narrower limits of this Appendix have not permitted describing every debatably relevant case or opinion, nor can brief summarization reveal the richness of

---

[418] See U.S. Department of Health, Education, and Welfare, The State and Nonpublic Schools, Misc. Doc. No. 28 (1958). This compilation sets out constitutional and statutory provisions relevant to aid. Though now somewhat out of date, it gives an excellent sense of the many parts of a constitution that may bear on the issue.

[419] For an excellent and still valuable analysis of the various types of constitutional provisions, see R.J. Gabel, Public Funds for Church and Private Schools 537-549 (Catholic Univ., 1937). See also A.P. Stokes and L. Pfeffer, Church and State in the United States 420-425 (Harper & Row, 1964).

analysis that often underlies the legal conclusions. In estimating the significance of these conclusions, the reader should be alert to the year in which they were stated. In this, as in all areas of constitutional law, time may produce changing notions of what a provision means.

PROVISIONS IN EACH STATE

ALABAMA

Art. XIV, § 263: No money raised for the support of the public schools shall be appropriated to or used for the support of any sectarian or denominational school.

Art. I, § 3: That no religion shall be established by law; . . . that no one shall be compelled by law . . . to pay any tithes, taxes, or other rate for building or repairing any place of worship, or for maintaining any minister or ministry . . . .

ALASKA

Art. VII, § 1: . . . No money shall be paid from public funds for the direct benefit of any religious or other private educational institution.

> *Note:* In Matthews v. Quinton, 363 P.2d 932 (Sup. Ct. Alaska 1961), a divided court held that allowing parochial school students to ride public school buses would be a direct benefit to the religious schools and was thus prohibited by the state constitution. The court acknowledged that the legislative history of the Convention reflected an intentional omission of "indirect" aids from the prohibition, but concluded that these were limited to services given by the state welfare department.

ARIZONA

Art. IX, § 10: No tax shall be laid or appropriation of public money made in aid of any church, or private or sectarian school, or any public service corporation.

Art. II, § 12: . . . No public money or property shall be appropriated for or applied to any religious worship, exercise, or instruction, or to the support of any religious establishment. . . .

> *Note:* The state supreme court, Community Council v. Jordan, 102 Ariz. 448, 432 P.2d 460 (1967), has sustained

the effective channeling of public funds through the Salvation Army for the purpose of emergency relief, holding that:

> "aid" in the form of partially matching reimbursement for only the direct, actual costs of materials given entirely to third parties of any or no faith or denomination and not to the church itself is not the type of aid prohibited by our Constitution. The "aid" prohibited in the Constitution of this State is, in our opinion, assistance in any form whatsoever which would encourage or tend to encourage the preference of one religion over another, or religion per se over no religion. 102 Ariz. at 454, 432 P.2d at 466.

ARKANSAS

Art. II, § 24: . . . no man can, of right, be compelled to attend, erect or support any place of worship; or to maintain any ministry against his consent . . . .

CALIFORNIA

Art. XIII, § 24: Neither the Legislature, nor any county, city and county, township, school district, or other municipal corporation, shall ever make an appropriation, or pay from any public fund whatever, or grant anything to or in aid of any religious sect, church, creed, or sectarian purpose, or help to support or sustain any school, college, university, hospital, or other institution controlled by any religious creed, church, or sectarian denomination whatever; nor shall any grant or donation of personal property or real estate ever be made by the state, or any city, city and county, town, or other municipal corporation for any religious creed, church, or sectarian purpose whatever; provided that nothing in this section shall prevent the Legislature granting aid pursuant to Section 21 of the article [which allows authorizations for the construction of private hospital facilities, aid to the physically handicapped in private institutions, and aid to institutions caring for orphans and abandoned children].

Art. IX, § 8: No public money shall ever be appropriated for the support of any sectarian or denominational schools, or any school not under the exclusive control of the officers of the public schools . . . .

Note: Bowker v. Baker. 73 Cal. App. 2d 653, 167 P.2d
256 (1946), upheld a school district's transportation of
students to parochial schools in buses for public school
students along the regular public school routes.

COLORADO

Art. IX, § 7: Neither the general assembly, nor any county,
city, town, township, school district or other public corporation,
shall ever make any appropriation, or pay from any public fund
or moneys whatever, anything in aid of any church or sectarian
society, or for any sectarian purpose, or to help support or
sustain any school, academy, seminary, college, university or
other literary or scientific institution, controlled by any church
or sectarian denomination whatsoever; nor shall any grant or
donation of land, money or other personal property, ever be
made by the state, or any such public corporation to any church,
or for any sectarian purpose.

Art. V, § 34: No appropriation shall be made for charitable,
industrial, educational or benevolent purposes to any person,
corporation or community not under the absolute control of the
state, nor to any denominational or sectarian institution or association.

Note: The state supreme court has held it constitutional
for a county to pay the expenses of an indigent inebriate
in a private institution. In re House, 23 Col. 87, 46 Pac.
117 (1896).

CONNECTICUT

Art. VII: . . . no person shall be compelled to join or support . . . any congregation, church or religious association. . . .

Note: In Snyder v. Town of Newtown, 147 Conn. 374,
161 A. 2d 770 (1960), appeal dismissed, 365 U.S. 299 (1961),
the Supreme Court of Errors held that furnishing bus transportation to parochial school pupils violates neither the
state nor federal constitution.

DELAWARE

Art. X, § 3: No portion of any fund now existing, or which
may hereafter be appropriated or raised by tax, for educational

purposes, shall be appropriated to, or used by, or in aid of any sectarian, church or denominational school . . . .

Art. X, § 5: The General Assembly, notwithstanding any other provision of this Constitution, may provide by an Act of the General Assembly, passed with the concurrence of a majority of all the members elected to each House, for the transportation of students of non-public Elementary and High Schools.

Art. I, § 1: . . . no man shall or ought to be compelled to attend any religious worship, to contribute to the erection or support of any place of worship, or to the maintenance of any ministry, against his own free will and consent . . . .

FLORIDA

Art. XII, § 13: No law shall be enacted authorizing the diversion or the lending of any County or District School Funds, or the appopriation of any part of the permanent or available school Fund to any other than school purposes; nor shall the same, or any part thereof, be appropriated to or used for the support of any sectarian school.

Declaration of Rights, § 6: . . . no money shall ever be taken from the public treasury directly or indirectly in aid of any church, sect or religious denomination or in aid of any sectarian institution.

GEORGIA

Art. I, § 1, Ch. 2-114: No money shall ever be taken from the public Treasury, directly or indirectly, in aid of any church, sect, or denomination of religionists, or of any sectarian institution.

> *Note:* It is a violation of the constitution for a city to contract to reimburse a religious organization, the Salvation Army, for its expenses in caring for paupers, the state supreme court held in 1922. Bennett v. City of LaGrange, 153 Ga. 428, 112 S.E. 482.

HAWAII

Art. IX, § 1: . . . nor shall public funds be appropriated for the support or benefit of any sectarian or private educational institution.

Note: The Attorney General has indicated that the Church College of Hawaii can not receive public funds, but has said that appropriations to transport both private and public school children are valid, Atty. Gen Op. 67-13.

IDAHO

Art. IX, § 5: Neither the legislature nor any county, city, town, township, school district, or other public corporation, shall ever make any appropriatrion, or pay from any public fund or moneys whatever, anything in aid of any church or sectarian or religious society, or for any sectarian or religious purpose, or to help support or sustain any school, academy, seminary, college, university or other literary or scientific institution, controlled by any church, sectarian or religious denomination whatsoever; nor shall any grant or donation of land, money or other personal property ever be made by the state, or any such public corporation, to any church or for any sectarian or religious purpose.

ILLINOIS

Art. VIII, § 3: Neither the general assembly nor any county, city, town, township, school district, or other public corporation, shall ever make any appropriation or pay from any public fund whatever, anything in aid of any church or sectarian purpose, or to help support or sustain any school, academy, seminary, college, university, or other literary or scientific institution, controlled by any church or sectarian denomination whatever; nor shall any grant or donation of land, money, or other personal property ever be made by the state or any such public corporation, to any church, or for any sectarian purpose.

Note: In decisions in 1917, 1918, and 1919 which have subsequently been followed, the state supreme court held that the constitution does not prohibit payments to church-related manual training and industrial schools for the care and maintenance of children committed there by courts. The opinions emphasized that the purpose of the payments was nonsectarian and that they did not exceed what was necessary for care of the children, apart from any religious instruction they might receive. When children of one denomination attended a school of another, the court noted that they were not compelled to receive religious instruction. Dunn v. Chicago Industrial School, 280 Ill. 613, 117 N.E. 735 (1917; Dunn v. Addison Manual Training School, 281 Ill. 352, 117 N.E. 993 (1917); Trost v. Ketteler Manual Training School, 282 Ill. 504, 118 N.E. 743 (1918); St. Hedwig's Industrial School v. Cook County, 289 Ill. 432, 124 N.E. 629 (1919).

INDIANA

Art. I, § 6: No money shall be drawn from the treasury, for the benefit of any religious or theological institution.

Note: In State ex rel. Johnson v. Boyd, 217 Ind. 348, 28 N.E. 2d 256 (1940), the state supreme court upheld payments to Catholic Sisters who were teaching in schools that had previously been parochial but were then being used as public schools. The apparent assumption of the opinion is that payment to parochial schools would violate the state constitution. The attorney general has indicated that the provision of school bus transportation for parochial school students does not violate the state constitution. Atty. Gen. Op. 1967, No. 3, p. 9.

IOWA

Art. I, § 3: The General Assembly shall make no law respecting an establishment of religion . . .; nor shall any person be compelled to attend any place of worship, pay tithes, taxes, or other rates for building or repairing places of worship, or the maintenance of any minister or ministry.

Note: In 1918, the state supreme court held it unconstitutional for a school district to pay public funds for the operation of a school deemed to be sectarian. Knowlton v. Baumhover, 182 Ia. 691, 166 N.W. 202.

KANSAS

Art. VI, § 6(c): No religious sect or sects shall control any part of the public educational funds.

Bill of Rights, § 7: . . . nor shall any person be compelled to attend or support any form of worship . . . .

Note: In a case directly concerned with standing, the state supreme court strongly implied that public school funds could not constitutionally be used to support sectarian schools. Wright v. School District, 151 Kan. 485, 99 P. 2d 737 (1940). In 1892, the court had declared grants to sectarian colleges invalid as promoting private interests. Atchison, T. & S.F.R.R. v. Atchison, 47 Kan. 712, 28 Pac. 1000.

KENTUCKY

Section 189: No portion of any fund or tax now existing, or that may hereafter be raised or levied for educational purposes, shall be appropriated to, or used by, or in aid of, any church, sectarian, or denominational school.

Section 5: . . . nor shall any person be compelled to attend any place of worship, to contribute to the erection or maintenance of any such place, or to the salary or support of any minister of religion . . . .

Note: In 1917, the state supreme court held invalid an arrangement whereby public funds were used, in effect, to pay the tuition of common school pupils instructed in a sectarian school. Williams v. Stanton School District, 173 Ky. 708, 191 S.W. 507. The court has upheld the provision of bus transportation for students including those in parochial schools. See Nichols v. Henry, 301 Ky. 434, 191 S.W. 2d 930 (1945); Rawlings v. Butler, 290 S.W. 2d 801 (1956). Compare Sherrard v. Jefferson County Board of Education, 294 Ky. 469, 171 S.W. 2d 963 (1942). It has also sustained the use of tax funds for hospitals under denominational control, but open to all people. Kentucky Building Commission v. Effron, 310 Ky. 355, 220 S.W. 2d 836 (1949). Compare Butler v. United Cerebral Palsy, 352 S.W. 2d 203 (1961).

LOUISIANA

Art. XII, § 13: .No appropriation of public funds shall be made to any private or sectarian school. The Legislature may enact appropriate legislation to permit institutions of higher learning which receive all or part of their support from the State of Louisiana to engage in interstate and intrastate education agreements with other state governments, agencies of other state governments, institutions of higher learning of other state governments and private institutions of higher learning within or outside state boundaries.

Art. XII, § 1: . . . . The Legislature may also provide financial assistance directly to school children of the state for attendance at private non-sectarian elementary and secondary schools in this state . . . .

Art. IV, § 8: No money shall ever be taken from the public treasury, directly or indirectly, in aid of any church, sect or denomination of religion, or in aid of any priest, preacher, minister or teacher thereof, as such . . . . No appropriation from the State treasury shall be made for private, charitable or benevolent purposes to any person or community . . . .

> *Note:* The provision of free textbooks to students at private and sectarian schools as well as public school students was upheld as consistent with Section 8 of Art. IV and an earlier version of Art. XII. Borden v. Louisiana State Board of Education, 168 La. 1005, 123 So. 655 (1929). The United States Supreme Court affirmed the judgment of a case following *Borden,* Cochran v. Louisiana State Board of Education, 281 U.S. 370 (1930), discussed in Section I of Appendix A. In 1932 the attorney general rendered an opinion that the predecessor of Art. XII forbade paying a teacher to teach high school subjects in a parochial school. Op. Atty. Gen. 1932-34, p. 291.

MAINE

Art. I, § 3 protects religious liberty and prohibits any legal preference between sects, but the Constitution contains no express limit on the use of public funds for sectarian institutions nor any general establishment clause.

> *Note:* In Squires v. Inhabitants of City of Augusta, 115 Me. 151, 153 A. 2d 80 (1959, the Supreme Judicial Court indicated in dictum that the Maine constitution imposes no greater barrier than the federal one to the provision of transportation for parochial school students, and that a properly authorized plan to that effect would be upheld.

In a recent advisory opinion, Opinion of the Justices, Jan. 15, 1970, four of six justices indicated that general aid to parochial schools in support of their secular educational function would be unconstitutional.

MARYLAND

Declaration of Rights, Art. 36: . . . nor ought any person to be compelled to frequent, or maintain, or contribute, unless on contract, to maintain, any place of worship, or any ministry . . . .

Note: Provision for transportation of parochial school students has been sustained, Board of Education v. Wheat, 174 Md. 314, 199 Atl. 628 (1938); Adams v. County Commissioners, 180 Md. 550, 26 A.2d 377 (1942). In 1966, the court of appeals held that public loans to hospitals owned or controlled by religious institutions are permissible. Truitt v. Board of Public Works, 243 Md. 375, 221 A. 2d 370. In the same year, it declared grants to sectarian colleges unconstitutional as a matter of federal law though acceptable under the state constitution. Horace Mann League v. Board of Public Works, 242 Md. 645, 220 A. 2d 51, appeal dismissed and cert. denied, 385 U.S. 97 (1966). See Section I of Appendix A.

MASSACHUSETTS

Section 148, Art. XLVI of Ammendments, § 2: . . . no grant, appropriation or use of public money or property or loan of public credit shall be made or authorized by the commonwealth or any political division thereof for the purpose of founding, maintaining or aiding any school or institution of learning, whether under public control or otherwise, wherein any denominational doctrine is inculcated, or any other school, or any college, infirmary, hospital, institution or educational, charitable or religious undertaking which is not publicly owned and under the exclusive control, order and superintendence of public officers or public agents . . . .

Note: The Supreme Judicial Court has advised the legislature that this provision does not preclude setting up a special authority which would raise its own funds and make loans to educational institutions including private and sectarian ones. Opinion of the Justices, 236 N.E. 2d 523 (1968), discussed in Section III of Appendix A. In a 1913 opinion, the justices advised that a predecessor provision, which unlike the present one spoke only of schools, did not preclude grants to sectarian institutions of higher education. Opinion of the Justices, 214 Mass. 599, 102 N.E. 464.

MICHIGAN

Art. I, § 4: . . . No money shall be appropriated or drawn from the treasury for the benefit of any religious sect or society, theological or religious seminary; nor shall property belonging to the state be appropriated for any such purpose . . . .

Note: The Attorney General has advised that the provision of bus transportation to parochial school students does not violate the state constitution. Op. Atty. Gen. 1963-64, No. 4177, p. 181 (1963).

MINNESOTA

Art. VIII, § 2: . . . But in no case shall the moneys derived as aforesaid [income arising from the school fund], or any portion thereof, or any public moneys or property, be appropriated or used for the support of schools wherein the distinctive doctrines, creeds or tenets of any particular Christian or other religious sect are promulgated or taught.

Art. I, § 16: . . . nor shall any money be drawn from the treasury for the benefit of any religious societies, or religious or theological seminaries.

Note: The Attorney General has indicated that a school board could not levy a tax for the support of a parochial school. Op. Atty. Gen., 159-B-10 (1933).

MISSISSIPPI

Art. VIII, § 208: No religious or other sect or sects shall ever control any part of the school or other educational funds of this state; nor shall any funds be appropriated toward the support of any sectarian schools, or to any school that at the time of receiving such appropriation is not conducted as a free school.

Art. IV, § 66: No law granting a donation or gratuity in favor of any person or object shall be enacted except by the concurrence of two-thirds of the members elect of each branch of the legislature, nor by any vote for a sectarian purpose or use.

Note: The state supreme court has upheld the loaning of textbooks to parochial school students as not a support of the schools. Chance v. Mississippi State Textbook Rating and Purchasing Board, 190 Miss. 453, 200 So. 706 (1941). For the possible applicability of Section 208 to colleges, see State Teacher's College v. Morris, 165 Miss. 758, 144 So. 374 (1932). In Craig v. Mercy Hospital-Street Memorial, 209 Miss. 490, 47 So. 2d 867 (1950), the court said that payments to a hospital in return for its keeping ten percent of its beds available for charity patients were not donations or gratuities under Section 66 and, in dictum, that they were not for a sectarian purpose or use.

MISSOURI

Art. IX, § 8: Neither the general assembly, nor any county, city, town, township, school district or other municipal corporation, shall ever make an appropriation or pay from any public fund whatever, anything in aid of any religious creed, church or sectarian purpose, or to help to support or sustain any private or public school, academy, seminary, college, university, or other institution of learning controlled by any religious creed, church or sectarian denomination whatever; nor shall any grant or donation of personal property or real estate ever be made by the state, or any county, city, town, or other municipal corporation, for any religious creed, church, or sectarian purpose whatever.

Art. I, § 7: That no money shall ever be taken from the public treasury, directly or indirectly, in aid of any church, sect or denomination of religion, or in aid of any priest, preacher, minister or teacher thereof, as such . . . .

Note: The state supreme court has held that it violates these provisions for public money to be spent to support parochial schools. Harfst v. Hoegen, 349 Mo. 808, 163 S.W. 2d 609 (1941). See also Berghorn v. Reorganized School

District, 364 Mo. 121, 260 S.W. 2d 573 (1953). The court
has also struck down the provision of bus transportation for
parochial school students, McVey v. Hawkins, 364 Mo. 44,
258 S.W. 2d 927 (1953), and the use of public school speech
teachers in parochial schools, Special District for the Education and Training of Handicapped Children v. Wheeler,
408 S.W. 2d 60 (1966), but in both instances it held only
that public school funds could not be spent for these purposes, without deciding if other funds might be so spent.

MONTANA

Art. XI, § 8: Neither the legislative assembly, nor any county,
city, town, or school district, or other public corporations, shall
ever make directly or indirectly, any appropriation, or pay from
any public fund or money whatever, or make any grant of lands
or other property in aid of any church, or for any sectarian
purpose, or to aid in the support of any school, academy, seminary, college, university, or other literary, scientific institution,
controlled in whole or in part by any church, sect or denomination whatever.

Art. V, § 35: No appropriation shall be made for charitable,
industrial, educational or benevolent purposes to any person,
corporation or community not under the absolute control of the
state, nor to any denomination or sectarian institution or association.

Note: The state supreme court has declared that art. V,
§ 35 forbids the public payment of salaries of secretaries of
private veterans' organizations. Veterans' Welfare Commission v. Department of Montana, 141 Mont. 500, 379 P. 2d
107 (1963).

NEBRASKA

Art. VII, § 11: No sectarian instruction shall be allowed in any
school or institution supported in whole or in part by the public
funds set apart for educational purposes . . . . Neither the
state Legislature nor any county, city or other public corporation, shall ever make any appropriation from any public fund,
or grant any public land in aid of any sectarian or denominational
school or college, or any educational institution which is not

exclusively owned and controlled by the state or a governmental subdivision thereof . . . .

Note: The state supreme court sustained the withholding of funds to a district in which the only school was in part sectarian. State ex rel. Public School District v. Taylor, 122 Neb. 454, 240 N.W. 573 (1932). In United Community Services v. Omaha National Bank, 162 Neb. 76, 77 N.W. 2d 576 (1956), it said, inter alia, that a state corporation could not give money to sectarian charitable organizations, even if the activities for which the money would be used were non-sectarian.

NEVADA

Art. XI, § 10: No public funds of any kind or character whatever, State, County, or Municipal, shall be used for sectarian purposes.

Note: In 1882, the state supreme court held that this section precluded a grant to a Catholic orphan asylum. State ex rel. Nevada Orphan Asylum v. Hallock, 16 Nev. 373. The Attorney General has since indicated that public funds may be used to support crippled children in a sectarian hospital if they do not receive religious instruction. Atty. Gen. Op. B-40 (1941). But home instruction to parochial school students by public school teachers is unconstitutional, he has said. Atty. Gen. Op. 209 (1956). In 1965, the Attorney General advised that funds might be accepted under the Elementary and Secondary Education Act of 1965, some of which would help students in parochial schools, but that they should be designated as federal moneys and kept separate from state funds. Atty. Gen. Op. 276. The clear implication is that such expenditures would be invalid under the Nevada constitution if made by the state.

NEW HAMPSHIRE

Part 2, Art. 83: . . . that no money raised by taxation shall ever be granted or applied for the use of the schools or institutions of any religious sect or denomination . . . .

Note: In an advisory opinion, the supreme court justices indicated that grants to hospitals, including sectarian ones, for the purpose, in part, of training nurses would not be barred by this section. Opinion of the Justices, 99 N.H. 519, 113 A.2d 114 (1955). The justices have also advised that it would be constitutional to set up an authority to make construction loans at advantageous rates to private schools and colleges, Opinion of the Justices, 99 N.H. 536, 114 A. 2d 801 (1955), but without commenting on the constitutionality of such loans to sectarian institutions. On Oct. 31, 1969 the justices advised that the loan of textbooks to parochial school students is constitutional. Opinion of the Justices in response to Request of the Senate, No. 5969.

NEW JERSEY

Art. VIII, § 4, Par. 3: The Legislature may, within reasonable limitations as to distance to be prescribed, provide for the transportation of children within the ages of five to eighteen years inclusive to and from any school.

Art. I, Par. 3: . . . nor shall any person be obliged to pay tithes, taxes, or other rates for building or repairing any church or churches, place or places of worship, of for the maintenance of any minister or ministry, contrary to what he believes to be right or has deliberately and voluntarily engaged to perform.

Note: Even before Article VIII, § 4, Par. 3 was made a part of the constitution, the state supreme court upheld public transportation of parochial school pupils. Everson v. Board of Education, 133 N.J. L. 350, 44 A.2d 333 (1945), affirmed, 330 U.S. 1 (1947), see Section I of Appendix A.

NEW MEXICO

Art. XII, § 3: . . . no part of the proceeds arising from the sale or disposal of any lands granted to the state by congress, or any other funds appropriated, levied or collected for educational purposes, shall be used for the support of any sectarian, denominational or private school, college or university.

Note: The Attorney General once advised that public school trucks may not be used to transport private school pupils, Atty. Gen. Op. 1921-22, p. 92 (1921), but more recently has indicated that school bus transportation for all pupils is permitted. Atty. Gen. Op. 1951-52, No. 5339 (1951).

NEW YORK

See Section III of Appendix A.

NORTH CAROLINA

Article I, § 26 of the constitution protects religious liberty; there is no prohibition on expending money in support of sectarian institutions or any general "no establishment" provision.

NORTH DAKOTA

Art. VIII, § 152: All colleges, universities, and other educational institutions, for the support of which lands have been granted to this state, or which are supported by a public tax, shall remain under the absolute and exclusive control of the state. No money raised for the support of the public schools of the state shall be appropriated to or used for the support of any sectarian school.

Note: For discussion of the definition of "sectarian school" see Gerhardt v. Heid, 66 N.D. 444, 267 N.W. 127 (1936).

OHIO

Art. VI, § 2: The General Assembly shall make such provisions, by taxation, or otherwise, as, with the income arising from the school trust fund, will secure a thorough and efficient system of common schools throughout the State; but, no religious or other sect, or sects, shall ever have any exclusive right to, or control of, any part of the school funds of this State.

Art. I, § 7: . . . No person shall be compelled to attend, erect, or support any place of worship, or maintain any form of worship, against his consent . . . .

Art. VI, § 5 is a special provision to allow the guaranteeing of loans to students receiving higher education; it makes no differentiation on the basis of the institutions attended.

Note: The court of appeals has held that it would violate the state constitution for a municipality to issue bonds or expend tax funds to establish a sectarian school. Findley v. City of Conneaut, 76 Ohio App. 153, 63 N.E. 2d 449 (1945).

OKLAHOMA

Art. II, § *5:* No public money or property shall ever be appropriated, applied, donated, or used, directly or indirectly, for the use, benefit, or support of any sect, church, denomination, or system of religion, or for the use, benefit, or support of any priest, preacher, minister, or other religious teacher or dignitary, or sectarian institution as such.

Art. XI, § *5:* . . . no part of the proceeds arising from the sale or disposal of any lands granted for educational purposes, or the income or rentals thereof, shall be used for the support of any religious or sectarian school, college, or university . . . .

Art. XIII-A, § *4:* Private, denominational, and other institutions of higher learning may become co-ordinated with the State System of Higher Education under regulations set forth by the Oklahoma State Regents for Higher Education.

> *Note:* The state supreme court has sustained contracts for the payment of public funds for the support of orphans in a sectarian orphanage, Murrow Indian Orphans Home v. Childers, 197 Okla. 249, 171 P.2d 600 (1946), but it has twice declared invalid public provision of bus transportation for parochial school students, Gurney v. Ferguson, 190 Okla. 254, 122 P.2d 1002, appeal dismissed, 317 U.S. 588 (1942) ; Board of Education v. Antone, 384 P.2d 911 (1963). Compare Oklahoma Ry. Co. v. St. Joseph's Parochial School, 33 Okla. 755, 127 Pac. 1087 (1912).

OREGON

Art. I, § *5:* No money shall be drawn from the Treasury for the benefit of any religeous (sic), or theological institution, nor shall any money be appropriated for the payment of any religeous (sic) services either house of the Legislative Assembly.

> *Note:* In Dickman v. School District, 232 Ore. 238, 366 P.2d 533 (1961), cert. denied, 371 U.S. 823 (1962), the state supreme court held the provision of free textbooks to parochial school students to be unconstitutional. The Attorney General has advised that the state might distribute federal funds under the Elementary and Secondary Educa-

tion Act of 1965 although such expenditures, insofar as they benefited parochial school students, would be unconstitutional if made by the state. Atty. Gen. Op. 1966-68, No. 6162, p. 14 (1966). Compare Atty. Gen. Op. 1966-68, No. 6359, p. 351 (1967). In 1968 Atty. Gen. Op. No. 6543, he indicated that scholarship aid to students in sectarian institutions of higher education would probably violate the state constitution, and suggested that the line between sectarian and non-sectarian institutions might be drawn in the manner of Horace Mann v. Board of Public Works, 242 Md. 645, 220 A.2d 51, appeal dismissed and cert. denied, 385 U.S. 97 (1966).

PENNSYLVANIA

Art. III, § 29: No appropriation shall be made for charitable, educational or benevolent purposes to any person or community nor to any denominational and sectarian institution, corporation or association: Provided, that appropriations may be made . . . in the form of scholarship grants or loans for higher educational purposes to residents of the Commonwealth enrolled in institutions of higher learning except that no scholarship, grants or loans for higher educational purposes shall be given to persons enrolled in a theological seminary or school of theology.

Art. III, § 30: No appropriation shall be made to any charitable or educational institution not under the absolute control of the Commonwealth, other than normal schools established by law for the professional training of teachers for the public schools of the State, except by a vote of two-thirds of all the members elected to each House.

Art. III, § 15: No money raised for the support of the public schools of the Commonwealth shall be appropriated or used for the support of any sectarian school.

> *Note:* In Collins v. Kephart, 271 Pa. 428, 117 Atl. 440 (1921), the state supreme court declared invalidate appropriations to a variety of sectarian institutions, including Duquesne University. See also Collins v. Martin, 290 Pa. 388, 139 Atl. 122 (1927). See Busser v. Snyder, 282 Pa. 440, 128 Atl. 80 (1925), indicating that non-sectarian private

institutions can receive grants that would be denied to sectarian ones. In a more recent case, Schade v. Allegheny County Institution District, 386 Pa. 507, 126 A. 2d 911 (1956), the court sustained payments for the support of neglected or dependent children in sectarian institutions, on the theory that support was a government duty and the payments were, in legal effect, to the children. In 1967, provision of bus transportation for parochial school children was upheld. Rhoades v. School District of Abington Township, 424 Pa. 202, 226 A. 2d 53, appeal dismissed, 389 U.S. 11 (1967).

RHODE ISLAND

Art. I, § 3: . . . no man shall be compelled to frequent or to support any religious worship, place, or ministry whatever, except in fulfillment of his own voluntary contract . . . .

SOUTH CAROLINA

Art. XI, § 9: The property or credit of the State of South Carolina, or of any county, city, town, township, school district, or other subdivision of the said State, or any public money, from whatever source derived, shall not by gift, donation, loan, contract, appropriation, or otherwise, be used, directly or indirectly, in aid or maintenance of any college, school, hospital, orphan house, or other institution, society or organization, of whatever kind, which is wholly or in part under the direction or control of any church or of any religious or sectarian denomination, society or organization.

Note: In Parker v. Bates, 216 S.C. 52, 56 S.E. 2d 723 (1949), the state supreme court said in dictum that this provision precludes the allocation of public funds in any manner to hospitals and health centers under the control of a sectarian organization.

SOUTH DAKOTA

Art. VIII, § 16: No appropriation of lands, money or other property or credits to aid any sectarian school shall ever be made by the state, or any county or municipality within the state, nor shall the state or any county or municipality within the state accept any grant, conveyance, gift or bequest of lands, money or other property to be used for sectarian purposes, and no sectarian instruction shall be allowed in any school or institution aided or supported by the state.

Art. VI, § 3: . . . No money or property of the state shall be given or appropriated for the benefit of any sectarian or religious society or institution.

> *Note:* In 1891, the state supreme court held that public funds could not be used to pay the tuition of students in a sectarian university, Synod of Dakota v. State, 2 S.D. 366, 50 N.W. 632. The Attorney General has advised that federal funds may be distributed for a lunch program in parochial schools. Atty. Gen. Report 1959-1960, p. 33 (1968), but has said that school districts may not reimburse room and board expenses of parochial school students, Report 1951-1952, p. 7 (1950), pay their tuition, Report 1920, p. 152 (1919), donate books to them, Report 1920, p. 182, or pay their transportation, Report 1957-1958, p. 217 (1958). But see the more recent and somewhat ambiguous opinion on tuition payments, Report 1967-1968, p. 167 (1967).

TENNESSEE

Art. I, § 3: . . . no man can of right be compelled to attend, erect, or support any place of worship, or to maintain any minister against his consent . . . .

TEXAS

Art. I, § 7: No money shall be appropriated, or drawn from the Treasury for the benefit of any sect, or religious society, theological or religious seminary; nor shall property belonging to the State be appropriated for any such purposes.

Art. VII, § 5: . . . And no law shall ever be enacted appropriating any part of the permanent or available school fund to any other purpose whatever; nor shall the same, or any part thereof ever be appropriated to or used for the support of any sectarian school . . . .

Note: The Attorney General has indicated that public funds can not pay for tuition in a sectarian school, Op. Atty. Gen. 1940, No. 0-2412, or assist crippled children to attend a denominational school, Op. Atty. Gen. 1940, No. 0-2832. He has also advised that public school buses may not carry parochial school students. Op. Atty. Gen. 1946, No. 0-7128; Op. Atty. Gen. 1941, No. 0-4220.

UTAH

Art. X, § 13: Neither the Legislature nor any county, city, town, school district or other public corporation, shall make any appropriation to aid in the support of any school, seminary, academy, college, university or other institution, controlled in whole, or in part, by any church, sect or denomination whatever.

Art. I, § 4: . . . . No public money or property shall be appropriated for or applied to any religious worship, exercise or instruction, or for the support of any ecclesiastical establishment . . . .

VERMONT

Ch. I, art. 3: . . . no man ought to, or of right can be compelled to attend any religious worship, or erect or support any place of worship, or maintain any minister, contrary to the dictates of his conscience . . . .

Note: Without deciding if the Vermont constitution had the same revelant scope as the federal one, the state supreme court invalidated tuition grants for parochial school pupils under the federal Constitution. Swart v. South Burlington School District, 122 Vt. 177, 167 A.2d 514, cert. denied, 366 U.S. 925 (1961). In Vermont Educational Buildings Financing Agency v. Mann, 127 Vt. 262, 247 A.2d 68 (1968), appeal dismissed, 396 U.S. 801 (1969), the court held that financing assistance could be given for the construction of facilities at a church-related (Catholic) college. It noted that, unlike the school in *Swart,* the college was not controlled by the denomination.

VIRGINIA

§ *141:* No appropriation of public funds shall be made to any school or institution of learning not owned or exclusively controlled by the State or some political subdivision thereof; provided, first, that the General Assembly may, and the governing bodies of the several counties, cities and towns may, subject to such limitations as may be imposed by the General Assembly, appropriate funds for educational purposes which may be expended in furtherance of elementary, secondary, collegiate or graduate education of Virginia students in public and nonsectarian private schools and institutions of learning, in addition to those owned or exclusively controlled by the State or any such county, city or town.

§ *67:* The General Assembly shall not make any appropriation of public funds, or personal property, or of any real estate, to any church, or sectarian society, association, or institution of any kind whatever, which is entirely or partly, directly or indirectly, controlled by any church or sectarian society; nor shall the General Assembly make any like appropriation to any charitable institution which is not owned or controlled by the state; . . . but nothing herein contained shall prohibit the General Assembly from authorizing counties, cities, or towns to make such appropriations to any charitable institution or association.

Note: In Almond v. Day, 197 Va. 419, 89 S.E. 2d 851 (1955), the state supreme court held unconstitutional a program to pay the tuition and other expenses of orphans of veterans at private and sectarian educational institutions. Since the decision, Section 141 has been altered as it applies to private nonsectarian institutions.

WASHINGTON

Art. I, § 11, Amend. 34: . . . . No public money or property shall be appropriated for or applied to any religious worship, exercise or instruction, or the support of any religious establishment . . . .

Art. IX, § 4: All schools maintained or supported wholly or in part by the public funds shall be forever free from sectarian control or influence.

Note: In 1943, a closely divided state supreme court held the provision of transportation for parochial schools students unconstitutional, Mitchell v. Consolidated School District, 173 Wash. 2d 61, 135 P. 2d 79. The Attorney General has advised that it would be unconstitutional to provide state funds to sectarian institutions of higher education but that it would be permissible to provide grants or loans directly to needy students at such institutions. Report of Atty. Gen. 1957-1958, p. 104 (1958).

WEST VIRGINIA

Art. III, § 15: No man shall be compelled to frequent or support any religious worship, place or ministry whatsoever; . . . and the legislature shall not . . . pass any law requiring or authorizing any religious society, or the people of any district within this State, to levy on themselves, or others, any tax for the erection or repair of any house for public worship, or for the support of any church or ministry . . . .

WISCONSIN

Art. I, § 18: . . . nor shall any man be compelled to attend, erect or support any place of worship, or to maintain any ministry, against his consent; . . . nor shall any money be drawn from the treasury for the benefit of religious societies, or religious or theological seminaries.

Art. I, § 23: Nothing in this constitution shall prohibit the legislature from providing for the safety and welfare of children by providing for the transportation of children to and from any parochial or private school or institution of learning.

Note: Section 23 was passed after the state supreme court had held the provision of bus transportation to parochial school students to be unconstitutional. State ex rel. Reynolds v. Nusbaum, 17 Wisc. 2d 148, 115 N.W. 2d 761 (1962). See also State ex rel. Van Straten v. Milquet, 180 Wisc. 109,

192 N.W. 392 (1923). In 1919, the court had upheld payments to veterans attending educational institutions of their
choice, including sectarian ones. State ex rel. Atwood v.
Johnson, 170 Wisc. 251, 176 N.W. 224. The Attorney General has indicated that the salaries of persons teaching only
in parochial schools can not be paid by a city school board,
18 Op. Atty. Gen. 374 (1929). See also the application of
this principle to funds received under the Elementary and
Secondary Education Act of 1965, 55 Op. Atty. Gen. 124
(1966).

WYOMING

Art. VII, § 8: . . . nor shall any portion of any public school
fund ever be used to support or assist any private school, or
any school, academy, seminary, college or other institution of
learning controlled by any church or sectarian organization or
religious denomination whatsoever.

Art. I, § 19: No money of the state shall ever be given or appropriated to any sectarian or religious society or institution.

Index

208

Biographical Notes

WALTER GELLHORN is Betts Professor of Law at Columbia University and a past president of the Association of American Law Schools. He is the author of many works on constitutional law and administrative law, including *American Rights: The Constitution in Action; Individual Freedom and Governmental Restraints; When Americans Complain: Governmental Grievance Procedures; Ombudsmen and Others;* and *Children and Families in the Courts.* Professor Gellhorn, who has had broad experience in government, is by presidential appointment a member of the Council of the Administrative Conference of the United States. He is also a Councillor of the American Bar Association's Section of Administrative Law and of the American Philosophical Society, a Fellow of the American Academy of the Arts and Sciences, and a member of the American Academy of Public Administration.

R. KENT GREENAWALT, a Professor of Law at Columbia, teaches Constitutional Law and has concentrated on the law of church and state. He attended Swarthmore College, where he studied in the field of religion, did graduate work in political philosophy at Oxford and was Editor in Chief of the Law Review at Columbia Law School. He was law clerk to Mr. Justice John M. Harlan of the United States Supreme Court. He is co-author of a supplement to *Political and Civil Rights In the United States* and has written numerous articles in areas of constitutional law. He has served on the Civil Rights and Federal Legislation Committees of the Bar Association of the City of New York.